The Complete

Bowhunting
Journal

BOWHUNTING PRESERVATION ALLIANCE

The Complete

Bowhunting Journal

How to Pick the Right Gear and Use It Efficiently

Rick Sapp

Skyhorse Publishing

A portion of what you spent for The Complete Bowhunting Journal has been donated to the Bowhunting Preservation Alliance to recruit new bowhunters and develop new bowhunting opportunities. That allows the writing of this book to contribute to a higher calling. All writers want to convey a truth about the world as they understand it. A writer who pursues a specific craft focus such as bowhunting, however, is tasked with the additional requirements that his or her work be informative and entertaining. It is a special bonus when the writing also serves a higher purpose. Thank you for your purchase. Good speed and great bowhunting forever.

— *Rick Sapp*

Bowhunting is like religion–once you've seen the "light," you want others to find that special sense of accomplishment and challenge that only bowhunting offers. The Bowhunting Preservation Alliance works to put archery into every community, invite every beginning archer to try bowhunting, and wants every bowhunter to find opportunities to hunt where they live. Your purchase of this book will help provide the means for us to spread the "good news" about archery and bowhunting and ensure that, long after you've left the woods, others will experience the adrenaline rush and genuine satisfaction shared by all who've hunted with stick and string. Thanks.

— *Jay McAninch,*
CEO/President, Archery Trade Association

Skyhorse Publishing books may be purchased in bulk at special discounts for sales promotion, corporate gifts, fund-raising, or educational purposes. Special editions can also be created to specifications. For details, contact the Special Sales Department, Skyhorse Publishing, 307 West 36th Street, 11th Floor, New York, NY 10018 or info@skyhorsepublishing.com.

Skyhorse® and Skyhorse Publishing® are registered trademarks of Skyhorse Publishing, Inc.®, a Delaware corporation.

Visit our website at www.skyhorsepublishing.com.

10 9 8 7 6 5 4 3 2 1

Library of Congress Cataloging-in-Publication Data is available on file.

ISBN: 978-1-62087-693-0

Printed in China

Table of Contents

Dedication

This book, THE COMPLETE BOWHUNTING JOURNAL, is cheerfully dedicated to the men and women who made it possible. The unsung heroes who lobby for hunting seasons; who volunteer to help at archery events; who are curious about their gear and begin to tinker with it; and who take care of the children while the spouse sits in a treestand. It is dedicated to those who measure trophy heads; who take their children to hunting expos and crest arrows; who pass up marginal shots and practice so that they can make a quick, clean kill. You are just the kind of people who make America great. Thank you!

— *Rick Sapp*

Introduction

Bowhunting is what makes us special, you and I, what helps define us. This subtle activity separates us from men and women who reflexively sit down to their dinner with only the vaguest idea of where their food came from, what was involved in blood and sweat, to bring their hamburger to the table.

I am extremely pleased to write the Bowhunting Journal, because it has allowed me to present six unique men and their stories. Within these true tales, I believe, there are glimpses of . . . if I can say this without boring you or making you laugh . . . our bowhunting genius. Listening to their stories and trying to present their passion on paper has made me a better writer. For that reason, and because I reckon each of them as a friend, I am grateful that they would share part of their lives with me and, thereby, with us all.

Del, who passed through the fire of his own mortality with a lust to hunt truly dangerous game.

Frank, the 79-year-old bear hunter, who was Fred Bear's first and, you could say, last employee.

Sonny, whose courage and ice-cold accuracy under extreme pressure saved his life.

Eddie, whose stubborn impetuousness killed him late one afternoon on the side of a Colorado mountain.

Bob, who has successfully hunted in the most formidable environments in the world.

Dan, who, defying every convention, passionately bowhunts whitetails.

The hunting stories are only part of our scheme in Bowhunting Journal, however. Each story introduces a section of this book and has something to say about our country and our sport, if I may call bowhunting a sport. The fact that we can hunt with so little social and governmental oversight, chase so many species, and in so many different manners, is truly incredible, and we ought to recognize that. The world is no longer a wild and untamed place. To have an opportunity to roam virtually unimpeded with the bow and arrow is an inconceivable blessing, one that is so rare on Planet Earth as to be . . . well, a real miracle.

One other thing must be said, especially as I am writing this during an election year. Our unique system of government and our delicately balanced social fabric allows us to choose among dozens, perhaps hundreds of bows and broadheads. This contagion of choice continually amazes immigrants. They encounter this "problem" first in the aisles of a grocery. In their home country, if they had a product available at all, they most often had no choice in size, style or price. Our peculiar way of life presents us with thousands of choices and allows entrepreneurs to flourish, and we lifetime residents take it for granted. We should not.

Bowhunting is a modern "Made in America" phenomenon. It is a cause for celebration.

The other aspect of the stories in THE COMPLETE BOWHUNTING JOURNAL is how they link us to our technological side. Some biofeedback as yet only marginally understood, has made us who we are: man makes tools and tools

Happy days! The author (right) and his friend Dan Smith of Renville, Minnesota bowhunt the Minnesota River bottoms after a snow storm . . . not long ago.

have made man. Sonny's story brings us into the world of broadhead evolution, for instance. Del's fragile insistence upon close encounters with animals that would kill and eat him introduces our discussion of archery mechanics. Frank's preferred world was a throwback to an earlier, but not necessarily simpler hunting style, and it contrasts with the one most of us now inhabit. Dan's commitment to speed, silent shooting and accuracy at any range pays off and initiates our discussion of archery accessories. Finally, I picture Eddie crawling slowly, like a spider across his cliff face, and becoming more desperate each time he shifts his compound bow upward; his story introduces us to modern bows.

Hundreds of individuals and bowhunting companies have generously helped develop the information for Bowhunting Journal, and right here I would like to thank them. I indeed stand on the shoulders of giants. If I got it right, I suspect that their explanations were patient . . . and probably repeated. If I did not, it was most certainly my fault for not asking the right questions.

Photo courtesy South Dakota Tourism

I have credited many companies and individuals with photos and information, and many more go unnamed. Because I was a social science major in college and not an engineer, I must work hard to explain some of the concepts that make bowhunting such a fascinating field. What could be cleaner than the long, arcing flight of an arrow? Certainly it is beautiful, but the dynamics behind that beautiful curve are devilishly contorted.

So, I have not mentioned every company or every individual who has contributed to this small volume and for that I apologize. Perhaps if we meet like this again in the near future, I will be able to make up for that failing.

Originally published in 2005, this volume was slightly updated in 2013 to bring the gear more in-line with today's shooting and manufacturing. The principles of archery equipment design and fine shooting remain the same as ever, but gear is like a river, continually in motion, continually changing—and in a market-based economy like ours, that is a healthy thing, a good thing. Great hunting ahead for all!

Rick Sapp
Gainesville, Florida

CHAPTER ONE

The Mechanics of Shooting

DEL'S DANGEROUS GAME

Men have not always hunted dangerous game. Of course, that depends on your definition of "men" and "dangerous," but for 99 percent of our lineage on Planet Earth, we hid and ran and climbed for our lives, narrowly escaping the fang and claw.

Man as Homo sapiens is not physically disposed as either a predator or, it may surprise you to learn, a prey species. Our canines are small, and our claws nonexistent. We are not especially fleet of foot. During our thousands of years of prehistory, our numbers were small and our fat content, until very recently, has been low. In our prime, we are no match for a small bear or a big virus.

The great cats and packs of hunting wolves of a million or so years ago–recently in the age of life on earth–surely thought of us as a meal of last resort. Individually we would have been easy to kill, but by that time, we had some skill at fighting back cooperatively. For all the aggravation then involved in killing and eating scrawny men and women, surely a fat

Connecticut's Del DelMastro would not admit that he is addicted to adrenaline, but he did stalk a black-maned lion taken in Africa after warning his guide not to shoot unless the lion was going to take him down. Perhaps we now hunt dangerous game for the same reasons we climb dangerous mountains, "Because they are there."

plains antelope would be easier and probably taste better as well.

Inside jokes in the lion pride must have sounded something like this: "Antelope taste better because they eat the green grass. God only knows what those humans have been eating, Simba. Anything that does not eat them first!" Ha. Ha.

Our unique physiology and brain specialization eventually gave us an advantage. Opposable thumbs and flexible fingers could shape any tool our complex brain could envisage. Dolphins are apparently brilliant intellects, and pigs truly not far behind them, but just ask one to put a point on a spear and they would be lost, and would probably whine about it. We hate whiners. Two more reasons why we eat them and they do not eat us. Anyway, the same brain that could imagine tools and defensive weapons shaped from rocks and sticks miraculously moved us toward language, a beautiful, rich vocabulary full of meaning and command.

Language and tools at last gave us dominion over the earth and the creatures therein. It was not that long ago, really–perhaps 25,000 or 30,000 years–that man became the ultimate predator on the planet. The date is significant, for the bow and arrow were invented then. Thus, the last of the giant cave bears and saber-tooth tigers died on our arrow points.

The bow gave us the ability to strike from beyond the reach of the leopard's lightning lunge. The flight of the arrow helped equalize our lack of speed as the opportunistic jaguar chased us through the jungle. When the bow at last arrived to replace the spear thrower, we began to hunt dangerous game. Sometimes we hunted bears and tigers to prevent them from hunting us first. At other times, their fangs and claws and pelts became tools in our religious ceremonies. Finally, perhaps, we hunted them just because they were there.

None of this was in Del DelMastro's conscious mind, however, when he booked a brown bear hunt on Kodiak Island. Del found an outfitter who served the remote, west end of the island around Karluk Lake. "Lots of bears," he was told, "big bears." That was good, Del thought, because he wanted the bears to be "on fish."

The recommended guide, Jeff Hirsch, did not at first please Del or his bowhunting buddy, Rich Chaffee. Jeff admitted that he had never guided a bowhunter . . . but he was willing to make the effort. Yes, he understood that they would need to stalk uncomfortably close to the giant bears. Yes, he would carry a significant firearm, and yes, he agreed, he would only use it if a bear attacked them.

"The index finger on the rifle trigger," Jeff thought, "is the ultimate combination of man's tools and intellect."

Jeff was about to learn a new lesson, or possibly relearn a very old one.

Del DelMastro does not claim to be a great hunter, but he is. The

Del DelMastro's record book brown bear fell to one arrow on Kodiak Island. Although his guide had never worked with a bowhunter, Del stalked to within 27 yards of the huge boar shortly before the end of his hunt.

Connecticut auto body repairman has indulged a vision of bowhunting around the world. One day when he is too old to run and climb and shoot, he says, he will retire to an overstuffed chair in a game room filled with lions and bears and deer and turkey, and spend his days reminiscing about all of those wonderful times. Thus, he has hunted America coast-to-coast, and has taken lions in Africa and red stag in New Zealand. At the turn of the millennium though, he had never been to Alaska, possibly because a brown bear hunt on Kodiak Island is easily twice as expensive as and infinitely more rugged than an African hunt for plains game, even dangerous game.

Del is not only a darn good hunter; he is driven to experience the outdoors. "Passionate" may or may not describe him, but deadly serious certainly does. He calls turkeys, stalks deer and bears, and takes black-maned lions on the ground. He thrills to get close to his quarry, and the more dangerous it is, the more he seems to relish it.

Dangerous game certainly has gotten close to him. In 1999, a stalking killer nearly took him out. The robust and energetic auto-body worker was felled; down, and down hard, too, but not out. The attempted murderer was something so small that he could not get a broadhead into it. That year, cancer robbed him of his left kidney.

Taking a trophy Kodiak bear was not the first thing Del thought of when the doctors told him he had narrowly escaped with his life. The first thing he thought of was how he wanted to live the remaining years of his life. After surgery, and the threat of radiation and chemotherapy, he determined that he would not hold anything back.

"I want as many people to know me as possible," he laughs. "When I went through the cancer, I realized I wasn't untouchable."

No longer married, with no kids and recently acquainted with the shadow of death, Del made a commitment to indulge his adrenaline passions. Lions and bears. Maybe a leopard. But certainly, dangerous game.

So Del told his Kodiak guide, "If I am going to hunt with you, you must promise that you will not shoot unless a bear has me down on the ground." Dangerous, indeed, but knowing Del, it was not bravado. It was simply his way of living life to the fullest.

The arrangements on Kodiak turned out to be a tiny trapper's cabin not much larger than a back-yard tool shed. The hunters and their guides were cramped and the Bay of Alaska's famously fickle weather turned foul immediately upon their arrival. It was cramped in the cabin. Doubly cramped, because of the mountain of gear the eastern hunters had packed and the addition of Jeff's Alaskan friend, Dale Routt, who was simply curious to see if a bowhunter could work the big bears from the close range they claimed, and live to tell about it.

Del woke in the darkness of the first morning to hurricane-force wind and rain slashing the little cabin. Intermittent hail beat against the roof and the temperature plunged. For 48 hours, the two hunters, their two guides and the unexpected guest were trapped inside a dark and freezing space smaller than Del's master bath. "All the more reason to choose an amiable hunting partner," Del thought.

Del spent the first four-and-a-half days of his $15,000 hunt hunched over a kerosene heater. When the weather broke, Rich harvested a bear with his rifle.

"Why wait around?" Rich asked. "We could be in that cabin forever." The 150-yard shot echoed across the lake and found its way into the dripping, fog-shrouded mountains surrounding them.

"Are you sure you want to hunt with your bow?" Del's guide asked. "That broadhead looks pretty small and these bears can weigh more than a thousand pounds. You'll be amazed how fast they are. You're welcome to use my rifle, if you change your mind."

Del lightly fingered the cutting blades and trocar tip of his 90-grain Muzzy head. "Maybe a one-inch hole seems small to you," he said, "but it's bigger than your bullet." That ended that conversation.

For eight days, Del and his guide cursed the Arctic fog and the wet, swirling mists as they climbed into the mountains around Karluk Lake to glass for bears.

Bears were not scarce. Bears were everywhere, especially along the streams where they caught and ate fish in an orgy of Ursus arctos gluttony. Not one was the great bruiser that Del had imagined or come half way around the world to hunt, though. Eventually, one part of his brain decided that it would return home before it took a small bear.

With the end of the hunt in sight, the men decided to hunt a different shoreline, and Del, Jeff and friend Dale hauled their boat out of the lake and man-handled it half a mile up a shallow, unnamed stream toward Lake O'Malley. The boat grated on pebbles scraped smooth by the last ice age, as men began to cross the Bering Strait to the New World. Salmon darted between their legs and fog swirled around them, obscuring the banks where the world's largest carnivore lurked in the head-high brush.

An instant before the boat floated free into O'Malley Lake, a biting wind blew the moisture-laden mist behind them and Del spotted the bear he had come so far to challenge. It was resting nearly 50 feet up a high-sloping cliff over their stream.

Grounding the boat, the guide checked his Weatherby and Del checked his McPherson .38 Special. This was not the time for a shell to jam or a sight pin to jiggle loose. Meanwhile, Dale kept his binoculars on the bear. This was no deer hunt. The animal they were preparing to stalk could kill all three of them.

Still, the bear had not seen them or it would have moved, and the three men scrambled through the thick brush, up the cliff toward it.

Once on top, Del and his hunting party began to snake their way through the alder thicket and silently approached the bear. Because of the eternally damp conditions, there was little danger of breaking a stick and because the men were well aware of the bear's speed, power and ferocity, they were not about to allow their boots to strike a willow stump carelessly. The breeze was quartering into their faces.

Closer and closer the men crept, until it was necessary for Del to drop onto all fours and slowly crawl through a bear-tunnel in the head-high brush. Bear tunnels are covered highways for the resident bruins. Pounded down daily by hundreds of generations of heavy bears, the only dangers were meeting a bruin face-to-face or gagging on the accumulated filth of a thousand seasons of bear scat and fish waste.

Periodically, Del would slip to one side and use his Bushnell Yardage Pro laser rangefinder to verify his distance to the bear. Seventy-five yards soon became 45 and finally, slowly stepping around a patch of alders at 27 yards, there was nothing at all between him and the massive creature.

The bear sat on its rump facing away from him and Del remembers praying for it to stand up and give him a quartering away shot. As if it were answering his prayer, the bear stood up. Del drew, placed the TruGlo fiber optic pin on its last rib and triggered his shot.

When the Carbon Express 300 arrow hit, the bear let out a soft grunt and spun completely around. It crashed away through the alders, bulldozing a new tunnel. Spinning once more, it fell headlong into a deep ravine. Del estimated that from the moment he triggered his Fletcher release to the moment the enormous bear collapsed was less than 40 seconds.

On their way home, Del and Rich spent several days recovering at the justly famous Great Alaskan Bush Company in Anchorage. After two weeks on Kodiak Island, that rustic city felt like Paris to the exhausted bowhunters.

"The better shape you are in before you go to Kodiak Island," Del says, "the more you will enjoy the experience. It's a rough place with terrible, erratic weather and heavy alder and willow thickets. When storms hit, which was frequently, we stayed in the trapper's cabin. The little kerosene heaters kept us from freezing, but in a way, it was almost as tough inside as outside in the gale-force winds and sleet. The Bay of Alaska is not what you would call a 'forgiving environment.' In the morning, the temperature can drop and you will think you are in the middle of a Badlands blizzard. By noon, the sun comes out and you can hunt in your tee shirt. Go figure."

With a 24-inch skull, Del's bear easily scored high enough to claim a spot in the Pope & Young record books. Guide Jeff Hirsch, who lives year-round in Palmer, Alaska, estimated that the bear was slightly shy of half-a-ton, but the hide and skull alone weighed more than 200 pounds. Following Del's shot, it took the three men the rest of the day to care for his trophy. Because bears are volatile and unpredictable omnivores with a lazy streak, who do not hesitate to lunch on their dead brothers, one of the three men stood guard with the Weatherby at all times.

Del's hands let you know that he has not spent his life at a typewriter or in a library. His hands are tough, permanently creased and stained. Scarred, but agile. What you might proudly call, "working man's hands." Del's are the kind of hands our ancestors possessed when they invented the bow.

A bear as enormous and powerful as a Kodiak can open an automobile like a soda can. It can smash a trapper's cabin, and kill and eat the huddled hunters like the cream filling in an Oreo cookie. Perhaps a bear of this size, with a brown bear's mental make-up, is capable of being gentle, if it is a female caring for cubs, but no bear that ever lived or ever will live on this earth could simulate the simplest work of Del's weathered hands.

This story has self-consciously mentioned Del's bowhunting gear. The purpose is not to promote specific companies, but to emphasize that this man selected particular tools, organized them into a marvelously functioning whole, and then used them to find and kill a dangerous animal four times his size. Except that they built their tools from natural materials, prehistoric bowhunters did precisely the same thing.

Many scientists believe there is feedback between our hands and our brain. The more we think about the questions our environment presents, the more restless our hands become: "Can we strap our gear to our back and climb the cliff without the bear detecting us?" The longer we employ our hands developing technological solutions to our problems, the more our complex, bifurcated brain expands and develops additional questions: "Is my 64-pound bow sufficient to cut cleanly through and kill this bear?"

Paraphrasing Mount Everest mountaineer George Mallory, Del DelMastro says that he went to Kodiak Island to hunt its famous bears, "because they are there." Mallory died on Everest's icy slopes in 1924 at the age of 40. As this story is being written, Del is off to hunt bull moose in the Yukon. Mallory might have lived longer if he had taken up bowhunting and stuck with lions and tigers and bears, which are, after all, safer than Everest. Just ask Del. Dangerous game challenges Del DelMastro for a predictable reason–a brown bear will kill you–and for a personal reason as well: during the past decade he has struggled with cancer. Fighting cancer is no different from bowhunting dangerous game. Understand your adversary. Build a trustworthy support team. Pay attention to detail.

DelMastro is as attentive to bow tuning as he is to doctor visits. Two pills after the evening meal with a glass of water mean precisely that, not one pill (because they taste wretched) with a sip of apple juice. In the same way, his draw length must translate precisely into 100 percent action-energy when he is shooting at a great bear, because the tolerances are so very close. And that is what this chapter is all about, close tolerances, getting your setup exactly right, because "close enough" just is not good enough.

GETTING PERSONAL

Bowhunting is an extremely personal activity. Resources are available to help you learn how to shoot and even some to help you learn to hunt, but your bow and arrows must fit you, not your best friend. A pro shop owner cannot build your muscles to handle a heavier draw weight. Your daddy cannot make your shot on a deer.

The beauty of hunting with the bow and arrow, and its ultimate challenge, is that it draws on inner resources that, at the moment of greatest challenge, you alone control.

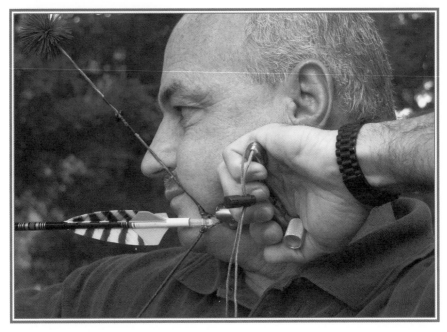

It is as important to get your draw length and draw weight just right when shooting a recurve as it is with a compound. A traditional bow is a little different, however, since there is no let-off and bowhunters rarely hold longer than a moment at full draw.

YOUR DOMINANT EYE

Bows are built to fit right- or left-handed individuals, but your choice–surprise–should be based on eye dominance, not on hand dominance! Just as you write, brush your teeth or eat with a fork, right- or left-handed, you also have a dominant eye, a master eye.

For most of us, hand and eye dominance are same-sided, but sometimes a right-handed person will have a dominant left eye or vice versa.

There are two ways to determine your dominant eye. First, with both eyes open, point your index finger at a distant object. Now, close your left eye. If your finger still points at the object, you have a dominant right eye. If your finger shifts to the side when you close your left eye, you almost certainly have a dominant left eye. For confirmation, point again with both eyes open and then close your right eye. If, while you are looking with your left eye only, your finger still points at the object, you can feel certain that your left eye is dominant.

The second way to determine eye dominance is a method many people find less optically confusing and it uses both of your hands. First, place your hands together at arm's length from your eyes, palms facing out so you are viewing the backs of your hands. Now, touch the tips of your thumbs and forefingers and swivel your hands together so that the "V" between your thumbs and your forefingers forms a hole. Pick out an object on the far side of the room and center it in the hole. Slowly move your hands together so the hole becomes smaller and smaller and, while you are doing this, bring your hands and the hole back to your face. You should end up with a small hole circumscribed by your hands in front of your dominant eye.

Your hand-eye coordination is simplified if your dominant eye matches your dominant hand. Then you simply choose a bow configured for your dominant side: a right-hander with a dominant right eye will choose a right-handed bow.

If your hand and eye dominance are mismatched, select a bow based on eye dominance rather than hand dominance. A right-hander will feel awkward at first shooting a left-handed bow, but in the long run you will shoot better and more comfortably this way. After a while, it will seem natural.

Most successful bowhunters sight with their dominant eye. Hand dominance in archery is simply performing manual operations directed by the brain. This allows them to aim with both eyes open, and that gives them better depth perception for distance estimation. To aim with your weaker eye, you need to close or cover your dominant eye.

DETERMINE YOUR DRAW LENGTH

The distance between the bowstring and the grip when you hold a bow at full draw or pull the string all the way back to what is called your "anchor point," is your draw length. This is a specific personal measurement determined by the length of your arms and the width of your shoulders, and it governs bow selection. Do not confuse your draw length with your ultimate arrow length. There is a relation, but arrows can be shorter or longer than your draw.

You can be measured for draw length at any archery pro shop or you can get a friend to help. If no special device is available at a pro shop, use a lightweight bow and nock an arrow onto its bowstring. Then, draw the bow. As you hold comfortably at full draw, have a friend mark the arrow directly above the pressure point (the "V" formed by your thumb and forefinger as you grip the bow) of the handle. This spot should be even with the center of the arrow rest hole (the rear hole if there are two) in the sight window.

Add 1¾ inches to that measurement to determine your standard draw length for a compound bow. If, for instance, your measurement is 28 inches from the string to the pressure point at full draw, your true draw length is 28 + 1¾ = 29¾ inches.

Most compound bows allow for some draw length adjustments–on some bows it can range from 26 to 31 inches on , for example. You can usually make minor adjustments (+/- 1/4-inch or so) to draw length by changing the end of the bowstring from one post to another on your cam or cams or by moving the string spool from one position to another. Adjustments of

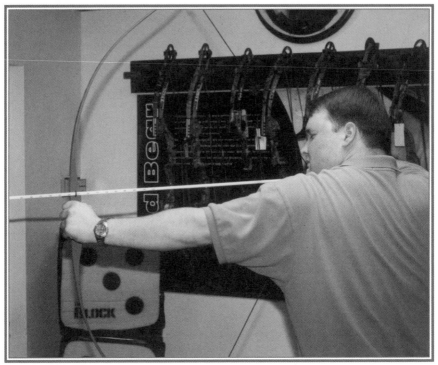

Determining your proper draw length is one of the most important personal settings in archery. Unlike a firearm, which people of different sizes and statures can shoot successfully, a bow must be precisely fit to your individual frame and shooting style. Most archery pro shops have draw-check bows, ultra-lightweight recurves with special measuring bars attached, for this purpose, but you can actually come close on your own or with a friend.

more than a couple inches require a different draw length module on the cam (usually, an easy job) or even a change of cams, as cams come in different sizes, but that is a more complex operation and requires a professional bow press.

If your bow does not quite match your draw length, make additional adjustments by twisting or untwisting the string. This can change the draw length by one-quarter inch. This is more complex than changing a module or even a cam, and should be performed with a bench-mounted bow press. You can also twist synthetic cables to change draw length. A combination of twisting or untwisting the cables and strings lets you tune your bow for your precise draw length.

Twisting the cables can throw a twin-cam bow out of time. This is not science fiction. It means the cams roll over unevenly. Some older style compound bows with metal cables have slotted harness attachments or yokes that allow for quarter-inch draw-length changes. These adjustments will alter your draw weight as well as draw length. Lengthening the string increases draw weight while shortening the string reduces draw weight. Expect the opposite for lengthening and shortening the cables.

Some archery coaches believe the average bowhunter shoots with too long a draw. If you began shooting with fingers and switched to a release, a low wrist grip and a string loop, you should experiment with dropping your draw length, perhaps as much as an inch to an inch-and-a-half.

If your draw length is too long, you must do one of the following to pull the string to the bow's valley: overextend your bow arm's elbow and push that shoulder unnaturally toward the target; or anchor far back, away from the front of your face, sometimes to the point where the hand is not even touching the face. Many bowhunters with too long a draw length take a stance that causes them to lean back, away from their target.

Reducing your draw length may improve your accuracy. A shorter draw turns you into the bow and target, produces a more relaxed stance and opens the distance between your chest and the string. In bulky cold weather clothing, this is a bonus. With the bow arm unlocked in this stance, there is also less stress on the elbow and triceps.

FIND YOUR BEST DRAW WEIGHT

One of the primary elements governing your choice of a bow and your ability to shoot well is peak draw weight, the maximum amount of pounds needed to draw the bow at your draw length.

You often see bowhunters struggling to draw their bow. Using extreme effort, they raise the bow over their head, grimace and strain.

If you have to raise your bow for leverage when you draw, you are pulling too much weight. If you cannot draw the string straight back to your anchor without trembling or hunching your shoulders with the strain, you are pulling too much weight.

Maybe it is macho to draw a heavy weight, but on the other hand, maybe making a great shot is even better. Reduce the draw weight on both limbs equally until you can easily draw straight back and then, as your shooting form improves, ease the bow back toward a heavier weight if that is what you need for the game animals you are hunting.

The best draw weight for you varies according to your physical build, strength and, to a certain extent, upon the size game you are hunting. You want to draw your bow without significant difficulty, hold your sights on target and pull the string straight back to your anchor without straining.

A hunting situation is a lot different from competition or practice. Uncontrollable factors in the field, such as fatigue, cold and "buck fever," take their toll on your body and your mind, and it becomes increasingly difficult to draw to your peak weight. If you must strain to draw when you are practicing, you may find you cannot draw at all under pressure. The solution

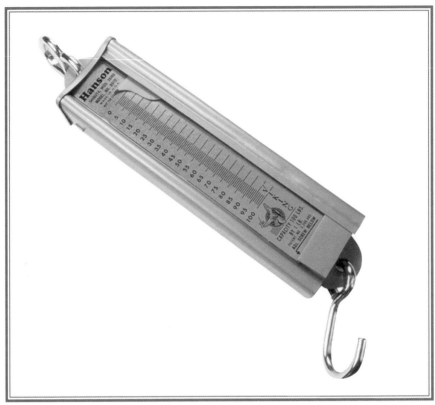

This hanging bow scale measures to 100 pounds in one-pound increments and it is found in most archery pro shops. Discovering your comfortable draw weight will ensure that you are not over-bowed, pulling too much weight. A 45-pound bow is adequate for taking whitetails under 30 yards. Unfortunately, too many bowhunters want to shoot more weight than they can comfortably handle. Whether it is 45 or 75 pounds, find a comfortable weight for your body size and shape, and learn to shoot it accurately.

is to buy a bow with a draw weight you can handle under any circumstances.

A smooth draw is not the only reason to choose a particular bow. Thousands of bowhunters suffer chronic shoulder and elbow injuries, such as tendonitis. Certainly, these "overuse injuries" can either be caused by or aggravated by repeatedly shooting heavy bows over a period of years. A comfortable draw weight also helps you steady your sight picture.

A too-heavy draw weight also contributes to "target panic." A heavy bow, particularly one coupled with light or poorly spined arrows in a set-up tuned for speed rather than shooting comfort, sends harmful vibrations throughout a bow and your arm and elbow. Modern vibration-dampening technology has greatly reduced bow breakage problems, but the greater the stress on a bow, the greater the potential for damage. (And yes, let the draw weight down if you are not shooting for a significant length of time.)

The results of good mechanics, attention to a well-tuned bow and smooth arrow flight! Oklahoma's Roger Raglin has taken more than 170 record-class big-game animals on four continents, and his 75 or so record-class whitetail bucks have been harvested in 21 US states and four Canadian provinces.

Modern compound bows drawing 60 to 70 pounds are heavy enough for all North American game animals except perhaps for musk ox and the greater bears. Draw weights above 60 pounds may give your arrows a slightly flatter trajectory, a benefit at longer and unknown distances, but–all things being equal and, truthfully, they rarely are–increasing weight does not significantly improve arrow penetration at a distance.

How do you determine a comfortable draw weight? You should draw a number of bows of differing weights and choose one you can draw easily. Remember that a bow that advertises a peak weight of 60 pounds is fully adjustable from 50 to 60 pounds. So, if 60 pounds is an effort, back the bow down five to ten pounds and work your way up to the point you feel comfortable. It is not recommended that you back bow weight down beyond ten pounds because efficiency then begins to suffer.

A peep sight may do more to improve your accuracy than any other bowhunting accessory except for a release aid. Peeps essentially serve as rear sight posts and, many believe when shooting with a release, make a positive anchor less important. Nevertheless, be certain to serve the peep so that it will not slide in your string and so that it comes back to your eye in the same manner each time. Peeps come in numerous aperture sizes, and because deer usually appear in early morning or late afternoon, bowhunters typically prefer a larger hole or aperture than 3-D competitors.

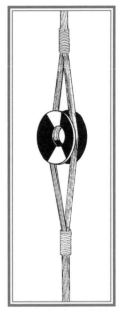

STEPS IN LEARNING TO SHOOT

Start by facing your target and then turn your feet about 45 degrees to one side: counter-clockwise for a right-hander and clockwise for a left-hander. This is the "open stance." It offers several practical advantages. First, it helps move the bow and string slightly away from your arm and chest. This is doubly important because a few slaps of the string on your forearm will be enough to make a strong man squeal. Second, if you are layering on a cold day, the string is less likely to hang up on your clothes. If it hangs up on the zipper or some fold of clothing, you will not hit what you are shooting at.

Sometime in your hunting career, you may find yourself gravitating toward a more closed stance. This stance gives you more power by aligning the bones, muscles and joints with the pull of the string, but it has the disadvantage of bringing the bowstring close to your chest and clothing.

For consistently good groups, you must draw to the same spot on your face every time. You can touch your middle finger to the corner of your mouth or lock your index finger with a release under or along the side of your jaw. Establish an anchor point that aligns your eye with the string. If your eye is to either side, left or right, your accuracy will suffer because you will be looking across your arrow and sights rather than at zero-angle.

Accurate hunters use a string-mounted peep sight. A peep is essentially a piece of black plastic with a small hole in it through which you align your pins with the target. The peep forces a consistent anchor position because otherwise you could not see through it. To find the correct place on the string to mount a peep, close your eyes, draw your bow to anchor and then open your aiming eye. Have someone slide the peep down the string to your eye, never the other way around (trying to mount it too low will interfere with your center serving), and then serve it securely into place.

Hold your bow with a loose, relaxed hand. If you are drawing too much weight, this will be impossible. Reduce your draw weight until you can draw without grimacing and gripping the bow with all your might. All that

Del DelMastro took his magnificent red stag in New Zealand. "That is one long trip," he says, "but the hunt and the scenery are unforgettable." And that is, in part, what it is all about.

expended energy is going to cause you to miss.

A wrist sling combined with a relaxed grip is a great combination, especially when you are shooting from a treestand. Relaxed, you can leave your fingers open, away from the riser as you draw, and shoot. The sling is not there necessarily to catch the bow after you shoot, although it will. A sling gives you the confidence that you will not drop your bow, and that confidence lets you hold the bow in the fork of your thumb and forefinger without torquing it, especially on follow-through.

Aiming, release and follow-through are one step, one set of body/mind mechanics. Get on target the same way each time. Either bring your sight pins up and count the distance as you go or bring them from the side or top. It does not matter as long as you make the action repeatable. If it is repeatable, it becomes more automatic, less error-prone.

Release the string or trigger your release smoothly and quickly when

15

your pin is positioned in the vitals. The longer you remain at full draw with your pin on target, the greater the chance you will experience target panic or feel muscle fatigue. Draw, aim deliberately, take a calming breath and shoot.

A relaxed, but disciplined follow-through is especially important. That means not consciously moving to look at the result. If you do this well, your arrow will always clear the set-up cleanly, no matter how excited you become. Your bow is naturally going to rebound following the shot, but the arrow is gone and . . . you are wearing a wrist sling.

Twisting your head following release to see where your arrow hits is called "peeking." This will cause you to begin to anticipate and will move the bow in a manner that is not conducive to good follow-through. As peeking gets to be a habit, your left-right accuracy will suffer.

BOW TUNING

The most daunting aspect of bowhunting is hitting what you are aiming at. Getting your bow ready is called "tuning." There seems to be a mystery

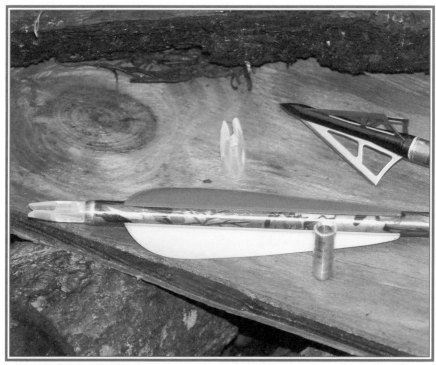

Half the battle of setting up and tuning a bow is realizing that you are not tuning the bow, but the arrow. Of course, you can time cam roll-over and adjust the cable guard for clearance and check for cam lean, but tuning is a matter of working with your arrows and arrow components. The object is to have your bowstring apply force directly through your arrow from the nock throat to the tip of your broadhead.

about bow tuning, but there should not be one. Anyone with a little time and place to shoot can tune a bow. Regardless of all the technical jargon, tuning for good shooting is not rocket science!

TUNE YOUR ARROWS

Arrows are the most important elements for good shooting. Only a couple of all the shaft sizes made have the correct "spine" (the amount they flex when shot) to shoot well from your 60-pound one-cam Parker bow. Select the proper arrow size, by referencing Easton's shaft-selection chart and plugging in your personal data: draw weight, draw length, the weight of your broadhead and type of cam (for a compound). You already know whether you shoot with fingers or a release.

When you purchase shafts or arrows, spin them over rollers and never shoot any shaft-broadhead-nock combination that wobbles.

Now, find the right arrow rest. Finger shooters should use a side-control rest. A finger-released arrow bends side-to-side as it leaves the bow, requiring left-right oscillation control. This horizontal "wallowing" results as the string moves forward and around your moving fingertips.

By comparison, arrows shot with a mechanical release oscillate vertically. This is called "porpoising" and requires a launcher rest. Fall-away rests are also excellent choices for a release because they offer superior fletching clearance.

Excellent string-release allows the string to move forward cleanly. How an arrow leaves the string affects down-range flight and penetration. An arrow that attaches to the string underneath a clamp-on nock point will not tune or shoot the same as one that is cradled within a tied-on release loop. Similarly, an arrow released by a high-friction three-finger release will not fly as well as one released by a bowhunter who drops pressure from a top or bottom finger before shooting. The greatest accuracy and easiest tune with a mechanical release comes from a soft, tied-on release loop. With fingers, the best shooters use a tab, not a glove.

Select your accessories and set up your bow as close as possible to "real" conditions before tuning. Any change you make will change the tuning process. Attach your bowstring silencers, install the D-loop, peep sight, kisser button, stabilizer, quiver, rest, sight, Limb Savers and any other accessories before you tune. Make a decision about draw weight and tune the bow to that poundage. Finally, do not change the length or weight of your broadhead or you will need to review what you have just completed.

PAPER TUNING

Shoot through butcher paper or newspaper stretched between uprights or across a frame to complete the tuning process. Bare-shaft tuning is arguably the most reliable way to use a paper frame to figure out if your arrow is coming straight out of the bow. With no fletching to straighten the arrow's flight, the farther it travels, the more it should move in the direction and orientation it started when it left the bow.

Shoot your first arrow through the paper from about three feet away. The target on the other side needs to be at least three feet behind the paper or your arrow will hit and flip to the side before it exits the paper. This will result in a false paper tear.

Your tuning goal should be to have a bare shaft fly straight into the target at 20 yards (although you will not begin shooting that far). If you can do that, you can comfortably assume that fletched arrows will come out of the bow straight, if there is no contact with your cables or arrow rest. If your arrow leaves the bow straight, the fletching should not have to work as hard to stabilize it and straighten out its flight. The minimal task remaining then is keeping the arrow on its flight path. If you tune with a bare shaft first, arrow flight problems should disappear.

To make bare-shaft tuning more effective, wrap very small strips of duct tape around the arrows where fletching was removed until they weigh the same as your fletched arrows. Also, do not mount broadheads on the bare shafts initially; use field points of the same weight as your broadheads. They are available, so why not eliminate one small tuning variable?

Take your time shooting. Think about posture and shooting mechanics.

Now, without moving from your position, check to see how the arrows are sticking into the backstop. If the shafts are not sticking straight in, they did not leave the bow straight and some adjustments are needed.

Begin by checking your arrow nocks from where you shot. If the arrows' nock ends are lower than the points where the arrows entered the backstop, your arrows are leaving the bow rear end low. You can fix this. Move the nock locator up on the string or lower the arrow rest's launcher fins. Either adjustment should have the same effect.

If the nock ends are high in the backstop, adjust your nock locator in the opposite direction. If your nock locator is too low, the arrows' nock ends will kick up when they come off the rest, causing them to be high in the target butt.

Adjust the nock locator up and down the string until your arrows leave the bow with the rear end neither high nor low, but straight.

Next, adjust for arrows leaving the bow with the nock ends to the left or right of the entry hole in the backstop. Move the bow's centershot by adjusting the arrow rest left or right. Continue shooting and moving the rest until the bare shaft's nock is on the same vertical left-right line as the entry hole.

Adjust both the nocking point and the rest to deal with "combination" tears. For example, for a tail-high and tail-right tear, move the nocking point down and the arrow rest to the right. Then, shoot again and continue tweaking rest and nock position as needed. The same tuning instructions apply to right-handed and left-handed shooters.

If your arrows do not respond with gradual tuning adjustments from three feet away, either your arrow is incorrectly spined and/or your arrow's vanes are hitting your arrow rest when you release.

To check for a collision problem, dust an arrow's vanes with powder and shoot the arrow into the target again, but without the paper. Scuffs in the powder or residue on the rest will let you know if and where you have a problem with rest clearance. Rotate your arrow nocks or try a different rest to cure this interference.

Designed to prevent any unwanted vane-rest contact, fall-away or drop-away rests are now popular with bowhunters. As a last resort for curing rest-vane interference, try shooting with feathers instead of plastic vanes. Feathers are a little noisy and prone to wilt in damp weather, but they do flatten on contact with any rest, thereby minimizing problems.

A special problem arises if you must move centershot away from your power stroke more than one-quarter inch to straighten shafts hitting severely left or right of the nocks. Changing arrow point weight might correct this by changing your arrow's spine, but if that is not sufficient, you might need to change draw weight or use a differently spined arrow.

After you tune shafts to enter straight into a backstop at three to five yards, shoot at ten and 20 yards. You might see, as you move back, that you need to do some additional tweaking. Shafts that are a little off at six yards will be off farther at 20 yards.

At 20 yards, gravity begins to work on your broadheads, so you should not tune for the height of the arrow nock to be the same height as the arrow's entry hole in the backstop. Because the arrowpoint is heavier and there is no fletching to raise it when you are bare-shaft tuning, the point gradually pulls the front end down. The entry hole normally will be lower than the shaft's nock by a couple of inches at 20 yards.

Tuning is no more complicated than adjusting your arrow rest and your nocking point. When an arrow tears a hole larger than the diameter of the head, shaft and vanes, you need to make some adjustments. Traditionally, a perfectly tuned bow is achieved when your arrows slice through the paper and leave holes shaped like a "Y" for three-vane arrows or an "X" for four-vane arrows. These holes should not be any larger than the broadhead and fletching, with no tear at all. All you want to see is the neatly cut "footprint" of the broadhead blades and vanes. But do not expect this result immediately.

Once you are shooting bullet holes from all three ranges, your arrows will be flying true, and remember that the purpose of going through all this effort is to hit what you are shooting at consistently.

EASY, COMMON SENSE TUNING REVIEW

For straight shooting, begin with straight, matched arrows. Spin check and weigh them before the season. Spin checkers are not expensive and they have multiple uses, from checking straightness, nock and broadhead alignment, and even cresting your arrows. Unless you want to buy your own grain scale, any pro shop can help you weigh your arrows and components. First, spin your arrows with no point or nock attached to make sure the shaft is straight. Then, progressively add elements such as fletching or cresting, the nock, the inserts and then your broadheads. It is a progressive system, but it is a logical system and it almost takes more time to write and read about it than it does to do it. It is easy to heat the insert glue in an aluminum arrow and turn the point until the arrow spins straight. (Do not overheat the shaft; heat it only enough to loosen the insert, because many composite shafts cannot be heated in this manner.)

Not every arrow you spin will be straight or well balanced, especially after a few sessions of pulling arrows out of tight foam targets or particularly uneven hay bales. Discard them or take them to a pro shop to be professionally straightened. Even then, mark these as strictly practice arrows. When you need to drill what you are shooting at, use your straightest and most balanced arrows.

The broadheads and arrowpoints you add to your arrow must be straight with the shaft. Do not be concerned about your broadheads being aligned with your fletching. That idea, truly, is irrelevant.

With broadhead-tipped arrows, you do want to get weight as close as possible to a standard. Some professionals say a "two-grain weight difference between arrows will cause a three-inch difference on impact point at 50 yards." We do not know whether this is true or not, the difference is so minute, but unless you are taking 50-yard shots at game–and this is not recommended–the difference is insignificant.

Your set-up should be tuned so an arrow consistently comes out on a straight path. Of course, the arrow will flex–this is called "archer's paradox"–as it leaves the bow, but it should flex along a straight path in the direction you want the arrow to fly. When the flexing stabilizes, the arrow will be headed straight toward your point of aim.

We are referring to your arrow being straight when it leaves the bow, not down range after the fletching has straightened it. If the arrow leaves the bow crooked and the fletching must move the shaft back and forth to correct it, the shaft might no longer be headed exactly toward the aiming

The elements of good form all come together with this Florida compound bow and release-aid shooter: wrist sling, proper hand grip, shock-absorbing stabilizer, shoot-through rest, properly spined carbon arrow and a cable guard positioned near the arrow to move the cables away from it just enough to ensure fletching clearance.

point, and it will certainly lose velocity and kinetic energy. Your fletching should not have to force an arrow around to straighten its flight, only keep it on the straight path it started on.

Most of us bowhunters spend some time tuning up our bow. We hit a paper plate consistently out to maybe 40 yards and then, just as we begin to feel confident before hunting season, realize our broadheads do not hit the target at the same spot as our field points. In fact, the arrows are only consistent in the erratic nature of their flight. With less than a week to opening day, we are frantic.

If this describes you, take a few minutes–again–to paper tune. Arrows that do not leave your bow straight probably cause this problem. Broadhead blades have a wider surface than a field point. Consequently, if the arrow begins its flight crooked, your broadheads will tug against the directional stability of your fletching. The broadhead (even a small, vented blade) will move the arrow more in the direction it starts before the fletching straightens it.

If arrows leave your bow straight, provided the broadheads are properly aligned with your shaft, you will no longer need to switch to broadheads before the season to adjust your sights. Both broadheads and field points now will impact at the same spot.

Essential bow set-up or shooting form problems cause some shooters to pull their hair during the tuning and sighting-in process. If you twist the bow, for instance, your arrows will not begin their flight straight. If you shoot a super-fast bow with arrows that are improperly spined for your draw weight, you could even have problems with bare-shaft flight. But with a little attention or perhaps some coaching, most people can adjust their set-up so arrows leave the bow just fine.

These few elements of set-up may greatly simplify bow tuning, improve arrow flight and, ultimately, your accuracy:

Install a string-loop. This inexpensive device, which can be made from string or metal, lets you release the string from directly behind your arrow. With a string-loop, you will not twist the string or pre-load the arrow to cause the arrow to leave the plane of the bow in a crooked manner.

Try a fall-away arrow rest. A fall-away rest holds your shaft in position for the first few inches of travel–the good ones are adjustable for length of travel–and then drops away before the back of the shaft and its fletching reach it. These rests typically use the forward movement of the cable guard or the downward movement of the buss cable to move the rest out of the arrow's path. They are especially useful if you shoot large, helical fletching. Finger shooters will have little trouble, because normal left-right arrow flex should move the fletched end of the shaft out and away from the riser.

Think about switching to carbon or composite arrows. Carbon shafts are not as critical to the cast of the bow and will generally fly straighter from a greater variety of set-ups than aluminum arrows.

Experiment with a release aid. Every testimonial says you will improve your accuracy with a release. There are several styles of string-holding jaws–double or single calipers, rope, bars or levers, ball bearings–and all work just fine. There is no solid evidence of different results from one style or another. Typically, rope releases are preferred in competition and almost any other style in bowhunting, as it takes a little more manual dexterity to hook a rope release and, under the pressure of a shot at an elk, this can be a daunting task!

Draw a slightly heavier bow. A heavier bow–heavier mass weight, not draw weight–gives you a steadier sight picture and tighter groups. If your bow is light, it will feel good as you carry it to your stand; but it also will float around as you aim. If your bow is light and you are struggling with accuracy, try a heavier stabilizer, but get its weight close to the riser or perhaps with a set of "V" bars, even behind the riser.

THREE SPECIAL TIPS

If you have arrow-flight difficulties you cannot seem to overcome, try numbering your arrows and shooting them individually. This will help you identify problem shafts, and a correction may be as simple as realigning the nock or broadhead.

Broadhead alignment is easily checked with a set of rollers or an arrow straightener with rollers. Simply position the tip of the broadhead on a reference line and turn the arrow on the rollers. Even small alignment problems are noticeable.

Several products are available to help you inspect your arrows for straightness. Some products helps you visually check your shaft's straightness, nock alignment, vane and feather balance and broadhead balance and alignment. More serious versions have smooth, nylon arrow rollers and a precision indicator gauge that lets you check and correct minor problems with aluminum arrows. This type of straightener is useless with carbon shafts except as spin testers for broadhead and nock tuning. If you are

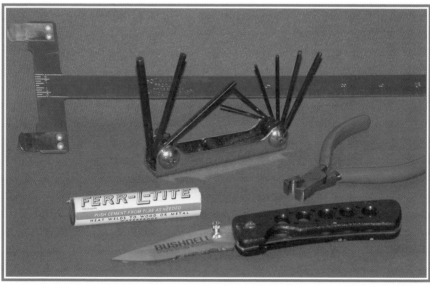

A few tools are vital to help you care for your bow in the field or in your basement workroom. A good sharp knife will help you cut serving threads and perform 1001 other archery chores, but should NEVER be used to separate bowstrings if, for instance, you are inserting a peep sight. A bow square will help you set up a nock point and check for centershot. A pair of nock pliers will help you adjust the nock point without damaging it. A set of hex keys will help you tighten and adjust accessories or your bow's weight. All are inexpensive and necessary.

serious about good shooting, you should use a spin checker and perhaps let your neighborhood pro shop buy the expensive arrow straighteners for frequent everyday use.

Look for a bow square with dual clips for nocking-point measurement and positioning. It works without having to move or remove any of your in-place accessories (peep, nock point locator, silencing whiskers, etc.). Spring steel clips hold the square in place while you make adjustments. This type of bow square is also useful for setting tiller and nocking point. A unique mini-square with a built-in 5/16-inch nock that screws into many arrow-point inserts, is useful as an instant visual check of your arrow nock in relation to the nock locator. It is especially handy for a day pack.

Archery coach and bowhunter Terry Wunderle says you can use your arrow rest to tune for centershot. First, shoot at a dot from ten yards and, leaving those arrows in the target, shoot at the same dot from 35 yards using the same sight pin. Your arrows will hit low, but if the low arrows are left of a perpendicular line from the top arrows, move the rest to the right. If the low arrows are to the right, move the rest to the left. Repeat the process until the bottom group is directly below the top group.

Wunderle says to select six matched and fletched arrows and then to equip three with field points and three with your broadheads. Shoot each broadhead at a separate dot and then shoot a field point at each dot. This is a quick process of adjusting your nocking point and draw weight so your broadheads hit in the same place as your field points.

With this shot-by-shot method, if the broadheads hit high, move the nock point up a little and try again. If they hit low, move the nock point down. If a broadhead hits left or right of the field point, adjust the weight of the bow. If the broadhead is to the right, decrease draw weight. If it is to the left, increase it. He says it should not hurt arrow flight if the broadhead is "a bit to the left side," but if it is to the right, it will certainly affect your grouping.

Several tools are available to help move your nock point without damaging your string or crimping the nock. There is a set of pliers specifically for putting a nock point locator on your string. These pliers have two cavity sizes for smooth crimping of different size nocks. Other types of pliers let you to remove or loosen the nock point without damaging the serving or the nock. Unless it becomes scarred in the tuning process, you can reuse the same nock a number of times.

The necessary tool in every archer's tool kit is a hex wrench set with multiple hex keys (or Allen wrenches) that can be positioned at any angle. Although the steel is not especially hard and the keys are prone to strip, they fit most archery accessories. A tool to look for should have eight hex keys, a flat-blade and Phillips-blade screwdriver, an open-end adjustable wrench and a three-blade broadhead wrench.

NAVEL-GAZING?

Many bowhunters seem discouraged with shooting the bow and arrow because they spend too much time worrying about paper tuning and cam lean and brace height and centershot and properly spined arrows. For deer hunters who shoot within their ability, hitting an eight-inch pie plate consistently at 20 yards is good enough. The pressure is to be exacting with your shot selection. Certainly, we must be conscious of the ethics of taking the life of an animal, but we hunt because we love to hunt, not because we love to take an animal's life or diddle with equipment.

Competition is different than hunting. In those games, pinpoint accuracy is how you define success and it is only natural to worry about the most microscopic aspects of tuning and shooting.

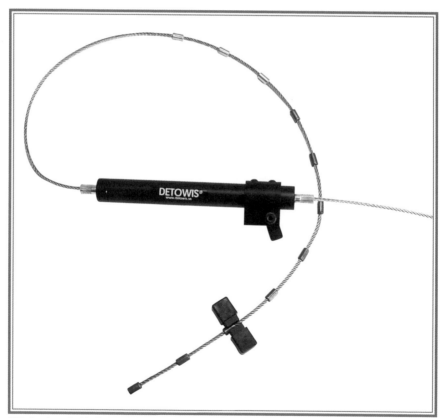

This backpackable bow press is an inexpensive tool that will allow you to perform many tasks in bow tuning and maintenance at home, without having to take your bow to a pro shop for routine string changing or twisting your string to alter the draw length.

It is widely believed that bowhunters have trouble hitting what they are shooting at, whether it is a live deer or a 3-D deer. I sometimes wonder if the primary problem with accuracy is that we spend too much time worrying about "tuning" and not enough time getting outside and having fun.

Virtually any adult bow sold today is capable of greater accuracy than is the person shooting it. So here is a rule of thumb for bow buying and accuracy: buy the bow you like, the one that feels good. Buy one you will be proud to shoot and, when you begin to tune it up and put on accessories, expect that you will find a comfortable level of accuracy. Then, go with it. Otherwise, the whole bow-tuning issue can drive you to drink and kill your passion for hunting.

Tuning a bow has less effect on your shooting accuracy than good quality practice. Although it is not recommended because it strains your bow, you can change a bow's tiller by as much as four to six pounds on either limb and still shoot excellent groups on the range. So you can quit worrying about the old argument that if your limbs are unbalanced they will fight each other, thus disrupting level nock-point travel in a significant manner, because they will not be affixed to the riser at the same angle or same weight. Measure your tiller, get the weight at the limb bolts close, and then forget about it.

Wheel or cam "timing" is about the same. Timing or wheel roll-over should be close (at least set initially to the manufacturer's recommendations) on a twin-cam or cam-and-a-half system, but this is irrelevant on a one-cam bow. If your wheel timing is the same on each shot, your arrows will strike in the same pattern. You can change centershot up to almost one-half inch and, with the bow in a shooting machine, it will fling arrows into the same holes at 20 yards as it did before you made the change.

To shoot accurately, pay attention to two straightforward ideas: select the bow that is right for you and then help your arrows leave the bow straight when you release the string. ■

CHAPTER TWO

A Bow for All Seasons

EDDIE CHEATS DEATH

Eddie says his experience changed him. Staring closely and, one could argue, intimately at death, as Eddie Claypool did one bluebird day in August 1989, would change most people. At the least, it would leave one with a terrifying memory. Claypool is 45 years old, but he was a mere 30 the day he died.

"I used to be a daredevil," he says. "I always like challenges. Things I knew better than to try, I did 'em anyway. I always got preached at a lot, but I sure have had some enlightening experiences." Mixing his tenses, Claypool is not sure whether he means he "used to be" or "still is" a daredevil.

As a kid, Claypool "raised a little Hell" with his buddies. "We climbed those 250-foot electrical towers and jumped trains," he says, not proud of those carefree days and his misbehavior, but not exactly apologetic, either.

Every summer, his father hauled the family to the mountains for a vacation. Twenty-four hours of two-way togetherness in a family car with plastic seats and no air conditioning to see the sights and look at the animals. Those trips left Claypool with an itch for the outdoors.

Claypool is a union pipefitter and the son of a pipefitter. His father taught him life around big steel. Chewing, scratching, pulling his own weight. Looking out for the other guy. Pipes an 18-wheeler can drive through. Hundred-ton tanks. Pumps, oil fields, refineries, power houses, chemical plants. "Pipefitter" is a blue collar job. A dangerous blue collar job, at that.

"I've seen men get electrocuted and some others fall and get crushed to death," Claypool says matter-of-factly. "You have to be careful all the time. A lot of time, there isn't any margin for screw-ups. For instance, it can take three weeks just to set up the move of a 100-ton turbine from a rail car to its cement platform."

From his dad, Claypool learned how to act around other tough, sweaty pipefitters. It's not a whiny bunch. He learned to work hard. It's man's work, intense and demanding, but it's a job with a little flexibility, too. While there is no secretary waiting with a mug of hot coffee, Claypool may start work in January and quit altogether when hunting season rolls around.

Claypool's father also taught him about the outdoors. Fishing was how Claypool, Senior got away from it all. Claypool picked up hunting on his own. When he discovered archery, he couldn't get enough of stalking white-tails in the hills of eastern Oklahoma.

Eddie Claypool is a self-described "elk-aholic" and he indulges his elk hunting passions in the Sangre de Cristo Mountain Range in southern Colorado at every turn. His trips often result in taking a bull elk, sometimes large and sometimes small, but whether or not he kills an elk, he says that every drive is worth the effort.

"In the '70s, there weren't many bowhunters out here," he recalls. "That's sure changed."

The venue for Claypool's lonely death was established by a rough-and-tumble upbringing and those relentless family vacations. He left home without telling anyone where he was going. He didn't leave a note or map.

"They'll understand."

The trip harbored more than its share of potential disaster. Like country boys daring each other to pee over an electrified fence, sooner or later somebody was bound to get hurt.

It's a monotonous 700-mile drive from Chouteau, Oklahoma, to the elk pastures in the Sangre de Cristo Mountains, especially alone, driving straight through. By the time he stopped the truck that day in 1989, it was afternoon and Claypool was already tired.

Glancing at his watch, Claypool took a deep breath, slammed the door of the truck, picked up his bow and headed straight up a mountain outside Alamosa, Colorado. He could have taken the easier but longer path around, but that would have taken too long, and after all those miles in the pick-up, he was impatient for action.

Maybe the fact that he was tired when he started explains why he refused to quit when he eventually reached the limits of his endurance. A more alert climber would have been aware of danger. Hours later, the realization dawned that he was going to die and that dying broken and alone on a mountain, clutching his bow to his chest, was not going to be romantic. It looked, in fact, like it was going to be extremely unpleasant.

"A climbing party of three is minimum," write The Mountaineers in the fifth edition of Mountaineering. And that's just the first rule Claypool broke.

The Sangre de Cristos are part of the eastern ramparts of the Rocky Mountains. They run north-south through Colorado, from Denver to Santa Fe, New Mexico, bordering the breathless immensity of the Great Plains. High, wild and dry, oil company geologists, free climbers, and spelunkers refer to them as "unexpectedly precipitous."

Claypool was alone in the Sangre de Cristos that August day when he fell to his death. He is a trophy bowhunter by avocation, a true "born-again bowhunter," and elk bone is his ultimate passion. Claypool had just driven 12 hours alone, as fast as he could, so that he could spend two days hunting elk. He planned to hunt every minute of daylight and then, 48 hours after arriving in Alamosa, drive 12 sleepless hours home.

To give him credit, he did not start out to go climbing. The first evening, he would be scouting, looking for a herd; searching for natural approaches like rockslides or sleeves of timber that would let him set up an ambush within 30 or 40 yards. He would be studying the terrain for concealment before he bugled

Lest you believe Eddie Claypool is only an elk hunter, the Oklahoma pipefitter also thrives on other bowhunting challenges, including big whitetail bucks.

and chirped. He did not start out to go climbing, it just ended up that way–with an out-of-body experience included. He carried his bow just in case . . .

The mountaineering handbook recommends a lot of things Claypool didn't bother with, so full of passion and bustin'-out-all-over "time-waits-for-no-man" energy was he. "Rope up on all exposed places." He didn't have a rope. "Never climb beyond your ability and knowledge." Pshaw. "Never let judgment be overruled by desire when choosing the route or deciding whether to turn back." Do they think they're dealing with librarians? "Leave the trip schedule with a responsible person." Old lady librarians at that!

Claypool set out on a hike and ended up in a mad scramble for his life. He didn't have a map or a compass; spare food, or water or flares; not even a first-aid kit. He should have died at the bottom of that mountain, but he did not. It was just dumb luck that kept him off the rocks.

Maybe his shoes saved him. Claypool hunts in lightweight, soccer-style "tennis" shoes. They have a soft, gripping rubber sole, especially at the toes. Toes are important in a steep free climb; strong, nimble toes. Then again, maybe living to tell about his climb did not have a whole lot to do with his shoes.

Maybe adrenaline saved Claypool. Adrenaline is a powerful chemical. It causes your heart to race and blood pressure to skyrocket. Ounce for ounce, adrenaline is the body's equivalent of white lightning.

Bowhunters know about adrenaline. It is what causes a mature, 200-pound man who has a family and a high-pressure job to tremble uncontrollably when a trophy buck stands just out of bow range, snorting and stamping its feet.

At times, hanging on the side of that mountain, Claypool's "stomach felt like it had butterflies." That was the effect of adrenaline and it saved Claypool's life. Adrenaline and a sheer stubborn-headed "beat your head against it until it falls down" stubbornness that good pipefitters possess in abundance.

The bowhunter wanted a shortcut up the mountain. Rather than climb the long, slow, safe route up the wooded slope, around the boulder field, and through the blow-downs, the Okie pipefitter looked up the steep slope from his Ford pick-up truck and decided that he would go right straight up.

Anyone who climbs or hikes in mountains learns that when you do need to go straight up, the best way is some form of zig zag. It saves energy, saves your legs, and saves your lungs. This climbing technique does not cause the avalanche of loose stones that can actually reach up the slope like a surging wave and undercut the climber, burying him beneath thousands of tons of sand and rock. Claypool didn't know that.

With nothing but his fanny pack and bow, Claypool slammed the door of the truck and took off at a frantic pace, more of a run than a walk. His objective was to glass for elk before twilight and, even Claypool understood, still leave some light for his return. Experience had taught him that the hour before dark was his best chance to catch the big ungulates moving out of the dark fir and thick stands of aspen into the open meadows. He was not worried about finding his way back. Like so many other possibilities, in his enthusiasm, he hardly gave it a thought.

Hunting at timberline can be an exhilarating, lonely, and exhausting experience, especially alone. At that altitude, the oxygen is thin. You suck in a lot more air to burn fuel than at lower altitudes, so you tire easily. Above timberline, the world changes. Comfortable, familiar environs quietly turn hostile. Except when it is near the horizon, the sun stares down unblinking and virtually colorless. A few stunted trees mark the boundary between life, as you know it in Choteau or Peoria, and the utter, barren waste of boulder fields clad only in primordial mosses and lichen. And there is the wind, always the wind. At 12,000 feet, the elements are perfectly harmonious and absolutely unforgiving.

If you are hunting alone above timberline and anything goes wrong, anything at all, no one is coming along to help, not ever. The utter isolation of the elements in the wilderness is overwhelming in the wind and the sun and the cold. There is no "alone" that is quite so lonely as timberline, except perhaps in a small boat on the ocean, and you are tempted to make promises of the "I'll do anything if . . ." variety.

If you are alone and kill an elk above timberline, the job of field dressing and quartering, caping, and hauling is also yours alone. And unless the weather is cold, the carcass will immediately attract a swarm of stinging, egg-laying insects.

At 800 or more pounds, adult elk are huge animals. You face miles of hiking with a heavy pack frame–you did remember to bring the frame, right? Otherwise you will not make it–and the promise of bears and coyotes and cougars, all interested in a free meal.

After the first trip carrying the heavy antlers and cape, all of the adrenaline from your successful shot, the blood trailing, and the photo taking has worn off. You are ready to call it a day. Nevertheless, you do the right thing and leave your bow behind to concentrate on the hindquarters; one trip each. You would not be human if you did not think, once at least, "That's enough! Leave the rest for the critters." And this on a well-planned trip.

"It is easy to get in trouble in the Sangre de Cristos," says Colorado wildlife biologist Dave Kenvin. "It's a long, narrow range of mountains. Dry and very steep. They range from 7,000 to 14,000 feet and I guess they are about the toughest mountains in the state."

Kenvin was a Colorado game warden for 20 years and remembers being called often for rescue duty. "Sometimes hunters, but usually mountain climbers," he remembers. "Sometimes we even got them out alive."

Dave Kenvin notes that in Colorado, visitors can buy a hunting permit over the counter. "We see people who drive all night to go hunting just for a day or so," he says, as if he knows Eddie Claypool. "They pick up their license and head right out. They go hard, really push themselves all weekend and drive home just in time to change clothes and go to work. Mostly younger people, young and tough."

Claypool was climbing like mad when his soccer-style tennis shoes slipped the first time. "Clumsy Okie flat-lander," he laughed. Hard on himself. Never a break. That was the roughneck way.

He cinched the fanny pack tighter and slung the bow uncomfortably over his shoulder. Grabbing roots and pushing off rocks kept him going up until he sensed that the angle of his climb was becoming awfully steep. Some automatic response, the balancing mechanisms in his inner ears maybe, adjusted his body to a smaller angle with the slope and he kept pumping. In those days, he had legs of steel, muscles as hard as the rock they were climbing.

"I felt like I'd been climbing for an hour, but it must have been more like 30 minutes when I looked around and there was the truck, way down below me, a tiny little spec. It seemed like it was right under me, like if I let loose, I'd fall right on top of it. I wondered how that could be. I looked up and couldn't see where I was going, so I just kept grabbing stuff and going up."

Thinking about elk in a green mountain meadow or in the ragged woods below timberline, Claypool continued fighting his way up. He reached and hauled and tried to make himself comfortable, with the bowstring pinching his shoulder, and at some point, his tennis shoes lost their traction. His hands and arms bore most of his weight, even though the strain on his hard pipefitter muscles was considerable.

He was easily 1,000 feet above the truck and half a mile distant longitudinally, climbing on a steep angle of loose soil and small rocks. Unstable and vegetation-free, except for scrub juniper and odd species of pink and orange mosses, Claypool felt like he was climbing in powder, without a solid toe- or finger-hold. One step up and a breathless, but thankfully short slide back.

Claypool hung there, suspended in space, like a spider caught in the open, waiting for a shoe to fall.

When he glanced around, the hair on his neck and arms stood up and he felt a chill. There was nothing below him except empty space. The slope he was climbing had disappeared. When he looked up, the mountain seemed to curve outward and merge, at some unfathomable distance, into blue sky and white, fluffy clouds. It was impossible, and that vertigo was the loneliest and most disorienting feeling he ever experienced.

With his face pressed into the dirt next to the bottom cam of his bow and his fingernails straining and digging for a hold, it occurred to Claypool that he had screwed up. For a moment, he regretted all those years of dare-devil histrionics. The showing off. The testosterone high after diving off train tracks the second before a speeding locomotive would have obliterat-ed him. Was it worth it, the need to prove himself in a tough, take-no-pris-oners crowd of steel workers and roughnecks? There was no one to watch him now, no one to slap him on the back when or if he made it. There was no one to understand and share the fear that began to well up inside him. No one to calculate the probability that he might die because he was so damn impatient.

He needed to be mindful of the time, because to his left the light was thinner as the sun dipped toward not-so-distant peaks. Claypool had always been in a hurry. It was his style. Fast Eddie. Pressing the limits. Impatient unless he was stretching himself, straining to break some rule, setting a "personal best." A faster car. A bigger bull. Now, when he had least expect-ed it, the bill for all that fun was presented for payment.

Claypool glanced down and realized that he could not save himself by going back. That would require a slow delicacy of movement or perhaps suddenly flipping his body 180 degrees to face out from the cliff for one long, controlled (he hoped) slide. He could not possibly do it. He would surely slip into an unmanageable fall or start a landslide, and he did not know about landslides, except it was a sure way to die. He did not have an interest in being buried alive.

Twisting to his opposite side, he looked up. The mountain seemed massive. Sullen and glowering, it was growing, sliding outward in a fright-ening arc above him. He could see it moving. A reverse climb might save him, pitons, ropes ... and all of it useless in the talus. Anyway, that was gear and experience he did not have. Going up was as impossible as going down.

As strong as Claypool was, he was not sure he had the strength to make the right decision. Every time he moved, the slope crumbled and he began to slide, sometimes just a quarter inch or a half inch, but the inexorable monotony of it began to terrify him. Like a dream where you fall but never actually hit the ground, or the pipefitter's special dream, where the black pipe as big as your house breaks its chains and ever-so-slowly begins to roll, and you cannot move out of the way.

Starved for oxygen, the muscles in his hands and feet ached. More than half of the bones of the body are in the hands and feet, and on this August afternoon, Claypool was straining them all to the snapping point.

He was trapped and he knew it, so he froze, clinging to that impossible slope. Just for a moment, he thought of home and the other passions in his reckless, self-absorbed life: his little girl, his wife, his work. But he was beyond "reasonable sensibilities."

He pressed his body tighter than ever against the mountain and held on.

He thought about dropping the bow, but he could not bring himself to do that. Breathing through his mouth, he gasped at the thin air almost 12,000 feet above sea level. His gloveless fingertips were bleeding.

Claypool does not recall how long he hung there. His mind conjured up images of a helicopter rescue and angels hovering around him. When he imagined the soft hands of God cupped beneath him, he darn near relaxed and let go. Still, every time he opened his eyes, there was nothing to see except the same blur of scree. He was too close to it to focus.

So Claypool prayed. He rested his forehead against the rock and begged for strength. At some point during that whispered invocation, he realized that if he was going to live, he would have to rescue himself. He would have to get moving no matter how frightened he was.

"I was shaking and afraid," Claypool recalls. "Somewhere there, I faced a death spirit eye to eye. I saw it and it did not blink. It was hair raising. How I got a grip and did not freeze up and die on that mountain, I don't know, but I did. It must have been God's work, because I sincerely believe I looked right at death, looked in its face and accepted that I was going to die up there."

Claypool gave up, but he didn't quit. Death was one thing; dying was something else. Death was oblivion; dying was a painful process and he didn't want anything to do with it. Not when there were still elk on the mountain.

He edged his left hand upward and groped blindly for a hold. The bowstring scraped in the scree, but he could not take care of it. If it broke and fell, well, he would buy another one.

With his face and body pressed tight against the slope, it was an enormous strain feeling for a spot without looking up. It was as if he were shaving with a straight razor, using a mirror that was ten feet away, and there were not many spots. Testing every niche against his weight, at first just a little and then with all of his 175 pounds, he slowly eased his right foot upward a few inches and dug in with the toes of his tennis shoes. Dirt and gravel cascaded down his shirt.

It was excruciatingly slow. He found tiny rocks that would hold his weight. Thin, miraculous little ledges of just a couple inches allowed him to take the strain off his bleeding knees and fingers. Narrow crevices allowed him to jam his toes inside for leverage. And finally, Claypool stopped looking down, stopped being afraid.

At the first pink of sunset, Claypool thought he would have to hang on the cliff all night. The going was so slow that his muscles were cramping. One serious cramp, a cramp in the major muscle of his calf or the arch of his foot and he might tumble down the cliff, squealing like a rabbit in the jaws of a coyote. One bad cramp and he was done-for. The air was cold now near timberline and he could feel his strength and will ebbing. He would never last through the night.

Then, without actually seeing it he sensed a narrow ledge just above him, almost within reach. A narrow slice of salvation. Not quite a walkway, but it was all Claypool needed. Incredibly, Claypool took an elk from a mountain meadow on that hunt. Black and blue and aching from the strain of the climb, his shoulders responded when called on to draw and make the trophy shot. Claypool could have done that with a recurve or a longbow, because he is committed to trophy hunting and elk are his passion.

Claypool believes that the man makes the bow. The bow only completes man the hunter and whatever style you choose to shoot, there is a superior bow choice available. A compound offers terrific engineering advantages, but a traditional bow is beautiful in its simplicity and will get the job done, too.

THE COMPOUND BOW

Today, most bowhunters shoot compound bows. Indeed, we tend to think of ourselves as "normal." This has not always been the case, though. Even now, thousands of bowhunters still enjoy the "hunting the hard way" challenge with traditional bows.

If Claypool had been hunting with a traditional takedown recurve that day, when he found himself overmatched by the Colorado precipice, he might have been able to take it apart and fold the limbs, riser and bowstring into his backpack. It would have made climbing a whole lot easier.

LET-OFF

There is no difference between a compound bow and a longbow . . . at least at the simplest level of design. They are both springs built to propel an object forward through the air.

Otherwise, the difference between compounds and all other bows is pronounced. A compound bow uses cams and cables to reduce the effort required to pull the string to full draw and hold it there while you sight at your target. This reduced effort is let-off. It allows you to draw and hold a compound much longer than you could hold a longbow or a recurve, which have no let-off.

Let-off is the key to understanding how a compound bow works and why this kind of bow is so popular. The cams near the limb tips of a compound bow act like pulleys. They allow you to hold a compound at full draw using less force than the bow's rated draw weight.

Begin with an average 65-pound draw weight bow, with a cam system that advertises 75percent let-off. You need to pull back the full 65 pounds of weight, but when you do, the cam or cams roll over and you are left holding only 25 percent of 65 pounds or 16 1/4 pounds at full draw. Most adults can hold that

Over the years, several companies have promoted an angled grip styling on the theory that when you naturally extend your arm and hand (with nothing in it), you realize that your hand and grip are not vertical. A right-hander will naturally have a clockwise tilt and a left-hander will have a counterclockwise tilt. Several bow manufacturers have introduced machined risers with arrow shelf cut-outs or offsets based on this concept, calling it a natural or ergonomic grip. The bow pictured is an older style McPherson Annihilator. (This mimics the "cant" or tilt of a longbow, where the arrow lays not on the horizontal shelf, but more in the "V" between the shelf and the riser. Shooting with feathers rather than plastic vanes minimizes deflection of your arrow off the bow riser.)

amount of weight for some time while they steady their breathing, select the proper sight pin and slowly squeeze the trigger of their release aid. Of course, you must still pull through the peak weight of 65 pounds, and that can be prolonged on some high-energy speed bows, but it nevertheless takes only a few moments before you reach full draw and peak let-off.

By comparison, to pull and hold your 65-pound recurve at full draw takes a continuous 65-pound effort. Neither recurves nor longbows have let-off, and holding one of them at 65 pounds for any length of time without shaking, and while maintaining a steady sight picture, is a difficult task, even for a strong person. Traditional bowhunters typically release the string almost immediately upon reaching full draw.

Cam design determines the reduction in draw force. In the early 2000s, 33 percent let-off was standard and 50 percent was thought to be the limit at which a bow would provide quality performance. Indeed, 50 percent let-off seemed high in its day.

Designs and materials have improved since then. Now, bows with let-off as high as 80 and 85 percent are common and, in the right hands, can achieve consistent, high-quality shooting performance. Compound bows with high let-off sell better than bows with low let-off, perhaps four-to-one. Today, the average bow is sold with 75 percent let-off, and manufacturers make optional modules for 65 and even 85 percent let-off. Some manufacturers include them with a bow purchase and others sell them as optional accessories.

When you are considering the purchase of a compound bow, you should be aware that some states, lobbied by advocates in the traditional archery camp, have adopted limits to let-off in the same manner that they have occasionally limited electronic shooting and hunting aids.

The Carbon G3 from Hoyt Archery is a good example of the trend to lower holding weights. Just 31.5 inches axle-to-axle with a 6.75-inch brace height, this 332 fps (ATA rated) speed bow is sold with their RKT Cam & 1/2 that gives about 80 percent letoff. You can buy a Carbon G3 in eight color and camo options.

Once you reach full draw, a bow with a lower holding weight is easier to aim and shoot effectively. That is conventional wisdom and it is true to a point, but high let-off bows are under such stress that they tend to be finicky with sharp draw-force curves. This means that if you allow the string to creep forward only slightly, your cams will want to snap over and let the arrow go immediately!

With a low let-off bow, say 50 or 65 percent, it is relatively easy to let down, not shoot an arrow after you come to full draw. You will feel the cams snap over and the bow will give your arm a jerk, but the strain is manageable. Let down a high let-off bow, however, and you should be prepared for a couple of difficult moments wrestling with the string. Hold the string securely with your fingers and consciously move your finger or thumb away from your release trigger or you could dry fire your bow. If you dry fire, you could damage it beyond repair and void your warranty.

Just like the precise grain weight of individual broadheads in a pack of three, let-off will not be an exact figure on most compound bows. It will vary slightly depending upon the modular arrangement of a bow's cam (or cams), your draw weight and draw length and the amount of string and cable stretch. Let-off may vary as much as seven percent above or below the advertised rating. So if you test your Bowtech Insanity CPXL on an accurate bow scale and find that your expected holding weight varies by half a pound or so when you ramp it up from 60 to 70 pounds, remember that this is essentially a normal condition of compounds.

ONE-CAM, TWO-CAM

For perhaps 25 years, from the moment Holless W. Allen applied for his patent in the late 1960s, bows with top and bottom cams were "normal." These wheels or irregularly shaped cams were machined or molded as mirror images of one another. Beginning in the 1990s, this twin-cam design fell out of popularity.

In about 1990, Matt McPherson's one-cam bow revolution gained momentum. His one-cam bows had a single, eccentrically shaped, machined cam on the bottom limb and a perfectly round, balance wheel, called an idler, on the top limb. This revolution was so complete that all manufacturers have produced one-cam bow designs. For a few years recently, it was difficult to find a high-performance twin-cam bow. Around 2005, at companies like Hoyt and PSE, twin-cam ("cam and a half") designs are quietly beginning to again dominate the line-up.

Although the one-cam revolution made most twin-cam bows seem obsolete, they were not without performance kinks. One-cam bows were slower than twin-cam bows and nock travel was inconsistent. Upon release, the nock and bowstring should thrust an arrow forward in a straight line. It took archery engineers several years to work through these difficulties, but today, one-cam shooting systems have "arrived" in both speed and consistency of performance.

Why did many bowhunters believe the one-cam bow was better than the twin-cam bow? With twin-cam bows, cams must turn synchronously to prevent the nock point locator, against which your arrow clips, from moving forward in an uneven manner. Synchronous cam movement is called "timing." On out-of-time twin-cam bows, the nock point locator moves forward through the power stroke with a wave motion, up and down. This provides less than excellent propulsion to your arrow, which flies erratically and takes longer to stabilize in flight.

In the early '90s, timing problems on were exacerbated on twin-cam bows as all-synthetic strings and cables replaced Dacron bowstrings and plastic-coated steel cables. Using materials like the early versions of FastFlight, all-synthetic systems may indeed have been "stronger than steel," but steel does not stretch. These new synthetic materials did stretch, and that compounded the difficulty of achieving straight-line nock travel.

One-cam bows eliminated these timing problems. If there was only one cam on the lower limb and a round idler on the top limb, obviously there could not be a problem synchronizing roll-over. By definition, a one-cam bow cannot go out of time with itself. (The wheel or idler on the top limb of a one-cam bow does not just provide a rolling surface with minimal friction, although that is important. It helps insure balanced limb action and straight-line nock and arrow travel.)

Today, many bowhunters have concluded that the nock-point-travel controversy was exaggerated. It may have been significant among competition archers, where the difference between winning and losing can be the breadth of a hair at 35 yards, and "line cutters" or fat shafts are often preferred to thinner arrows for that reason. This kind of shooting precision is impossible to achieve in the field and is not necessary in actual hunting conditions.

Why then do you visit a mass merchant and find two-cam bows in boxes on their shelves, when you and most friends bought one-cam bows from a sporting goods store? Mass merchants deliver a huge volume of goods effectively, but at lower prices because they provide no service, support or advice that is trustworthy beyond the simplest concepts. As demand for twin-cam bows declined, the price that manufacturers could command for them fell. Enter the useful mass merchant.

Traditionally, there have been three wheel or cam styles for twin-cam bows. In the early '80s, manufacturers built bows with precisely round wheels and simply offset the axle holes from the center to imitate lobed cams and give you let-off. In the mid to late 1980s, wheels were largely supplanted–except on entry-level compounds–by more powerful oblong cams which often had dramatic lobes and cutouts, and which delivered greater arrow speed. Because the rim of a cam has two tracks–one for your bowstring and the other for your cable–you could describe a bow as having soft, medium or hard cams, depending on their shape and expected performance, and you would be understood on shooting ranges and in pro shops across the continent.

SOFT CAMS: These cams are often called energy wheels. They have a round lobe over which the bowstring travels in its groove, and a smooth but irregularly shaped lobe for the cable in its groove. On energy wheels, the rounded string lobe is what gives you the smooth, easy pull. The oval cable lobe lets you wring more speed from your bow than a fully rounded lobe. According to archery engineering expert Norb Mullaney, soft cams store about one foot-pound (ft-lb) of energy for each pound of draw weight. This means a 70-pound bow stores about 70 ft-lb of kinetic energy. That is enough to win 3-D competitions and to hunt big game.

MEDIUM CAMS: Both string and cable sides of these cams have oval lobes. These cams are more dynamic, but they still allow a relatively smooth draw. Medium cams allow more energy storage and more speed than energy wheels. As a general rule, Mullaney says, medium cams store approximately 1 1/4 ft-lb of energy for each pound of peak weight. Consequently, your 70-pound bow stores around 87.5 ft-lb of energy.

HARD CAMS: Think of hard cams as hatchet cams because they have a severely elliptical shape or lobe on both the bowstring and cable sides. Archery engineer Mullaney says these cams can potentially store as much as 1 1/2 ft-lb of energy per pound of draw weight, if properly tuned. With hatchet cams, your 70-pound bow can potentially store more than 100 ft-lb of energy. Twin-cam bows built with two hatchet cams can be very fast. They can also be very difficult to shoot well, and so they are not recommended for beginners.

UNDERSTANDING A DRAW FORCE CURVE

An engineering drawing called a draw force curve represents the total stored energy in a compound bow from its rest position to full draw . . . and even beyond. It also represents the increasing muscle strength you need as you pull to full draw; how far you must pull at peak draw weight; and how rapidly the bow lets-off and by how much.

On the horizontal X-axis, a draw force curve plots inches of draw length, while on the vertical Y-axis it shows pounds of draw weight. The area beneath the resulting curve (and you can construct a draw force curve for any bow) is

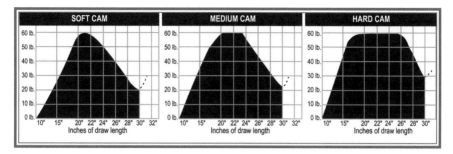

Force draw (or draw force) curves tell us a number of things about our bows. They give us a pictorial representation of the energy our bow stores at full draw, the point at which our cam reaches peak draw, at which it begins the let-off and the valley at our given draw length. The above diagrams represent hypothetical bows.

the total stored energy or foot-pounds (ft-lbs) that could possibly be sunk into your arrow when you shoot. No bow actually imparts 100 percent of its stored energy to an arrow, but the more efficient your set-up is, the greater the percentage of energy transferred and the greater your broadhead's impact power.

The effort required to draw a bow with energy wheels or soft cams builds gradually, peaks sharply and then slides gradually into the "valley," the point where the holding weight is least and let-off is maximized. Acclaimed archery entertainer and trick-shot artist Bob Markworth shoots a bow with this style soft cam at a low draw weight because it is easy for him to manage as he shoots balloons out of his assistant's hand!

You can draw any compound bow beyond its valley, but it is not recommended. Pulling up the back of the valley, or against "the wall" as it is called, causes the bow to shoot inefficiently as thrust against your arrow increases, then decreases, and at last increases again before it leaves the string. This herky-jerky motion does not promote smooth arrow flight.

With hard cams, your drawing effort will increase sharply, last perhaps for 10 inches at peak weight, and then drop rapidly into a short, steep valley. Unlike a bow with soft cams that drop you smoothly into the valley, if you are unused to shooting a hard cam, you will feel a distinct and unpleasant jerk when a hard cam drops into its valley.

What this means is that bows with hard cams require greater and more prolonged effort to pull to full draw or to draw through the draw force cycle. Bows equipped with medium cams, fall somewhere between the two twin-cam extremes of soft, round cam, and hard cam.

Hard cams typically give you greater arrow speed than soft cams, but for the reasons mentioned above, many bowhunters find them less pleasant and more difficult to shoot accurately, especially if trophy deer cause even the slightest buck fever. A hard cam's short valley, a couple inches or so, demands that you hold the bow at full draw with discipline. The slightest bit of let-down or anticipation can either cause you to release prematurely or else change the arrow's impact point by several inches, even at short range. Beyond a short-range shot, that is enough to miss completely.

Increased speed causes quite a few problems. Fast bows are more temperamental than slower ones. Slight flaws in your release are exaggerated by the manner in which your arrow absorbs energy. In other words, "columnar loading" (the mechanics of applying an energy vector only to the base of an arrow shaft rather than unevenly throughout its length) initially makes the nock end of your arrow want to fly faster than your broadhead end!

Finally, without attention to dampening the noise of a shot, a well-tuned hard-cam bow will be noisier than a soft-cam bow. Why? Hard, angular cams transmit a greater amount of energy to your arrow . . . but also to the bow. This causes vibration, noisy vibration, and what is known as "riser buzz" and "tennis elbow."

Because it is a high-energy system and leaves some of that energy within your arm and the bow after a shot, a fast, radical, hard-cam bow built with a single-cam or twin-cams requires continuous maintenance and tuning. So, if spending time paper-tuning your equipment and checking it regularly at your work bench is not a problem for you, a hard-cam bow may be just right. For long shots at unknown distances, the increased arrow speed and flatter trajectory of hard-cam bows certainly offer advantages. Again, expect that the trade-off is more time spent tuning your set-up.

The average bowhunter who limits himself or herself to 20 or 30 yard shots will probably be more successful and perhaps happier, too, with a soft- or a medium-cam bow. Although they will launch arrows slower, they are quieter, smoother-shooting and easier to keep tuned.

YOUR BOW'S PARTS
(AND THEIR ROLE IN SUCCESSFUL ARROW LAUNCH)

THE RISER

The central section of a bow is its riser or handle. Your bow hand serves as a pivot, linking the riser's stability and the potential energy in the connected system to your muscles. The riser or handle is the mechanical basis of your shooting system and your shooting success. Besides a handgrip, it provides anchor points for the bow limbs or their mounting brackets, and mounting holes for accessories such as your arrow rest, cable guard, stabilizer, sights and perhaps some silencing elements as well.

More than 90 percent of all adult hunting bows have risers that are machined from a solid bar of aluminum. The aluminum in your bow riser may originally have been soda cans or aluminum window frames, because a high percentage of today's aluminum is recycled. Do not worry, though, as these recycled aluminum bars are identical in composition and properties to a virgin billet.

Wood and then magnesium were the original choice for bow risers. Holless Allen, the man who patented the compound bow, built his risers from wood. Wood has been readily available and it is easy to work. It has a warm feel, and laminated wood risers are beautiful. Today, wood has virtually disappeared from the compound-bow market, replaced by various metals and even carbon composite.

Tom Jennings immediately understood the potential of Allen's ideas. After he negotiated with Allen for a license, he began manufacturing and enthusiastically promoting compounds, earning the title "Father of the Compound Bow." Jennings experimented with wood, but moved quickly into production with metal risers because of metal's inherent strength and internal consistency.

Die-cast magnesium dominated the handle market for practically 20 years. It is light in weight and very durable. Nevertheless, molds for magnesium handles have been excessively expensive and only a few foundries would manufacture bow handles for the industry, which is, after all, quite small. The time between the initial order and getting a bow to a pro shop's shelf was also excessive. Therefore, once a manufacturer settled a bow design, it was betting that it would sell enough bows to pay for the mold, plus manufacturing, promotion and administration expenses . . . and still make a profit.

Except in the traditional field and with very rare exceptions, aluminum

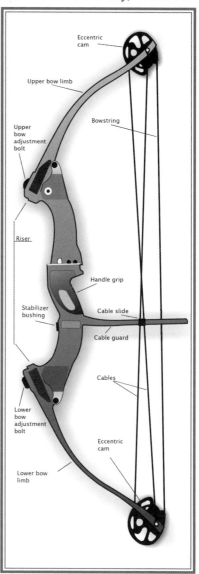

Eccentric cam

Upper bow limb

Bowstring

Upper bow adjustment bolt

Riser

Handle grip

Stabilizer bushing

Cable slide

Cable guard

Cables

Lower bow adjustment bolt

Eccentric cam

Lower bow limb

risers rule. With a programmable CNC cutting machine, the entire bow (except perhaps for the fiberglass limbs, and several companies now manufacture their own limbs, too) can be built in the manufacturer's own facility, rather than buying cams from Oklahoma and magnesium risers from Michigan. These milling machines are expensive, but bow-handle designs may be changed daily if necessary to stay abreast of customer demand and no molds are required.

Although some new risers have features of two styles, bow risers are either straight, or reflexed, or deflexed. On straight handles, the limb pockets at the top and bottom of the riser lie in a direct line with the handle. You can place a straight edge on the limb pocket screws, for instance, and they will fall in line with the riser grip pivot point. On deflexed bows, the limb pockets are designed behind the grip; the riser bends out and away from the shooter, thereby giving a long brace height. On reflexed bows, the limb pockets are out in front of the handle so that the center of the bow arcs backward, toward the shooter. At one time, this gave shooters short brace-height bows, but with the advent of parallel limb designs, the brace heights can be quite long even on short axle-to-axle bows.

Compounds with deflex risers are generally reserved for beginner bows or bows for recreational shooters. The Fred Bear Brave Warrior, a true beginner bow, has this styling. With higher brace heights, deflex-handle bows are popular starter bows. They are easy to tune, easy to shoot, easy to learn with and more forgiving of novice errors in form. They are also slow, however, often launching arrows at 200 fps or even less (in the case of a starter bow, sometimes far less). A high brace height contributes to introductory ease by giving arrows a little more time–and we are talking milliseconds–to straighten out before the arrow nock leaves the string and passes by or through the arrow rest. On their own, deflexed bows will usually tip back toward the shooter's face after a shot, and for this reason alone, most people shooting deflex-handle bows need a stabilizer to regulate the bow's in-hand balance.

While some very short bow designs defy the accepted rules because of the advent of "parallel limb technology," bows built with straight or reflexed handles typically have lower brace heights than bows with deflexed handles. (Measure brace height from the curvature of the grip, the grip pivot point, between the thumb and forefinger to the string when the bow is at rest.) Some highly reflexed, short-limbed bows have brace heights less than six inches, compared to straight bows with brace heights of seven to eight inches. Traditionally, straight- and reflexed-handle bows are faster than the deflex species.

Bow engineers are now able to give bowhunters the forgiveness of a

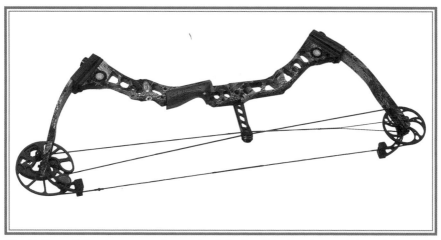

The Mathews Outback was a good example of significant design changes in bows in the early 2000s. It is short (31 1/2 inches, axle to axle) and fast (rated by Mathews at 308 fps IBO). Multiple let-offs are available: 80 and 65%. This bow's short limbs have moved toward a parallel and horizontal position. Harmonic dampening elements are incorporated into the riser and the string suppressors at cam and wheel to diminish string oscillation: both help reduce noise and vibration. The Mathews approach to preventing interference between the arrow fletching and the cables is a new style, high-mounted ball bearing-mounted roller guard.

longer brace height and the speed that comes with a dramatically reflexed handle. One such bow, the Mathews Outback measured a scant 31 1/2 inches axle-to-axle, but this reflexed riser bow is rated at 308 fps IBO with a remarkable 7 5/8-inch brace height. The Mathews team designed the riser to accept very short limbs, Mathews "most parallel limbs ever," by increasing the take-off angle in the riser's machined limb pockets.

Bows with low brace height are typically faster because, although it sounds counter intuitive, they have longer power strokes. The arrow stays longer on the string and accepts or loads a greater amount of energy. For example, the 38-inch axle-to-axle Mathews Conquest Apex 7 has a superior320 fps speed rating (70 pounds, 30 inches, 65 percent let-off, 350-gr. non-fletched arrow) while its brace height is a full 7 inches. A bow like the Conquest with a 30-inch draw length and a 7-inch brace height will have a power stroke three inches longer than a deflex-handle bow with a nine-inch brace height. A power stroke that much longer will shoot significantly faster.

A bow with even a slightly reflexed riser and higher limb take-off angles, has the benefit of greater arrow speed. Reflexed and straight risers also have excellent balance in your hand. To say that they will remain standing straight up in your hand following a shot or even tip forward slightly–which would be ideal–without the use of a stabilizer is straining to make a point, but their tendency to swing back quickly and pop you in the eye is lessened.

Bow mechanics once claimed that low brace heights of reflexed bows reduced the stability of your arrow, because the arrow "has less time to straighten out in the time between leaving the string and clearing the arrow rest." This is no longer the rule. Recent bow and cam designs have moved tirelessly in the direction of rapidly stabilizing arrows.

Not long ago, many bow risers were machined with an exaggerated offset or a "cut-out" by the arrow shelf because bowhunters used overdraws. Overdraws were an intermediate solution to arrow speed, allowing bowhunters to shoot shorter, lighter and therefore faster arrows, before manufacturers caught up with consumer demand.

The former AR series aluminum risers from Archery Research, a former division of PSE, moved in this machining direction. With an overdraw, short arrows and broadheads that normally extended an inch in front of the handle were being drawn behind the shooter's hand. Very short arrows with less weight and faster speed was the theory. (Sometimes, the broadhead was even drawn behind the bow riser in line with the shooter's wrist, a very tricky and dangerous set-up.) Offset-riser designs gave bowhunters a great deal of leeway to adjust for centershot and assured broadhead and fletching clearance.

Today, with increasingly sophisticated short, fast bow designs, offset risers are less important and manufacturers have moved away from them. In addition, a deep offset challenges the material strength of a 6061-T6 machined aluminum riser.

Above the riser's arrow shelf is the sight window. You aim through this zone. For 20 years, the rule was, short axle-to-axle bows have short sight windows and longer bows have longer sight windows. This often forced archers who shot with sights to change their anchor so they could see their top pins. The design principle has changed. One such bow had a full, eight-inch sight window even though it was only 34 inches axle-to-axle. If you anchor below your chin and your peep sight is served high, six inches or more above the nocking point, you could have difficulty using a pin sight on a short bow. When shopping for a bow, verify that you have selected one with a sight window that will not obscure your top sight pins, the very ones you most need for those close, 20-yard shots.

When you anchor at the corner of your mouth or above, this effectively moves your peep downward on the string toward the nock point. In this instance, then, you can probably manage with a short sight window. With a release, you can theoretically anchor anywhere as long as your peep and pins are in perfect alignment and wherever you choose to anchor does not change from shot to shot.

THE UNDER-APPRECIATED GRIP

Randy Ulmer is a terrific bowhunter and a world-class 3-D champion. Placing your hand on the grip, Ulmer says, is one of the most important and

Whether you prefer a grip that is thinner or thicker, to shoot consistently and accurately, you must position your hand exactly every time you draw. Many bowhunters and 3-D competitors prefer to remove the grip supplied by the manufacturer and hold their bow with their hand on its aluminum keel, perhaps wrapping the keel with leather or moleskin for warmth and so that it will not slip against their skin.

least understood steps in shooting a bow well. The primary pressure point between you and the bow is the grip, and it should be perfectly in-line with the center of the two bones of your forearm.

What's more, Ulmer says, you can easily locate the exact spot. "Bend the wrist of your bow hand slightly and use the index finger of your other hand to press firmly on the palm at various points. Stay relaxed. Your wrist will fold or hinge when you press on every spot except the one that is perfectly in line with the forearm. That is the point that should feel the greatest contact pressure against the grip at full draw. Any other hand position is more likely to introduce tension and torque."

When you draw and aim, keep your hand relaxed fully, because "tension not only has the effect of turning the bow when you release the string; it also creeps into your bow naturally. Trying to force your hand to stay open will create just as much shot-destroying tension as clenching it closed."

You must be diligent to place your hand on the grip exactly the same way every time. If you spend an extra two or three seconds to ensure consistent hand placement, Ulmer believes it will eventually become instinctive.

From his hundreds of hours in the mountains hunting elk and his hundreds of competitive events, Ulmer observes that many bowhunters buckle their wrists and even slide their hands around on the grip as they pull the string. This may put them in a more powerful position for drawing the bow, but it undermines consistency. "Once your hand and wrist are set in place, leave them alone. If you can't do that, you're probably shooting too much draw weight, or you're not placing your hand correctly in the beginning."

The grip portion of a riser varies and some companies specialize in custom grips. If you remember how often you have watched people stand at a practice line and shift the bow in their hand searching for their precise pivot point, like golfers getting set on the tee before they swing, you begin to understand why grip is so important.

Allen's original compounds had bulky wood risers. Many bows since then have had similarly thick grips, but not recently. We often hear that grips have gotten smaller over time. True . . . and not true. Some of the original Jennings compounds and many early Astro and Bear bows were built with thin metal risers and plastic grip sleeves or side-plates. Compounds with wood risers–the Browning Safari and Jennings (by Bear) –often had big, meaty grips, but recurves drawing even 65 and 70 pounds do not.

To shoot comfortably, a grip must fit comfortably in your hand and feel natural. This is a subjective, personal decision. Remember that on cold days you may wear a glove on your bow hand, and on warm days your hand may swell.

Many bowhunters believe that thick grips contribute to erratic shooting. With a handful of bow riser, they say, there is a tendency to twist or torque the riser before and after a shot and it is harder to duplicate your precise hand position. At the highest level of 3-D shooting, competitors rarely use a thick grip. Indeed, they often remove any wood or plastic grips and simply wrap the "keel" of the riser with leather for warmth.

This is not universally true, but manufacturers often outfit high-end compounds with attractive checkered wood grips, while their low-end and novice or beginner compounds come with hard plastic grips. On the other hand, several versions of a plastic/rubber grip that is not hard, but not quite soft either, are used by many companies.

BOW LIMBS

Around 2000, expensive bows were built with laminated wood or limbs. The multiple layers of dyed wood looked sharp, classy. The most expensive bows had recurved laminated limbs, things of beauty. Only inexpensive models had solid fiberglass limbs.

Now, every high-performance hunting bow has solid fiberglass or carbon matrix foam limbs. Limbs that appear to be laminated are only alternating wraps of black and white fiberglass yarn.

Fiberglass limbs are molded from layers of Corning yarn or even a mat, and submerged in a resin bath. They are practical and practically indestructible, but they are also short and ugly, their graceful contour painted in a camouflage pattern on all sides. But who cares about ugly if they work? The extremes of heat, cold and moisture that plagued laminated wood limbs and caused them to occasionally fail, especially if those limbs became even slightly damaged by being dropped or banged up, are not the slightest problem for an ugly glass limb.

In the late 1990s, manufacturers experimented with incorporating carbon into bow limbs. Carbon would theoretically improve the performance of thin limbs by acting as a "stiffener." This would allow limbs to be thinner without sacrificing strength.

Sheets of carbon are quite expensive, however, so sometimes, there's no more carbon than the scratch of a No. 2 pencil–enough to allow a clever advertising copywriter to claim "Carbon Limb Technology!" It sounded space-age, but a solid shaped limb of fiberglass actually proved to be more durable and, given the direction of bow development toward parallel limb technology, more powerful and efficient. Now magazines publish bow reports that barely mention a bow's limbs at all.

Another fad that recently disappeared is the recurved limb. Recurved limbs gave compound bows an appearance similar to a traditional recurve bow. These limbs may have had more eye appeal in their curves, but in terms of performance, solid straight limbs deliver more energy to your arrow and stand up better to the rough handling of a hunting season. Straight limbs are easier to manufacture from a fiberglass blank from Gordon or any other supplier–you can do this yourself in your garage with a router and sander–and are more durable.

All limbs on a compound bow appear to curve, but only recurved limbs are built with a curve. Straight limbs curve because they are under tremendous pressure, even at rest. (If you do not believe this, grip an adult compound bow at its ends and try compressing it between your hands. Unless you are extraordinarily strong, you cannot do it!)

Split or quad-limb bows have been around for years. One such bow, the TSS (Total Shooting Systems) QuadraFlex with angular split limbs was briefly popular in the early '80s. The technology practically disappeared for a dozen years.

Split limbs have less mass and so weigh less than solid limbs. Some archery engineers have suggested that because quad limbs are lighter, they deliver energy more efficiently through the bowstring. After all, a bow limb–not the riser or even the string–is the action element of a simple lever or spring. These engineers further suggest that well-balanced split limbs offer advantages in balancing forces at the limb tips, because the harness splits about six inches below the idler or cam on the upper limb and the twin upper and lower limbs can act independently to equalize the pressure.

Unless you are a bowhunter and a 3-D competitor who is seriously interested in winning cash on 3-D tournament venues, the difference between solid and split limbs is probably irrelevant. Split or solid, the style limb makes little difference in your shooting. A solid, pultruded limb may give you greater arrow speed, a few extra fps, and will probably be more durable over the long run.

Realize that there is nothing "split" about split limbs. They are not cut or split off a larger chunk of fiberglass, but are molded "as is," in the same manner as a solid limb. So the new rule is to buy what looks and feels good to you.

Regarding the movement toward parallel limb technology that many bow manufacturers experimented with, PSE Engineering Manager David Kronengold says it is "market driven." On the other hand, there is a perceptible difference in the feel of this type bow in the shooting hand and arm. Most bowhunters who shoot "parallel limb" bows attest that they feel or sense less shock in their hand and arm. Kronengold says the force vectors in the moving limbs tend to cancel each other out because of their opposing nature. Rather than the limbs moving synchronously forward, they spring up and down, thereby eliminating some of the felt energy, the shock left behind in the bow after the arrow has absorbed all that it can.

CABLES AND STRINGS

Early compound bows used Dacron strings and steel cables. Dacron worked well for 70-pound bows with 60 to 75 pounds of stored energy, but as cams became harder and archers insisted on greater arrow speed and more kinetic energy delivery down range, Dacron proved to be inadequate for the load.

Not many bow companies use steel cables or Dacron strings any longer except on low-end bows. According to Brownell, Dacron has a single-strand breaking strength of about 50 pounds, whereas more complex synthetic materials have much higher breaking strengths. Western Filament's Spectra, for instance, has a 90-pound single-strand breaking strength. Brownell's Dyneema D-75 has a 125-pound single-strand strength, and S-4, a 165-pound single-strand strength. By reducing weight, string diameter and string stretch, all-synthetic systems can increase arrow speed by as much as 10 fps. With new generation synthetic materials like Fast Flight, 450 Plus and DynaFlight 97, the bow-tuning process has been simplified . . . and, paradoxically, made more difficult.

Early Fast Flight (95-pound single-strand breaking strength, .015-inch diameter) string-and-cable systems developed a poor reputation because the strings and cables continually stretched and so the tune of the bow (mostly twin-cam bows then) could never be guaranteed. Fast Flight and others of these man-made materials do stretch to some degree, especially in hot weather.

The number-one problem with early "new generation" string materials was not stretch, however, but creep. These string materials were so slick that they would slip beneath the end servings. Improved manufacturing techniques have mostly eliminated that problem and today's all-synthetic riggings are more stable.

Regardless of the material, any bowstring sold on a compound bow comes with a string designed and manufactured to standardized lengths. According to the Archery Trade Association, "Compound bowstring length shall be designated by its stretched length as determined by placing the string loops over 1/4-inch diameter steel pins and stretching with 100 pounds of tension. Measurement is taken from outside of pin. Tolerance is + 1/4 inch after 20 seconds under tension load."

In an effort to eliminate string and cable stretch, manufacturers in the '90s experimented with a material called Vectran, which although it does fray, does not stretch. This fraying became quite a serious problem, though, causing Vectran strings to break after just a few thousand shots.

Seeking the best of both worlds, string makers braided materials like Fast Flight with Vectran to make durable, low-stretch string materials called 450 Premium and S4. Today, many bows use one of these materials, or even Fast Flight, for their strings and cables, but many have moved to materials like BCY 452, which has the same strength as 450 in half the diameter.

Here are some of the names you hear used: 450 Plus (total stability with no creep. Good arrow speed; no fuzziness), 452 (very smooth; half the size of 450 Plus; fast, small diameter and no creep), DynaFlight 97 (the original high-strength Dyneema; rugged, low creep, very durable), Formula 8125 (high speeds with low creep and stretch; smaller diameter than Dyneema) and Dyneema '02 (designed for recurves; strong, low creep and stretch with extra-light smooth wax).

Among string makers, the following general rules apply:
• The higher the number of strands, the faster your arrow;
• Larger diameter strands yield slower arrow speeds than thinner strands; and
• The best combination for speed and durability is a small string wrapped by a thick serving.

If you attach your release aid directly to your string, it is a given that your serving will eventually break or wear out. It is not a matter of if, only when. Therefore, you need to be familiar with the methods required to reapply the string's center serving.

A simple serving jig and a spool of replacement material are all you need. A common replacement serving is BCY Halo, which is 100 percent braided Spectra and is nearly three times stronger than #62 Braid, the traditional center serving. You have to serve Halo tight to keep the slick Spectra solidly in place on your string, but its extra durability makes it worth the additional attention required. (Finger shooters love the way the slick-feeling Halo slips off the fingertips. As if it were oiled.)

Once you have your string re-served, use a liquid lok to hold the new serving material in place. When it dries, this adhesive prevents slipping and separation. Use a lubricant over the end serving where it slips into the grooves of the cam to prevent wear damage there. Both products are useful to maintain a resilient bowstring.

It is also a good idea to use an over-wrap that goes on the end serving of your string or buss cable to protect the serving from damage by the rotating cam. Serving damage is a problem with many hard-cam designs and particularly so on large single cams. It can be applied by hand, but is best applied with a serving jig.

CABLE GUARD

A cable guard prevents interference between arrow fletching and cables by holding your bow's cables to the side. You do not want this rigid rod to stretch the cables any farther than is absolutely necessary or excessive wheel lean and unnecessary torque can result.

Some type of cable guard is standard on all compound bows, but they come in several styles and varieties. Typically, it is often a rod of either solid carbon or steel. Steel rods can be offset and may also be adjustable. Your cables move along it in a grooved plastic or Teflon slide that either slips over the rod or is held in place by the intense side pressure of the cables. Teflon or some Teflon composite is an ideal surfacing material for a cable slide because it minimizes friction during the shot.

The cable guard is positioned between the axles in the center of the bow. With most bows, however, this is not possible, though, so the guard is positioned either above the arrow rest by one to three inches or below the rest by a half dozen or so inches.

There is a safety factor as well as a technological factor to keep in mind when you look at cable-guard placement. High-mount guards were standard until the early '90s, when low-mount guards became the norm, perhaps for no other reason than a change in style. Let go of a bow riser (not the string, the bow—do not laugh, it happens) that has a high mount, above the rest guard, and it can slam back and hit you in the face with disastrous results. Let go of a bow that has a low, below-the-rest guard and it can slam back and hit you in the chest, leaving you with a sore spot.

Nevertheless, the best spot for the cable guard seems to be the high-mount position, as from there an adjustable rod can move the cables aside just enough to prevent interference and yet remain close to the arrow. Minimal side movement of the cables means minimal torque on your cam and idler, thus minimizing cam lean. The result is, of course, accurate shooting.

Is a carbon cable guard better than a steel rod? Carbon rods are always straight, but steel rods can be straight or designed with a bend or offset. Both will flex and return to their original position for thousands of shots, leading us to conclude that either steel or carbon are entirely adequate. Under "normal" shooting conditions, though, carbon should retain its strength and flexibility for a greater length of time than steel.

The only new approach to moving the cables aside in many years is

Mathews' Roller Guard. Is it smoother or do the machined wheels eliminate the friction of cables sliding through a Teflon cable saver or slide? Does it minimize the possibility of cam or idler lean? Mathews claims that the answer to these questions is yes, even though no other manufacturers have yet followed the one-cam innovator's lead.

BOW LENGTH

Even as the cams have gotten larger, compound bows have shrunk in the past ten years. Not very many years ago, bowhunters wanted a long, forgiving 42-inch bow. These days, they willingly testify that a short axle-to-axle bow gives them increased maneuverability in ground blinds and on

An alternative approach to the cable-guard function. Its hinged, low-mounted, swing-arm cable guard swings back as the bow is drawn. This movement incorporates a slight lateral off-set to prevent cable interference with your arrow's fletching. The ideal position for the cable guard is immediately next to your arrow, as this position torques the cables and thus your cams as little as possible. However, this position causes some design problems and archery engineers have numerous options for your consideration.

treestands. It also increases arrow speed, they say, and bowhunters appreciate that greatly. Around 2005, the average length of a bow is probably 33 or 34 inches axle-to-axle and some models barely measure 31 inches!

Big news. Not! Short bows are faster than long bows, but it is not just because they are short. For any given draw length, the wheels on short bows are larger than on longer bows. This increases roll-over speed at the rim, at the string. Leverage is in play.

For every action, there is an equal and opposite reaction. We have long known that short bows are more susceptible to hand-applied torque than longer bows, probably because the longer and heavier bows are more resistant to twisting. Experienced bowhunters who understand tuning and good shooting form will be able to enjoy the lightweight maneuverability of a short axle-to-axle bow. If you are a novice or a hunter who does not understand or care about the fine points of tuning, you might find that a short bow gives you more shooting challenges than it conveys in benefits.

Finger shooters need longer rather than shorter bows. When the string is pulled to full draw on a short bow, there is an acute angle between the string and your arrow. This angle makes you move your fingers away from the nock point, because it pinches them uncomfortably, even if you drop one finger below and behind the string. The severity of this finger pinch depends on your draw length, but with bows shorter than about 38 inches, you should consider using a release.

Most estimates say that only 10 to 20 percent of bowhunters still shoot with fingers. A bow measuring 40 or more inches will make it easier for these finger shooters to become proficient.

PHYSICAL WEIGHT

Manufacturers are gradually squeezing out the ounces by lightening the riser, but the physical or mass weight of a compound bow usually falls in the three-and-a-half to four-and-a-half-pound range. Loaded with accessories and a full quiver of arrows, the weight can climb to seven or eight pounds. All this makes little or no difference if you hunt from a treestand or a ground blind. If you are hiking through the mountains of Colorado glassing for elk day after day, however, a heavy bow can become an obstacle to your enjoyment and success. Some of the new (but not yet well accepted) carbon-handle bows weigh less than three pounds.

Your fatigue during a day spent hiking the Rockies for elk should not influence your decision between a heavier or lighter bow. (After all, we are only talking eight to ten or so ounces and just cutting out a few high-calorie desserts could take care of that!)

The essential difficulty with a light bow is how it handles the kinetic energy that remains after the arrow absorbs its 75 percent. For a fast, high-

Taking giant Rocky Mountain elk while bowhunting alone is Eddie Claypool's specialty, but once a bull is on the ground, a tremendous amount of work must be done. His penchant for hunting miles from any road aggravates the situation. Typically, his shot will find its mark just before dark. Then, he must blood trail the bull, field dress it, hang the huge quarters in a tree (if possible) and pack out the head and antlers.

end bow, that means that 15 to 20 ft-lb of energy are left in the bow to become riser buzz and shock, vibration and noise. That is equivalent to dropping the bow from chest height. After an afternoon of shooting practice, this makes a difference in how your elbow and shoulder feel, and in whether you must retighten all of your accessories, because they are subjected to screw-loosening vibration.

Heavy bows absorb leftover energy more easily than light bows. Given the same amount of stray energy, a lighter bow makes more noise and rattles your sight pins and arm much more than a heavier bow. So if you opt to purchase a lightweight bow, look for solid, stable accessories to help you deal with leftover energy. Be aware, too, of Loc-Tite to help keep your sight and arrow rest properly, but not necessarily permanently, in place.

CAMOUFLAGE AND COLOR

Function comes first. A precision shooter in rainbow colors beats a mediocre machine in any camo pattern. Many companies offer the same bow and accessories in both competition colors and camo.

Two types of camo patterns are routinely applied to bows, a manufacturer's own pattern or one of the mass-marketed patterns from Bill Jordan's Realtree and Advantage and Toxey Haas' Mossy Oak. If a salesman hands you a bow in an odd pattern, with a name you do not recognize, "Skunk Mask with Leaves" or "Elk Tails in the Quakies," it is a proprietary camo applied by the manufacturer.

A good non-reflective camo pattern that matches the vegetation tones in your area and is well-applied to a bow's riser and limbs makes it feel like it is a natural part of a hunting situation. With new patterns emerging every year, you can find bows in every major and many unknown camouflage patterns.

Camo is important because it helps you blend into your hunting environment. It can be a confidence booster perhaps, but deer and other big-game animals do not care about the camo pattern on your bow. Millions of trophy game animals have been taken with solid green and solid black bows before the old World War II green or Jim Crumley's original Trebark camo were thoughtfully applied to our hunting bows.

COMPOUND CARE

Treat your bow like a fine shooting instrument, and it will perform like one. Treat it with care.

Any bow benefits from an occasional check-up. Excessive heat can damage it, whether the riser and limbs are made from wood, fiberglass or a carbon composite. Never leave your bow in the trunk of a car or hang it on the gun rack of your pick up truck to be exposed to direct sunlight. Heat causes the glue between laminates to crystallize and lose its bonding strength. It also causes your stronger-than-steel string and cables to stretch.

If it becomes overheated, your bow can lose its ability to shoot entirely. Most manufacturers would give you some credit on a replacement bow if it was not old and you have the original sales receipt, but every bow owner's manual explicitly warns against such careless treatment. Read the fine print!

Blowing dust adheres to the oil around the axles and, in extreme cases, can actually increase your draw weight and reduce arrow speed. To prevent this when you are using your bow often, lightly oil the axles and wheels every now and then. Use lightweight machine oil or a Teflon-based lubricant like Super Lube. Super Lube does not react with rubber, plastic, wood, leather, fabric or paint, so it is an ideal archery accessory. There are other oil products for your bowhunting gear. Be sure you wipe away any excess oil, because too much oil can be as harmful to superior shooting as too little oil.

Do not believe that modern strings perform well without waxing. Not true. Eventually strings and cables fray from the extreme tension of a shot and from rubbing against branches and other abrasive surfaces. To reduce this fraying, lubricate your string and cables with beeswax. Every archery sales outlet carries bowstring wax and one tube should last for years. Remember: Even modern synthetic, high-tech strings must be kept waxed.

The last thing you need on a hunt away from home is equipment problems and your "stronger than steel" bowstring is the most delicate part of your bow. If you nick a string with your broadhead or a knife or if you detect any visible fraying, you should replace it. It is a darn good idea to carry a spare bowstring, one that is set up exactly like the current one on your bow. Next to the spare string, carry a simple bow press. Some bows allow you to relax the limbs enough to change the string with only a hex wrench, but most do not.

When you shoot a bow, your arrow can absorb as much as 80 percent of the energy released by the limbs, leaving only 20 percent in the bow itself. If you dry-fire a bow by drawing and releasing the string, with no arrow on the string, the bow and your hand and arm will absorb 100 percent of the energy. This can be as much as 100 ft-lbs, and the stress of vibration through the limbs, handle, cables and string can blow your bow apart and give you a serious case of "tennis elbow." Dry-firing not only voids your warranty, but it can also hurt you if the shock causes the bow to blow apart.

Launching under-spined lightweight arrows produces a similar effect to a dry-fire, because light arrows absorb a smaller percentage of your bow's potential energy. To be safe (and to shoot well), you must adhere to the manufacturer's suggested spine recommendations. Then, oil the axles and lubricate your bowstring occasionally and:

• Avoid smearing insect repellents on the surface of your bow.

The chemicals in these products can damage the finish.
- Carry a spare shot-in bowstring and a portable bow press when on a trip.
- Carry a set of Allen wrenches and tighten your accessories before hunting.
- Check the bowstring before shooting. Frayed strings should be replaced.
- Keep your bow out of the heat. Laminated parts can come apart after only a few hours in a hot vehicle.
- Store your bow in a cool, dry area out of direct sunlight. Do not hang it by the string or cables, only by the riser. Better yet, lay it on a flat surface or store it in a bow holder.
- If you are not going to be shooting for a month or more, relax the tension on the string and cables by backing out the limb bolts before storing your bow.

TRADITIONAL BOWS

Recurve and longbow shooters are a vigorous minority of bowhunters. The hunter who carries a stick bow is typically a more experienced archer who has shot a modern compound and is looking for an additional challenge. Some people choose stick bows because they appear to be simple and beautiful, without the mechanical advantages that make a compound bow powerful. Except for a few home-made "self bows," bows made from a single stave or stick, all longbows and most recurves are still wood laminate and they can be works of art. Instinctive shooters are also drawn to traditional bows for their light weight and smooth (no cam roll-over bump) draw.

A strong group of hunters identify with traditional equipment and methods. The opportunity to shoot and to associate with other traditionalists both sets these shooters apart and includes them in a like-minded and friendly atmosphere. The "traditionalists" thus become whom they choose… and that, in part, is defined by who they are not.

Few hunters would suggest that traditional equipment is easier to master and use effectively than the more complex but labor-saving modern gear. Longbows cannot be tuned and sighted with anything remotely approaching the same precision as compounds, and they require more force to hold at full draw. Chances are your 60-pound longbow will reach 60 pounds before full draw with no let-off, while a comparable 60-pound compound bow with 75 percent let-off requires only 15 pounds of holding force.

Recurve bows have limbs that curve back toward the front of the bow. The string is therefore nocked or hung around both limb tips, but it actually lies against the limb itself. Most longbows, on the other hand, have limbs that form a smooth curve like the arc of a new moon toward the string.

Should you shoot a recurve or longbow? It is a matter of personal preference with a good bit of influence from our bowhunting friends. The recurve is probably the best choice for a bowhunter who is already familiar with modern compound bows. Except for the mechanical advantage of let-off, the compound and the recurve are similar in some respects. Both have pistol-style grips and, with some carefully chosen models, their performance characteristics can be comparable. With practice, basic proficiency with a recurve is easily attainable for those making the transition from "modern" equipment.

Although the longbow is fun to shoot, once you are accustomed to it, it is a more difficult transition for an archer accustomed to a compound. The longbow will feel extremely light, and the handle style is quite different. Before turning to the longbow, most shooters first gain experience with a recurve. Many experienced traditionalists, however, enjoy shooting both types of stick bows.

Occasionally, if he has his Colorado tags right, nature blesses Eddie Claypool with a mule deer such as this superb 5x5 trophy buck.

RECURVES

Modern recurve bows are fast, quiet, stable and a pleasure to shoot. Each limb on a recurve has two power curves. This gives the recurve more potential energy and faster arrow speed than the longbow, which has a single power curve for each limb. Some recurve bows are even comparable to compound bows in speed, although admittedly at the lower AMO ratings of 200 to 225 fps range, not the 260 to 315 fps range. The recurve also draws smoother, typically has less "stack" and has less hand shock than the longbow. ("Stack" is an informal or experiential measure that indicates that a bow reaches its maximum weight long before you reach full draw.)

Recurve hunting bows are available in lengths from 46 to 72 inches, but the most popular lengths are 60 and 62 inches. Bows below 58 inches are typically for specialty uses, or for young people or shooters with short draw lengths. Shooters with draw lengths exceeding 30 inches prefer bows longer than 64 inches. Because of the limb design, a short recurve is more comfortable to shoot than a short longbow.

When choosing a recurve bow, the general rule is to match the bow length to your individual draw length. If your draw is less than 27 inches, you will want a bow in the 56- to 58-inch tip-to-tip length; 28 to 29 inches require a 60- to 62-inch bow; 29 to 30 inches, a 62- to 64-inch bow; and more than 30 inches of draw length, a 64- to 66-inch bow.

Choosing a bow length, consider your personal preferences and how you will use the bow. Bowhunting open country or stalking allows the use of a longer bow. Because of the possibility of banging against a stand or maneuvering in a tree, stand hunters generally prefer a shorter bow, as do those hunting thick cover. Some archers prefer the feel and comfort of a longer bow; others like the balance and maneuverability of a shorter bow. It is entirely a personal decision based on the indefinable concept "how it feels" or perhaps how it works for you.

Recurves come in solid one-piece or in take-down models. Take-down longbows are available, too, but are rare, perhaps because there is a sentiment among traditionalists that the take-down or take-apart concept goes against the traditional grain. One-piece bows have a fixed length and bow weight, while take-down recurves consist of three sections–two limbs and a riser–and take-down longbows break at the grip.

One-piece bows have a more traditional appearance that some archers prefer, and they are generally lighter and balance better than take-down bows, but the take-down recurve is considerably more versatile. By changing limbs on some take-down bows, you can alter length and draw weight, a distinct advantage for a beginner or an expert who may want one set of limbs for deer hunting and a heavier set for elk or a lighter set for bowfishing for carp. A newcomer who begins with a 64-inch, 50-pound bow, for example, may decide after a year or two that a 62-inch, 55-pound bow is a better fit. Rather than buy a new bow, the archer can simply purchase a new set of limbs and mount them on the original riser.

The length of the riser determines the length of the sight window, and this in turn usually determines the type of sight you use. Of course, most committed traditional bowhunters do not use a sight, but the length of the riser is important to your aiming method. The riser is basic to the design and "feel" of the bow.

A longer riser section gives you a longer sight window. This affords a better view of the target, but these days a longer riser usually means shorter limbs, which will affect the way the bow shocks your hand when you shoot. For this reason, many traditional shooters prefer the combination of a short riser and longer limbs. If the bow is canted slightly to the side when shot, a longer sight window is unnecessary. You can best select the correct length for you by shooting many bows with different riser lengths and choosing the one that feels best for your individual shooting style.

Recurve limbs are usually fiberglass and wood laminates and risers can be made from a wide selection of materials, from lathed and laminated wood to machined aluminum to carbon composites. While some modern recurves do have machined or die-cast risers, metal risers are most often used for competition bows. Most hunting recurves–and all longbows–have wood risers, either solid or laminated, and these are often customized with handsome inlays. Most recurve risers accommodate the use of arrow rests, stabilizers, sights and a bow-mounted quiver, similar to those used on compound bows. Of course, whether these are actually attached or not is strictly a personal decision.

It is impossible to overemphasize the importance of selecting a traditional bow that you can draw and shoot comfortably. The most common archery error may not be shooting form, but choosing a draw weight that is too heavy and expecting that with a little practice you can grow into it. The average man can manage a traditional bow in the 45- to 50-pound range, while women should begin with weights in the 30- to 35-pound range.

When you first begin shooting a recurve (or a longbow), a reasonable draw weight for you is particularly important. Drawing a moderate-weight bow, beginners can be taught to shoot well in just a few sessions; using bows that are too heavy, they may give up and never learn to shoot correctly.

LONGBOWS

You rarely saw a longbow in the field until just a few years ago. Today, the longbow is a common sight in hunting camps and on archery ranges. For many, the longbow represents a return to the roots of archery.

Longbows do not shoot as far or as fast as recurves or compounds, and they require more practice for an archer to achieve and maintain proficiency. They are also rougher in the hand and produce a good deal more hand shock, but these "primitive" characteristics are precisely what thousands of devotees of traditional archery find appealing.

The longbow is not without its merits. Because they use longer limbs with a single curve, longbows are particularly stable launching platforms. Often equipped with specially braided Flemish strings, they are also very quiet. Many archers find the combination of stability, silence and tradition ideal for hunting and recreational shooting.

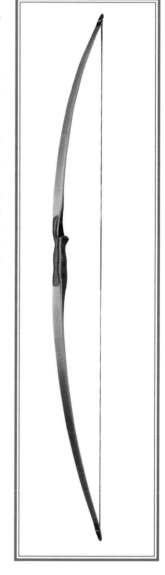

Of course, there are three additional reasons for a longbow's silent shooting signature. First, few traditionalists hang accessories on a longbow; they are not built for modern accessories, and so there is very little shake, rattle and roll after a shot. Second, the longbow does not power up an arrow like a compound bow; the kinetic energy is significantly less. Finally, with an ultra-light bow and no accessories, the soft tissue of your body absorbs a much greater level of shock when you shoot.

Although today's longbows are sometimes built with modern materials, including fiberglass and new laminate bonding agents, there is a tiny segment of the longbow fraternity that builds and shoots the self bow, made entirely of a single piece of wood. Self bows can be beautiful in the eccentricity of their wood grain and the irregularity of their lines, but they are slow and easily damaged.

Because a longbow limb has a single power curve–as opposed to the recurve's double curve–the limbs must be longer in order to achieve the necessary efficiency to launch an arrow with even close range penetrating power (kinetic energy). The most popular longbow lengths are 66 and 68 inches, but modern materials are now making it possible to create 62- and 64-inch longbows that have excellent

This all-wood longbow comes in lengths of 63, 66, and 69 inches. It can be built in practically any draw weight from 35 to 75 pounds.

performance. If treestand hunters switch to longbows in any significant numbers, shorter bows will likely become increasingly popular and more readily available through other than custom manufacturing outlets.

The ideal tip-to-tip length for your longbow depends on your draw length. Keep in mind that the typical longbow shooter's draw will be about one inch less than with a recurve, and about 1 1/2 to 2 inches less than with a compound bow. This reduced draw is a function of stack, the longbow's tendency to come to maximum weight early. Without sights, the longhunter just lightly touches his lips or cheek before releasing. Draw lengths exceeding 29 1/2 inches are rare.

Draw length to bow length recommendations, such as those that follow, are based on an average shooter and a longbow of standard modern design. If your draw length is 26 inches or less, a longbow that is no longer than 66 inches in length will probably fit you; from 27 to 29 inches of draw length, a 66-inch bow is about right; and if your draw is more than 29 inches, you might want to shop for a 68-inch or longer bow.

Most longbows are sold in a one-piece design, even though several two-piece take-down models are commercially available with fine performance characteristics. Athough traveling with a 66-inch longbow is awkward, and can easily be hazardous to the integrity of the bow, take-down longbows make up a minority of the total longbow market. In contrast to the take-down recurve, which is targeted first at versatility and second at convenience, the take-down longbow's appeal is primarily convenience, making the bow shorter and easier to manage when its owner is not hunting.

Longbow limbs are fiberglass and wood laminates, and there has been much debate among manufacturers about the best combination of these materials. Limbs incorporating bamboo, maple, yew, Osage, black locust, hickory, tamarack and other woods are all available. Although some materials draw easier than others and some transfer less hand shock, in truth there is little difference in the performance of these laminate materials. This is because most of the limb power in today's longbow comes from the fiberglass, not the wood. In the modern longbow, performance is determined mostly by bow design and quality of construction. Self bows, on the other hand, which are made without fiberglass, are significantly affected by the choice of limb material.

Longbows are less efficient than recurves or compounds, and this causes some bowhunters to make the mistake of compensating by choosing an overly heavy draw weight. Truly a beginner's mistake. The poor shooting that results from being over-bowed should not be blamed on the longbow.

YOUTH BOWS

Do we truly mean "bows for kids" or "short-draw bows"? Both phrases have their defenders, but women–and certainly young people–typically have shorter draws and draw lighter weights than their spouses, fathers or male friends who introduced them to archery. So besides being available in draw lengths in the low 20-inch range, the weight range for beginner or youth bows is lower too, often topping-out at about 45 pounds, the minimum recommended for deer hunting.

When you go shopping for a youth or short-draw bow, look for one with a draw weight close to your youngster's physical strength. If they can comfortably pull a 40-pound bow, select one with an advertised weight that peaks at 45 pounds. As young people grow in strength and confidence, you can usually tune this bow up in weight or even change modules to achieve a greater draw weight.

A bow is usually most efficient shooting at or just below the peak draw. It puts most of the energy of a shot into the arrow. Shoot at the low end of the acceptability scale–say 42 to 45 pounds on a bow that peaks at 55–and your youngster may experience sloppy and inconsistent performance and, for a novice shooter trying to get it right, that can be a game breaker.

Lightweight bows will be easier for a novice shooter to haul to the range or into the woods in your footsteps. For their sake and yours, do not just give them a hand-me-down adult bow and try to make it fit unless they are very close to you in size and strength. Unless the second-hand bow you are jury-rigging for them has some special significance, it will not make a young person happy. Guaranteed.

Smaller bows with short brace heights are going to be difficult for your youngster to shoot well. Before you buy, shop around in the catalogs available in local pro shops or sporting goods stores.

Statistically, you shoot a release, but should a novice learn with a release aid or fingers? In the long run, if they enjoy archery and stick with it, it may not matter, but it is probably preferable to begin their shooting with fingers, as very small bows, just barely larger and more powerful than toys, are not readily designed for release-aid shooting. They can learn so much with simple equipment that it is a shame to burden them with mechanical devices before they are prepared and understand the basics of shooting and hunting.

The question of let-off assumes you will start your young shooter on a compound bow, but this is not necessarily right for everyone. Superior small-to-medium recurves are available, and to learn the fundamentals of archery–breathing, stance, terminology and safety–this may certainly be the preferred way to go.

THE GENESIS BOW

The 36-inch axle-to-axle Genesis bow, originally crafted by Matt McPherson's Mathews Archery, has an innovative cam that eliminates let-off and fits all draw lengths, from 15 to 30 inches. A Genesis may be the place to start your kids and spouse, because anyone can shoot it. McPherson's idea was that you could buy a single bow at a reasonable price–$150 or so–and the entire family could use it to become interested in archery.

Practicing what he preaches, bowhunting rock and roller Ted Nugent teaches his son, Rocco Winchester, to shoot and hunt. Young people need equipment sized to their dimensions and, most important of all, the interest and attention of a big person in their life to serve as a guide.
(Photo courtesy Ted Nugent)

The Genesis is the first bow to accommodate youth and adult archers alike. Since it eliminates let-off, the Genesis stores and releases energy comparable to about a 35-pound recurve, when the Genesis set at 20-pound peak weight. It has a lightweight machined aluminum riser and a machined aluminum Genesis one-cam system with aluminum idler. The brace height is 7 1/2 inches. These bows also have composite limbs, a molded grip and a stainless steel cable guard. The Genesis looks very much like a modern one-cam bow, but it is strictly for learning. ■

CHAPTER THREE

The Importance of a Good Arrow

A BOWHUNT IN HELL

Bob cannot see the trees, even though he is aware that they are sweeping by at dizzying speed. He cannot see the water or the boat either, for that matter. It is pitch black and the unbalanced rocking motion, combined with the outboard fumes, is making him nauseous.

The boat's motor growls at the overhanging jungle scrub as if it is beating a safe passage through the dripping green maw of nature raw in tooth and fang. Occasionally, something slaps at his bow, or drops onto his hat or splashes against his face. He does not want to guess what those things might be.

For a half century, Bob Markworth has given archery demonstrations around the world. He performs live, on stage and on television. His passport is stamped with entry and exit visas from 75 countries. Markworth has seen much of the world and he is not an easy man to frighten.

Nevertheless, on this dark June morning in early winter south of the equator, he grips the gunwale of the rusty steel boat so hard that he loses feeling in his right hand. As the flat-bottom craft careens around corners that he cannot distinguish in the pre-dawn light, he never loses his hold. With his other hand, he holds his bow tightly against his chest.

Even though the natives are friendly and his Australian companions casually boisterous, Papua New Guinea is a hellhole.

In the close, sodden air, the roar of the engine pushing the boat north over the Bensbach River is hypnotic. A bat or perhaps a giant insect fleeing some unseen jungle predator flutters against his face, startling him. After that, Markworth hunches down on the seat and holds on, praying for the nightmare ride to end. That and the unexpected tilting and shifting to avoid what the outfitter warned him would be underwater snags or saltwater crocodiles, and Markworth does not know how much longer he can hold on without screaming.

Then, as suddenly as the malevolent tropical darkness had enveloped the lodge the evening before, the speeding boat bursts from the frowning jungle's hold. Even from his low position on the water, Markworth senses that they have entered an open savanna. The silhouette of low trees far to the east hints of sunrise.

The boat driver, who had flung the little hunting party up the river at breakneck speed, cuts the engine. For a minute, silence roars in

Markworth's ears like a horde of locusts and then, softly, the grassland around him begins to reveal its abundant, exuberant life.

Except for the lost river lodge, its half-overgrown landing strip and the steel boat in which he sat, there is no opportunity of civilization for hundreds of miles in any direction. Papua New Guinea is a land of 700 strange languages. A land of yams and jungle and the most primitive people left on earth, a people who still cut off the heads of outsiders, boil them and hang them, badges of honor on the pillars of their thatched huts and longhouses. New Guinea is a land of warriors who steal women and practice bloody rituals that the government has failed to stamp out. If Markworth becomes separated from his party, loses his way in the jungle . . . God help him.

The bowhunters nickname their native guide "Robert," because his actual name is unpronounceable and translates into "He who bites the tails off water rats to frighten his sisters." Robert is a tall, ungainly man who speaks no English, who smiles often, but who never takes his eyes off the other men. Accustomed to foreign hunters, perhaps, he makes himself understood with a grunt, sly smile and a hand signal.

Now, as Robert eases the boat to shore, Markworth regains his composure. When the bowhunters jump onto the bank, an astounding abundance of wildlife presents itself: rusa deer, wild boar and wallabies feed on the savanna. Flocks of birds call to one another and wing their way in all directions. The scene is primeval and Markworth has never seen anything like it.

If God had suddenly drawn aside the veil to the Garden of Eden, it could not have appeared more fertile and abundant with life. Pelicans skim down the river while magpie geese, scrub turkeys, long-legged storks, ibis and cormorants, bush fowl and cranes, cassowaries and dancing brolgas fly beneath the occasional shadow of a white-headed fish eagle. For many creatures that crawl and fly and swim, this indeed is paradise.

Stunned by the raw elegance of the prairie, Markworth and his Aussie friends shoulder their packs and bows, and follow Robert toward the jungle edge. In spite of the terrifying ride through the dark, a few minutes of daylight and solid ground awaken the hunting party to its possibilities. The deer, which had fled into the forest, will soon return, and the wild pigs, rooting for grubs and tender roots in the short-grass prairie, will now be searching for a place to lie down.

Long before they reach the edge of the jungle, the hunters sense the warm breath of decay. The wholesome forest mold of America is thousands of miles away and Markworth feels unaccountably alone and foreign, assaulted by odors that have no referent in his memory.

Robert leads the group deeper into the jungle until Markworth and the others have entirely lost their way. If the native deserts them, they will almost certainly perish.

In mid-stride, one foot raised, Robert freezes. Immobile and silent, he slowly crouches into the mud and motions for Markworth to come forward.

Holding his bow carefully in front, Markworth moves up beside his guide, forcing his eyes to see and his brain to understand what the strange forest might tell him. For a moment, there is nothing. Then he senses an almost inaudible series of splashes, no more than a small fish in a shallow pool. He cocks his head and hears a soft grunt. Pigs!

Markworth slips his pack and sees, barely 25 yards in front of him, the snuffling black form of several jungle pigs. The large one, black as the river passage, with wickedly curving tusks, is certainly a boar. Incredibly, although the tangle around their almost indistinguishable thread of a path is thick and impenetrable, Markworth has a clear shot and so he takes it. The aluminum arrow buries to the fletching behind the boar's shoulder.

In terror at the sudden pain, the pig squeals and spins around, snapping at the arrow's protruding shaft before it thunders toward the deeper swamp.

Bob Markworth (right) and his Australian hunting friend Mark Burrows with two jungle pigs taken along the Bensbach River of Papua New Guinea. Few outsiders travel to the island of New Guinea, which, although not cut off from outside contact, is nevertheless considered one of the most primitive areas on earth.

Markworth nocks a second arrow and rises from his kneeling position, but Robert touches his arm and motions for him to be still. For a full minute, and then two, both men simply stand silently and listen. The pigs have disappeared and even the birds have fallen silent.

Finally, Robert grins and claps Markworth on the back in his best "hale fellow, well met" fashion. Although the jungle pig has disappeared and Bob's natural inclination is to wait a half-hour before following it, Robert strides confidently into the dense cover of liana and thorny leaf palm. The pig lies crumpled at the base of a mangrove thicket, no further than 20 yards distant from its encounter with Markworth's arrow. The broadhead and shaft have sliced the pig precisely behind the shoulder blade and plunged forward through its heart and lungs. No tracking is required to find this black boar.

That night, the hunters feasted on roast boar and drank native palm wine. Robert's friend Kapara, as unsteady as the lodge's white guests, insisted upon demonstrating his own archery prowess. Kapara's bow was a primitive split-bamboo longbow and his featherless shafts more resembled ungainly bamboo spears than arrows. He had tipped his two arrows with massive steel broadheads, laboriously hammered from sheet metal. At any distance those wicked, rusting heads would be deadly, but Kapara's ability to deliver them on target was inept at close range and miserable beyond ten yards. Perhaps it was the wine.

The next morning, Markworth braced for yet another harrowing boat ride. He remembered the crocodiles lazily spread along the bank like fallen trees and so slid, as far as was possible, toward the center of the boat. A shot of whiskey might have steeled him to the dark, but there was none and when he burped, the taste of the evening's palm wine was sour in his mouth and throat.

This day's quarry was to be the native variety of deer, the small and elusive rusa stag. At some time, in the wine-addled hours of the previous evening, Markworth had apparently invited Kapara to hunt with him.

When the lodge owner interpreted the offer, Kapara jumped up. "Yes, I will come!" he shouted.

Now, as Robert pointed the boat toward Kapara's village, Markworth was certain his generous offer had been a mistake. On the bank, Kapara's fire sent flickering tongues of light into the ominous, sucking blackness of the hovering jungle.

Holding on tight and offering a silent prayer, Markworth endured his second trip up the mouth of the river. All he was conscious of was the unexpected lurching of the boat, the gasoline fumes and the utter blackness of the Bensbach.

In the comfortless light of early morning, Robert finally drew the boat toward shore. Not 25 yards in front of the bowhunters, a huge pig snuffled and grunted in the tall grass.

Seizing his bow and two arrows, and ignoring the possibility of lurking crocodiles, Kapara threw himself overboard. Wading ashore, the eager hunter shook himself like a dog and trotted off to intercept the pig.

Before the boat had fully grounded against the muddy bank, though, the hunters observed Kapara in full flight. Apparently, the aggressive pig had sensed the native hunter's approach and wheeled in Kapara's direction. Perhaps it could not distinguish the man through the grass, but it had become aware that something was amiss and rather than patiently wait for its adversary, it had charged.

In the cool light of morning, with the jungle pig not far behind, Kapara sprinted away from the boat and salvation across the uneven ground, his bow and two arrows nowhere to be seen. And the pig was gaining on him. In the boat, the hunters shouted, urging him to speedier flight. Without a rifle, they could only watch and hope that the villager saved himself.

It soon became clear that the fleeing man had set a course for the edge of the jungle. With the pig at his heels, Kapara hurled himself toward the first tree he came to. Arms outstretched, he grasped the branch and hauled himself upward, legs kicking and body obviously straining. There he hung, unable to pull himself onto the branch, a few precipitous feet from terrible hurt. Below him, the enraged pig danced and gnashed its tusks in frustration, unable by only inches to reach the bare flailing feet above it.

En masse, the hunters grabbed their bows and ran to help their stranded comrade, certain that they would feast on this pig at supper.

Kapara was suitably chastened, but within hours, his courage returned. Spying a group of wallaby on the park-like grassland, he indicated that he would like to stalk the miniature kangaroo. Although Papua New Guinea prevents non-residents from harvesting wallaby, locals who relish their dark, stringy meat consider the smallish marsupials superb game.

Kapara led Markworth through a tangle of mangrove and onto the tree-less savanna. Flocks of birds, deer, wallaby and the occasional pig were everywhere. Markworth feared some additional disaster and felt responsible for the native hunter. Kapara was athletic, however, and he stalked effortlessly toward the herd.

His bow in one hand and his camera in the other, Markworth trailed Kapara. Time after time, the New Guinea hunter stalked to within 30 or 40 yards of a wallaby, only to have it bound away and resume feeding at some distant point on the wide savanna. A shot at such a distance would have been easy with Markworth's modern equipment, but Kapara's bamboo bow and crude spear-arrows were so inaccurate that they were barely lethal at any distance.

Instead of using any semblance of a proper arrow shaft with feathers attached for guidance, local hunters used a short, thick cut of bamboo

Kapara and the wallaby he took by stalking to very close range and imitating non-threaten-ing animal behavior. Kapara's split-bamboo bow and awkward arrow can clearly be seen in the picture. Behind him is the Bensbach River of southwest Papua New Guinea and the wide plains that Bob Markworth says were so filled with game and birds, they reminded him of a Garden of Eden.

tipped with a homemade metal arrowhead. The arrow was not unlike a crude version of a Watusi war spear. As an arrow, it was ungainly and inca-pable of flying straight or fast or far. Although he did not know how to ask, Markworth imagined that the native arrow was tipped with some nefarious poison brewed by the village shaman.

In his final stalk, Kapara dropped to the ground and began crawling, slowly and submissively, in the open, toward a wary wallaby. Occasionally he would stop, and pull at the grass or slap the ground with the palm of his hand to imitate the thumping noise a wallaby will make with its large hind foot. Although he must have kept his quarry in his peripheral vision, the native bowhunter never appeared to make eye contact.

Kapara's tactic seemed to lull the wallaby. Several of them even hopped toward him, as if the strange, hump-backed animal, now so obviously devoid of threat, puzzled them.

The wallaby with the greatest curiosity or least fear finally hopped too close. Moving in exquisitely slow motion, the native hunter raised his bow with its clumsy arrow, bent slightly forward toward the apprehensive animal and, in one swift motion, drew and released. The ungainly shaft wobbled for-ward and stabbed the wallaby in the chest where its steel head stuck and held.

A native dugout canoe, hollowed from the trunk of a downed tree, rides just inches above the surface of the Bensbach River in New Guinea. American bowhunter and archery entertainer Bob Markworth had flown there to hunt the island's feral hogs and Rusa deer following a nightclub performance in Australia.

For nearly half an hour, Kapara chased the wallaby around the prairie. When it finally collapsed, the bowhunter drew his sharp, homemade knife and dispatched it. By New Guinea standards, this was fair chase and a proud Kapara would feed his family.

STRAIGHT ARROW

In the jungle of Papua New Guinea, Bob Markworth's hunting friend, Kapara, learned that a bow and well-developed hunting skills are practically useless without a good arrow. The arrow drives home your point; it delivers your message.

Although Kapara might disagree, for us, an arrow is an assembled shaft plus the required components, such as a broadhead and steering feathers. Except for some bowfishing shafts, which may be solid and very heavy, are tied to the bow via a string and are typically shot a short distance, hunting shafts are hollow and lightweight.

Obviously, a shaft has two ends. On the front, you mount a point, sometimes directly onto the shaft and sometimes via an insert. Toward the rear, you mount stabilizing fletching, and on the very butt end, a notched "nock" that holds the shaft on your bowstring.

UNDERSTANDING YOUR ARROW

Arrow shafts are measured and graded by their "spine" or stiffness. This is an important term to understand because manufacturers build

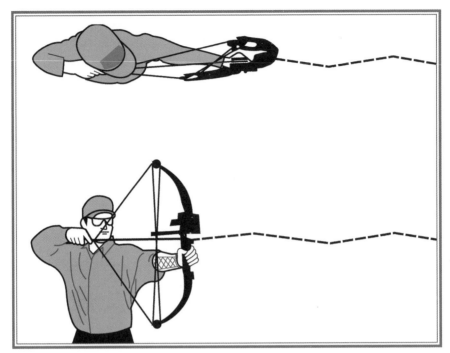

Your arrow immediately responds to the manner of your release. A finger release (top) causes your arrow to swing around your moving fingers as the string bursts forward, and this imparts a side-to-side effect to your arrow in the horizontal plane, called "wallowing." Shoot with a mechanical release aid and your arrow is given its forward motion in part by the nock set—hence the emphasis on straight-line nock travel—and this causes "porpoising," or up-and-down movement in the vertical plane.

arrows in many different spines. For perfect arrow flight, you must match the right arrow size and spine to your bow.

According to the Archery Trade Association, spine is the amount of bend in an arrow shaft caused by a specific weight placed at its center while the shaft is supported at the ends. In addition, the recovery characteristics of an arrow permit it to bend and then return to its original shape while in flight. This definition fits any type of arrow: wood, aluminum, carbon or composite.

An arrow shaft bends as it leaves the bowstring, recovering to its original straight shape several yards down range. This is called "archer's paradox." Its spine is a measure of how much it bends. All arrows from every kind of bow bend when they are shot (with the possible exception of those from Kapara's bow). Some bend more than others. Your job is to minimize that bending so your arrow rapidly achieves stability. If bending occurs at the right frequency before the arrow straightens, its path can be true; otherwise, it will fly poorly.

Shafts released by a mechanical release aid flex in a vertical plane, parallel to the long axis of the bow, while those released with fingers flex in a horizontal plane, perpendicular to the long axis of the bow. A shaft that is correctly spined for your bow set-up will flex less and recover more quickly than one of improper spine. As you are tuning for hunting season, this is an important factor.

For best arrow flight with your hunting set-up, you will need the arrow shaft with the correct spine. To understand how important spine is to good practice groups, shoot arrows that are mismatched. Identical arrows fly much differently from your 45-pound bowfishing recurve than they do from your 70-pound one-cam hunting bow.

When you release the bowstring, you still have power over the bow, but the arrow is gone and out of your control. Like words hastily spoken, you cannot recall the arrow. Therefore, it is critical to find the arrow that flies best from your set-up. This is why arrow-shaft manufacturers offer a fairly bewildering array of sizes and instructions for determining the proper spine.

Each arrow-shaft manufacturer publishes an arrow-shaft selection chart. These are designed to help you match a specific spine (or perhaps as many as three) with the finished arrow's length, the point weight you use, your draw length, the draw weight you are shooting and the type of wheel or cam the bow has, if any: round, hard twin cam, one-cam or recurve. If your arrows are not grouping well, consult the arrow chart for the brand you are shooting. Your shafts may be spined incorrectly for your draw weight. Manufacturers who develop new arrows and stay abreast of emerging bow technology routinely update their arrow charts. Check with a pro shop for current information.

Although one will be most highly recommended, several arrow sizes will normally fly smoothly from your bow. If you are fortunate enough to have a full-line archery dealer in your neighborhood, you may be able to test several size shafts to learn which flies best.

An arrow's spine rating is determined by its wall thickness, diameter, length and the weight of the head, but diameter has the greatest influence.

Usually, the larger the diameter and thicker the walls, the greater the spine. However, a larger diameter arrow with a thin wall can be made stiffer (and lighter) than a smaller diameter arrow with a thick wall.

Shorter shafts will be stiffer than longer shafts. Obviously, a 32-inch 2213 shaft will flex much more than a 26-inch 2213 shaft.

Heavy heads reduce an arrow's spine. A 32-inch 2213 aluminum arrow with a 125-gr. broadhead will flex more than an identical arrow with a 100-gr. head.

Many other variables also affect spine and can change the way your arrow behaves when it is shot. Large fletching, for example, stiffens an arrow in flight. An arrow rest's spring tension setting can affect arrow flight enough to effectively change spine value. And, of course, the way you release the arrow can affect its spine; arrows released with fingers bend more than those shot with a release.

Consider a 30-inch aluminum shaft with a manufacturer's spine rating of 2315. That number, 2315, is printed on the arrow. The first two numbers indicate the shaft's diameter in 64ths of an inch. This arrow is 23/64 inches in diameter, about a third of an inch. The second two numbers tell you its wall thickness in thousandths of an inch, in this case 15/1,000-inch. The manufacturer says this shaft weighs 350 gr. By contrast, a 30-inch 2413 aluminum shaft with a diameter of 24/64-inch and wall thickness of 13/1,000-inch from the same manufacturer weighs 312 gr. Although these shafts have comparable spine, one outweighs the other by 11 percent, and that is significant from a point of view of energy the arrow absorbs when you release the string.

Typically, any given carbon shaft will work over a wider range of spine sizes than will aluminum shafts. This means it is easier to choose the correct spine for a carbon shaft than for an aluminum shaft.

SHAFT SIZE AND WEIGHT

After you make a spine selection, your next consideration is weight. All things being equal, for speed, your best selection will be a lightweight arrow, probably built on a carbon shaft. Lightweight carbon arrows fly faster and with a flatter trajectory than comparably spined aluminum arrows. That is the good news, but that is not every consideration.

No arrow ever absorbs all of a bow's stored energy and lightweight arrows absorb less than heavy arrows, which may absorb as much as 80 percent of a bow's deliverable energy. This means lightweight arrows leave more energy behind in vibration, shock and noise, so you feel a shot much more in your hand and your arm, your bow set-up must be checked more frequently to be sure it does not fall apart, and your shot is noisier. The noise of a 300 fps arrow needs to be dampened and a variety of accessories are designed to help: string silencers, limb pads, extra padding or "socks" in the bow's limb pockets, shock-absorbing stabilizers and so on.

It is an arguable point, but because they absorb less energy, lightweight shafts may not penetrate as well as heavier shafts. This complicates your selection of broadheads. Penetration is not a factor for a competitor shooting at a foam target or a Spartana grass matt, but for a bowhunter aiming at flesh and bone, it is crucial to a generous blood trail.

Light aluminum shafts have thinner walls, and are not as durable as heavier shafts. Although several very good arrow straighteners exist, once the shaft has taken a crease, it is impossible to remove it completely. Never use it again for bowhunting.

A final consideration is that ultralight, high-speed arrows tipped with broadheads are more temperamental than heavier and slower, but more stable arrows. Unless your shot is perfect, very light arrows are likely to react instantly to any variation other than ideal shooting conditions.

The old rule recommended nine gr. of arrow weight for every pound of draw weight. For a 60-pound bow, you shot a 540-gr. arrow. Given modern bow and arrow construction and today's emphasis on a light, fast arrow, modern bowhunters have discarded the old rule. Nevertheless, using draw weight to determine arrow weight is still appropriate. Today, six grains of arrow weight per pound of draw weight is acceptable.

MEASURING ARROW SPEED

We measure arrow speed and rate a bow's performance two ways. Understand the two systems and you will have a standard against which you can tune your own shooting system. Keep in mind that published bow speed is usually the peak arrow speed a company's can achieve. Do not imagine that you can shoot the bow at this speed without a lot of effort.

"Bow speed" is the speed of a properly spined arrow shot from that bow and it is measured in feet per second (fps). A bow shooting 300 fps has become the standard for manufacturers and bowhunters. 300 fps is fast. We usually do not relate it to miles per hour (mph)–in the same way we do not measure the family car in feet per second–but an arrow traveling that fast is moving 1,080,000 feet per hour. That is an awfully big number, but if you were traveling 300 fps–204.55 mph–in the family car, your children would be bug-eyed in terror.

The original speed rating was called "AMO" and it has always been the lesser of the two measures. AMO stands for the Archery Manufacturer's and Merchants Organization (now known as the Archery Trade Association, and some manufacturers are now designating speed as ATA), and it oversees equipment standardization and lobbies in support of bowhunting. The AMO rating is the speed the normal archer will attain with minimum effort. A bow is AMO rated at 30-inch draw length, 60-pound draw weight and a 540-gr. arrow (nine grains of arrow weight per pound of draw weight).

The newer and faster "IBO" speed rating is named after the International Bowhunting Organization, which sponsors 3-D tournaments. Think of the IBO rating as the maximum speed your bow can produce under ideal conditions when the set-up, including the arrow, is perfect. IBO speeds are determined with a 30-inch draw length, a draw weight of 70-pounds and a lightweight, 350-gr. arrow (five grains of arrow weight per pound of draw weight).

Lighter arrows (five grains, not nine) at heavier draw weights (70 pounds, not 60) fly faster. A typical high-end hunting bow will shoot 223 fps AMO. The same bow tested on the IBO scale shoots 300 fps. It will take a significant amount of tuning, tinkering and proper equipment selection to make your arrows fly at that speed.

THE CHRONOGRAPH

You measure arrow speed with a chronograph. Most pro shops and many clubs have one. 3-D tournaments will have one available to ensure that competitors shoot to standard. (Both ASA and IBO limit arrow speed to 280 fps.) Chronographs are not expensive and they are accurate, especially with a three-shot average.

A chronograph clocks how long it takes your arrow to pass over a photoelectric circuit actuated when the arrow interrupts a beam of light. This chronograph style can be adjusted to the length of an arrow and it auto-matically resets. The ProChrono Digital from Competition Electronics is powered by a single nine-volt battery and will give readings from 22 to 7,000 fps in temperatures from 33 to 100 degrees. It is lightweight, easy to set up and has an error of plus or minus a couple of percentage points.

The Shooting Chrony works on the same principle, measuring with a 99.5 percent accuracy. The Master Chrony uses a 16-foot phone cord to con-nect it to a digital display unit and optional printer. The value of a separate readout and printer is that you can move the display away from the actual shooting.

The Arrowspeed RadarChron by Sports Sensors is a small Doppler radar that uses microwave technology (high frequency, short wavelength 5.8-giga-hertz energy) to measure arrow speed. Unlike optical chronographs, the short-range microwave operation of the Arrowspeed cannot be affected by background light or shadows. The Arrowspeed is 2.5 inches by 3.69 inches and weighs 2.7 ounces. It is powered by a three-volt camera battery and has a plus-or-minus two percent error range between 150 and 450 fps.

MEASURING KINETIC ENERGY

Arguably, kinetic energy (KE) is an important concept in bowhunting because it is one of our few relative measures of penetration. Without pen-etrating ability, you simply have no hunting ability. Penetration with a broadhead-tipped arrow means slicing and bleeding, because that is how an arrow kills a game animal. With clean shots to the vitals, good penetration means a good blood trail and a dead game animal within minutes.

It is no longer arguable whether you want a broadhead to pass completely through an animal or to remain inside it. When pre-historic bowhunters shot big game, their flint arrowheads certainly remained inside the animal, but these hunters often used poison because their arrows did not pack enough KE to kill a deer or a giraffe quickly by hemorrhaging alone. Bow and arrow dynamics are different today. The idea that a broadhead should remain inside an animal and continue to cut its insides as it runs is discredited.

The penetration standard today is an arrow tipped with a super-sharp broadhead that passes cleanly and quickly through an animal. This gives you an entry hole and an exit hole, both leaking blood. Because most deer

Eland are the largest of the African antelope and bulls can weigh up to 2,000 pounds. To take one of these trophies requires an arrow that delivers greater kinetic energy than is needed to take a 150-pound whitetail buck. Hunting consultant and "journeyman bowhunter" Rick Valdez has successfully taken most of the world's big-game animals and many small ones as well. He harvested his African eland in July 2001 while hunting with Nico Lourens Safaris and shooting carbon arrows and mechanical broadheads.

and bears are shot from treestands, it is important to have that lower exit hole for blood to drain as the heart pumps.

How much kinetic energy is enough? There is no standard, but the larger the game animal, the greater the KE required for a quick, clean kill. For a 100-pound deer, 40 to 50 foot-pounds is sufficient; less is acceptable with precise arrow placement. For larger, heavier animals like elk or caribou, you should step up your on-target energy delivery. A dramatic increase in KE is required for Cape buffalo or brown bear.

The formula for calculating kinetic energy in foot-pounds is speed (in fps) squared, multiplied by total arrow weight (in grains, including your broadhead), divided by 450,240. A foot-pound is the energy required to raise one pound, one foot against gravity. Under laboratory conditions, you would think that an arrow with 50 foot-pounds of KE should penetrate twice as far as an arrow with 25 foot-pounds. Penetration is a complex result of many factors however, and it is not that simple.

Studying the formula, many bowhunters assume that a fast light arrow will give them greater KE, but the formula is deceptive in several respects.

A light arrow absorbs less energy than a heavy arrow and, depending on the size, number and orientation of your broadhead blades and type of broadhead, it may retain its energy longer in flight!

Here is an example. Let us say you are shooting 250 fps with a 500-grain Easton aluminum shaft, which includes a 100-grain broadhead and the insert. What happens if you switch to a 400-grain Carbon Force arrow with a 75-grain head? You pick up about ten fps, but the heavier projectile delivers 69.4 foot-pounds of KE while the lighter (but faster!) arrow gives you 60.0 foot-pounds. The lighter projectile has 16 percent less energy at chronograph or point-blank range than the heavier projectile!

At close range, say ten to 20 yards, this should not make a difference, but what about longer distances? Again, conventional wisdom suggests that the heavier arrow will retain more energy at 30 or 40 yards.

In his book Idiot Proof Archery, archery coach and bowhunter Bernie Pellerite argues that this is not so because the larger, heavier arrow is subject to greater resistance or drag than the smaller, lighter arrow. A smaller, lighter shaft with a mechanical head in his experiments retains greater energy at 40 yards because it encounters less resistance than an arrow with fixed blades.

Conventional wisdom also says that another way to increase KE is to increase your draw weight. Increase just five pounds and you can pick up about 10 percent in energy and gain speed and a flatter trajectory.

We also know that stiffer, straight-flying arrows out-penetrate wobbly arrows. For deepest penetration, your arrow's energy must be directed down the centerline of the shaft, because when a flexing arrow hits game–unless it is flying perfectly and hits perfectly straight-on–the shaft whips to one side. This diminishes the energy available to drive the shaft through your quarry. In perfect flight, all energy is centered behind the broadhead.

Walking or running animals cause arrows to lurch sideways on impact. The broadhead enters, the shaft whips to one side, and penetration suffers. For best penetration, never shoot at a running animal. Unless your bow is extra-heavy, you will probably fail to shoot completely through it.

Unfortunately, there is no formula for determining what game animals can (or should) be hunted with any particular bow set-up. In the field, too many conditions interfere with precise measurements. Nevertheless, Easton has published the following recommendations which, they note, are intended only to be a guide. If you have any doubt about your own set-up, err on the high side and remember that while heavier arrows absorb more KE, resistance slows those heavier set-ups and reduces the KE available to drive your shaft completely through an animal. Undoubtedly, the ideal size and weight arrow is the one that you can put successfully on target within your own shooting range.

KE (FT/LB) OF YOUR SET-UP	SUITABLE FOR HUNTING
Less than 25	Small game: rabbit and squirrel
26–41	Medium game: pronghorn and deer
42–65	Large game: black bear, elk, and wild boar
66 and higher	Big Game: African plains game, grizzly, and brown bears

SHOULD YOU SHOOT ALUMINUM OR CARBON ARROWS?

Aluminum or carbon? Each type shaft has its proponents and detractors. "Carbon has unquestionably grown in popularity," says Deb Adamson at Easton, which manufactures Easton aluminum and Beman carbon shafts. "Carbon shafts are excellent and the price has fallen in the last few years, but assuming they come from the manufacturer straight (a carbon shaft cannot be straightened) it is going to be hard to beat a carbon shaft for speed, accuracy and durability. An arrow shaft is what delivers your broadhead on target, so we do not believe you should economize there. Buy quality and that means an exacting level of straightness with tight-fitting components."

Aluminum arrow shafts have been the standard for years, only recently being overtaken by the carbon revolution. Aluminum arrows are consistent in size and weight, thanks to precise manufacturing tolerances. They are formed by drawing aluminum tubes across a mandrel until they meet exact specifications for diameter, wall thickness and weight. The shafts are then straightened to tolerances as fine as .0015 inch.

The straighter they are, the more they cost, but how straight is straight enough? Usually, competitors want supreme, ultra-straight grades. For bowhunting, medium grades are fine.

Aluminum shafts are available in more than 50 sizes, with diameters ranging from 14/64 to 26/64 inch, and wall thickness from .011 to .19 inch. Within this range, everyone who shoots a bow can find a good shaft, one with the correct combination of spine and weight, from ultra-light for speed to ultra-heavy for maximum launch energy.

Any aluminum arrow can bend and break and the thinner the wall, the more susceptible it is to damage. Aluminum arrows with thick walls, however, hold up well under hunting conditions. Within a limited range, aluminum shafts can be straightened and reused for practice, not for hunting.

A standard feature of aluminum shafts is the use of head and nock inserts made of aluminum, plastic or carbon. Aluminum inserts are anchored with hot-melt glue. Carbon inserts, which weigh 10 to 15 gr. less than aluminum, may be installed with epoxy . . . or are of the press-fit style that can be used without glue because they fit so tightly inside the tubes.

Aluminum arrows come in a multitude of camouflage designs and colors to fit every bowhunter's taste. They are also less expensive than carbon shafts.

Carbon arrows may be all-carbon or composite or even aluminum covered by multiple wraps of woven carbon matt. These shafts are characterized by relatively small diameter and light weight; even at their maximum length and stiffness, they are lighter than aluminum. Carbon allows you to keep kinetic energy delivery high and gives you a speed advantage, too.

Carbon shafts bend, but do not stay bent, so you will never need to straighten them, and they can break if they hit a hard object. The biggest problem for carbon may come from being struck by another arrow at a target butt. Unlike aluminum, a carbon shaft that is chipped or creased is unusable and should be discarded, because splinters of carbon are extremely sharp and even a small shred of ingested carbon, if an arrow were to fracture in a game animal, could be deadly.

Arrow penetration tests using different types of foam targets give carbon arrows the edge over aluminum arrows with comparable spine, due primarily to carbon's smaller diameter. Larger-diameter shafts drift a little more in a crosswind, too.

Although dot and 3-D shooters prefer larger aluminum shafts called "line cutters," many bowhunters argue that slender carbon shafts, offering less surface resistance, do penetrate better. Others say the hole made by a broadhead is so much larger than the shaft diameter that penetration is unlikely to be affected by shaft size.

Carbon's small diameter has caused rest-clearance problems on older style shoot-through rests. With a larger diameter shaft, a rest's launcher arms can be spread apart, allowing lots of room for fletching to clear. With carbon shafts, support arm tips must be placed close together. Fletching must line up perfectly to slip between the arms.

In the early 1990s, carbon shaft design was in its infancy. Heads and nocks were occasionally attached with outserts, which slipped over the end of the shafts. That technology has been refined and today's inserts help with consistent arrow flight and ease of changing heads.

Initial thinking behind carbon arrows was that they were tough, flexible and would help bowhunters pick up arrow speed. In recent years, even many traditional archers have switched to carbon arrows. One reason for such a strong movement to carbon is their stiff spine in relation to weight. Traditional archers prefer wood shafts, but a recurve shooter with a long draw often has difficulty buying adequately spined cedar shafts. Plus wood arrows are expensive and difficult to find with good, straight grain. With carbon, you get plenty of spine at any arrow length.

A second reason for the move to carbon is the small diameter of carbon arrows. Unlike compound bows, not all recurves and longbows are cut past center. This makes carbon attractive, because a small-diameter shaft lays closer to the bow's centerline than a larger diameter wood or aluminum shaft.

Early carbon arrows were almost prohibitively expensive. The development of new grades of carbon, however, and new manufacturing methods have put low-end carbon shafts in a price range comparable to the best grades of aluminum.

Cedar arrows have a strong following among ardent stick bow shooters and some archers believe wood is a superior arrow material because it has flexing qualities similar to carbon that make arrows forgiving. Nevertheless, solid wood arrows do not perform as consistently as aluminum or carbon because they are heavy, the direction of grain must be consistent and they are hard to re-straighten if they bend.

Even hand-selected cedar varies greatly in density and weight, and cedar shafts must be methodically matched for spine. Well-matched cedar shafts can be shot accurately from stick bows and they can be painted and fletched handsomely.

Although, quality wood arrows cost more than any other shaft material, they have a brittle reputation and their durability is less than desirable, even when completely waterproofed. In addition, they can absorb water and warp in wet weather.

CARBON SHAFT SAFETY

Carbon shafts are suitable for any hunting application. If carbon arrows are abused, hit by other arrows or slapped against hard objects, however, damage to the carbon fibers can occur. Carbon arrows should always be gently flexed and twisted end-to-end as well as visually inspected for delamination or splitting before shooting. A damaged shaft could fail on release and hurt you or others.

When you set up a bow to shoot carbon, be sure to check your rest settings, specifically prong spacing to insure your arrows will not fall through. Be aware also of your arrow's position during the draw to avoid having it fall off the rest, as it could become jammed between the rest and riser. An arrow jammed between the rest and riser or between the prongs of the rest will fail.

Carbon hunting arrows could break or delaminate after being shot into an animal, resulting in sharp splinter-like fragments left inside its body. A break may occur inside an animal and not be immediately obvious after you recover it. These fragments will be harmful if ingested, so use extreme caution when field dressing game. In the past, manufacturers have recommended that you remove flesh in the immediate area of the wound, clean the area surrounding the wound, and dispose of any meat that might contain carbon splinters.

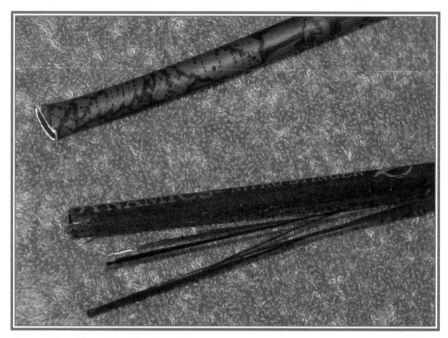

Factors that differentiate aluminum from carbon/graphite arrows are how they bend, how they break, and the potential results. All shafts bend slightly as they leave your bowstring, even wood. An aluminum arrow will bend and can be repaired—some—but the result of hitting a rock will most likely be a broken shaft, and a broadhead and insert driven down into the fore-end as much as an inch. Bowhunters occasionally find broken aluminum shafts when they field dress a game animal. Stepping on a shaft or hitting a tree may give it a permanent crease, too. In either case, the arrow should be discarded. A carbon shaft, on the other hand, will bend a great deal and still recover fully. If a carbon arrow shatters as it passes through a big-game animal, and this is exceptionally rare, harmful carbon splinters can remain inside the body cavity. Unless they are removed before the meat is packaged and prepared for the table, these splinters can be deadly. While carbon shafts resist the dings and dents you find in oft-used aluminum arrows, they should also be discarded if damaged.

SHAFT ACCESSORIES

Once you have chosen between carbon or aluminum and made a properly spined shaft selection for your draw weight and style of bow, you must attach things to that shaft: fletching to steer it, a nock to hold it on the bowstring and some type of arrow point and insert. Every shaft type has its own set of options, and your archery club or pro shop can guide you through the selection and set-up process until it becomes second nature.

Whatever you choose, unless you have the pro shop set everything up or you buy ready-made arrows, your new arrow shaft will be useless. Wood arrows must be tapered, and there are special tools for both ends. Carbon and aluminum shafts must have lightweight threaded inserts installed for standard practice points or broadheads. The inserts should fit tightly and should press absolutely straight into the shaft; rotate them to be sure that any glue used completely encircles the insert; finally, press them onto a flat surface to be sure they are fully seated. Unless you buy the correct size insert for your arrow, all bets are off, and if you glue the insert in crooked, your chance of hitting what you are shooting at dramatically decreases. With the increasing popularity of carbon, there has been a major push to standardize. Around 2005, main-line carbon shafts use carbon inserts of the same style as aluminum shafts, but the two are not interchangeable because of the differing shaft sizes.

The beauty of the broadhead insert is that it allows you to screw in and then remove arrow points as often as you desire. On the back end, you can experiment with different types of arrow nocks or even use one of the relatively new, stick-on tunable nocks that rotate to give you the best fletching-arrow rest orientation.

The arrow nock is critical to shooting performance. Nocks attach to the rear of your arrow shaft to hold it on the bowstring. They should snap on the string snugly, but not so tight that they hinder arrow flight when you release. Bowhunters who shoot release-aids often say they prefer nocks to be a little tighter than finger shooters. This keeps arrows from falling off the string after contact with the jaws of a release.

Consistency is crucial for successful bowhunting. Your arrows should fit the string identically and release with equal force. Once you find a nock that fits your bowstring and snaps on and off perfectly, use the same brand and size on all arrows.

Two types of nocks are preferred, but the one-piece nock that is glued directly onto a swaged shaft is being replaced for both aluminum and carbon shafts by press-in nocks that are easy to rotate for fletching clearance over your rest. To rotate a glue-on nock, you must melt it with heat and then cut it off.

You must put the nock on the shaft straight. A crooked nock pushes arrows slightly sideways when you release, causing your arrow to fly erratically. If one arrow consistently hits wide or high, immediately check the nock for straightness. In the field, you can cradle the arrow on a smooth surface like the "V" between your pinched together fingernails and blow on the fletching to spin the arrow. If there is any wobble in the nock, replace it. Inexpensive arrow spinners are available from Apple Archery to help you check nock and broadhead straightness. This simple step can significantly improve your accuracy.

Arrows are sized by stiffness or spine, to help you decide which shaft will fly best with your set-up. Unless the shaft is wood, the manufacturer's spine index is roll printed on it. The Easton 2213 aluminum shaft has a diameter of 22/64 inches and a wall thickness of 13/1,000 inch. These shafts are drawn from 7075-T9 aluminum and have a weight tolerance of + 1% and a straightness of + .002 inches. The Gold Tip graphite XT Hunter has a weight tolerance of + 2 gr. per dozen and a straightness tolerance of + .003 inch per shaft. This arrow weighs 8.2 gr./inch with a .400-inch spine, an outside diameter of .295 inches and an inside diameter of .246 inches. You must add components to a bare shaft to make it a useful arrow, but every component you add will change its performance. It is a conundrum. This means that for ideal flight and broadhead delivery, you must take exceptional care building and maintaining your arrows: inserts and nocks must be applied in a straight line and broadheads must spin true, indicating that the force applied comes in a single direction with no torqued side vectors.

FLETCHING

An arrow's feathers or vanes give your shaft stability in flight. Ideally, it should begin to rotate, like a bullet fired from a rifled barrel with twisting internal lands and grooves, as soon as it clears the riser.

Man has used bird feathers to stabilize arrows since he began shooting the bow. Feathers are not as popular now as they were just a dozen years ago because we rely so heavily on plastic vanes. Some archery pro-shop owners believe that 90 percent of all arrows shot today use plastic vanes.

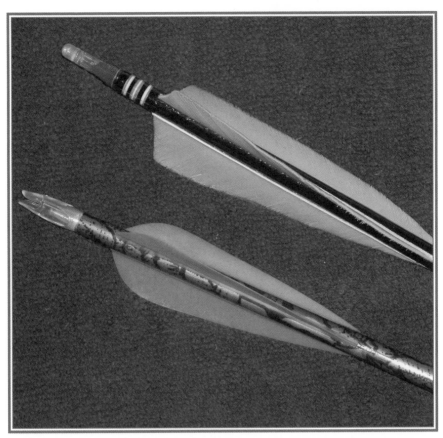

Among the other choices you make in developing your individual bowhunting set-up is whether to shoot arrows fletched with vanes or feathers. Plastic vanes made from urethane, vinyl or Mylar, are more durable and quieter than feathers. Feathers, taken from the wings of white pen-raised turkeys and dyed, are more forgiving of shooting-form errors and incidental contact with your arrow rest or a branch. They also weigh less than vanes; hence, arrows fletched with feathers are a few feet per second faster than arrows fletched with comparably sized vanes.

SPEED

Arrow speed is a big issue. Even small, custom bow manufacturers say prospective buyers ask what speed their bows can attain. Many people do not know that, among all the other variables, arrow fletching makes a difference in speed and feathers weigh less than plastic vanes. Bob Link at Trueflight says, "If you use feathers, there is less mass to accelerate and less wasted energy. Feathers save as much as 40 grains weight over full-length plastic vanes, and if they hit your arrow rest or bow riser they less interference. This also contributes to higher arrow speed."

Finally, feathers provide superior guidance, which helps prevent yawing

These two photos on the previous page compare typical anchor positions of a finger shoot-er and a release shooter. The amount of string contact with the release agent–fingers or mechanical release–is apparent and this helps understand archer's paradox or the bending of an arrow in the horizontal plane around the bow riser when released with fingers. When released with a mechanical release, the arrow flexes vertically from the columnar loading applied to your shaft. Finger shooter Gene Goldacker, a bowhunter and NFAA competitor, anchors with the knuckle of his thumb at the point of his jaw, rather than a more typical anchor with the tip of the index or middle finger at the corner of the mouth. For true align-ment, his kisser button is pre-set to touch the tip of his nose and the string comes back to touch his lips also. This gives him multiple checks on his anchor in addition to the peep sight. Release shooter Jeff Hopkins, a bowhunter and world class 3-D champion, anchors behind his jaw. Jeff draws the string to the exact position each time by bringing it back to touch his nose and the corner of his mouth. Jeff also uses a peep sight.

and fishtailing–erratic oscillations that add drag and slow an arrow down.

"On typical equipment," Link says, "independent tests confirm a five-feet-per-second gain as the arrow leaves the bow."

And how about down range? Velocity testing by archery engineer Norb Mullaney has shown that comparable feather-fletched arrows are still traveling four feet per second faster than plastic at 29 yards. Therefore, at usual bowhunting ranges, feather-fletched arrows travel faster and have flatter trajectories than plastic-fletched arrows.

STABILITY

Feathers stabilize arrows better and faster than vanes. A feather's surface has a regular, rippling roughness that causes a periodic disturbance in airflow over it. Trueflight calls this "grip." When an arrow "yaws" or flexes to the side, grip helps realign it faster than a smooth plastic vane.

The weight savings with feathers also helps stability. Any weight added to the rear of the arrow makes the arrow less stable. Add too much weight on its rear and the arrow will try to fly down range butt first.

Finally, as fletching crosses the arrow rest following release, you will experience occasional incidental contact even on a well-tuned bow. Feathers fold down out of the way, and then pop back up. Plastic vanes, because they are more rigid, bounce the rear of the arrow out of alignment. This deflec-tion causes substantial arrow swing and is aggravated by a plastic vane's weight and lack of grip.

YAWING

"Yaw" or "porpoising" is caused by columnar loading of the shaft and thrust applied in the vertical plane. For a microsecond, the end wants to go faster than the middle and the heavy head is least responsive to movement in any direction. The result is yawing or vertical flexing, sometimes called porpoising.

While the arrow is yawed, aerodynamic forces push it away from where you aimed it. Due to the more sluggish straightening ability of plastic vanes, the arrow oscillates from one yawed condition to another and this flexing costs speed, range and accuracy. While the condition gradually decreases, feather faithful believe feathers decrease it faster than vanes. What's more, the penetration of a yawed arrow is lower than a straight arrow. Yawing dissipates energy away from straight-line penetration.

THE FEATHER RECORD

A feather's ability to fold down if it hits something eliminates the large initial reaction after contact. A feather's light weight and "grip" adds to an arrow's stability and brings it into straight flight quickly. The combination of all these advantages means good arrow flight is more readily achievable with feathers. Thus, a feather-fletched arrow tolerates a range of bow variables and some errors in shooting form. Feathers also make tuning easier.

Feathers fly well even with variations in spine, bow weight and form of release. In the field, not many variables are controllable. Small variations in form are normal. Time, terrain, obstacles, cross winds . . . all these things add variation. A feather-fletched arrow simply tolerates variations better than vanes.

Because most of them shoot off a solid and unforgiving arrow shelf, traditional archers overwhelmingly shoot feathers. A minority of recurve shooters use a flipper-style rest and cushion plunger. This minority uses low-profile vanes, but their shafts are quite small and they tend to be expert in shooting form with a flawless release.

Feathers give traditional bowhunters control. Their feathers certainly hit the bow's riser at the shelf area before lying down flat, thereby causing remarkably little arrow flight interference. Feather adherents argue that the same thing happens when a shot hits or passes close to a branch.

According to Gateway Feather, bowhunters who consider using feathers rather than vanes often ask, "What orientation feathers should I use, left-wing or right-wing?" and "I shoot right handed. Should I use right-wing feathers?" Feathers from a turkey's left wing and right wing grow in mirrored curves and archers concerned with eliminating any possible source of error are interested. By all accounts, whether you use left- or right-wing feathers is not an issue that makes any measurable difference, because arrows do not being to spin until they are clear of the bow.

"Right-wing feathers, those with the little edge we call a 'catch lip,' have the lip on the left and rotate the shaft clockwise," Link says. "Left-wing feathers, with the 'catch lip' on the right side of the base, rotate counter-clockwise as seen by the shooter."

The big knocks on feathers are that they soak up moisture and are noisy. A rain-soaked feather changes your shooting dynamic because the weight is greater and a wet feather will not respond as quickly as a vane or a dry feather. However, several waterproofing agents are available to prevent their soaking up moisture.

Vanes shoot quieter than feathers. In a quiet wood, you can hear the flight of a feathered shaft, notes Roger Grundman of Flex-Fletch. Today, because bowhunters are doing everything possible to silence their shot, this is an issue. Vanes have very little "whistle" or flutter. On the other hand, the soft s-s-s-s-s sound of an arrow might only be a bird in flight or the wind rustling through leaves.

VANES

Bowhunters who want the latest gear and greatest arrow speed typically switch to vanes, but Link wonders if this is their best choice. "High-performance set-ups mean more energy and lower flight times," he says. "Stability and solid guidance are even more important. Any errors in form or equipment imperfections will be magnified. Less time is available for your guidance system to work."

While it is less of a problem today, plastic's flexibility and stiffness can change with variations in temperature. Plastic becomes more rigid in cold weather and more flexible in hot weather. This affects arrow flight and bow tuning.

Ultra-slow motion film shows that when an arrow is shot, plastic vanes ripple and flap as if the shooter were shaking a towel. This begins immediately due to the low strength-to-weight ratio of plastic, and it continues as the arrow plunges down range. The same film shows feathers quickly regaining an upright and stabilizing posture, even at high speed.

Plastic vanes cost less than feathers and are easier to mass-produce. Feathers grow on white birds and are plucked and cut by hand; the bases are ground and the feather is dyed. These manual operations cause feathers to cost more than plastic.

FLETCHING PARTICULARS

You want the smallest fletching that will keep your arrow's weight and friction profile at a minimum. Larger fletching stabilizes better, but at some point, the large vanes develop too much drag and cause, rather than cure, a problem with arrow stabilization.

"In general," Link has written, "a five-inch, three-fletch or four-inch, four-fletch will give excellent results on hunting arrows. High-speed bows shooting wide, heavy heads may require something in the 5 3/4-inch length." This may no longer be true.

These days, bowhunters with fast bows are shooting a stiff arrow. The arrow is tipped with a lightweight head, perhaps even a mechanical head with very little profile, not a "wide, heavy" broadhead. A four-inch, three-fletch configuration is standard, and plastic vanes are the public's overwhelming choice because they are bright, cheap and easy to work with. It is rare to find a bowhunter shooting four-fletch arrows.

Bowhunters argue about everything, including the best fletching shape, especially at its rear end. Conventional wisdom says for just the right amount of drag to steady your flying arrow, an offset (glued on straight, but at a slight angle to the centerline of the shaft) or helical (curved slightly around the shaft) mount works best to add gyroscopic stabilizing and help the shaft rotate. Helical and offset fletching produces more rotation and stability than straight-mounted vanes.

Whether you shoot low-profile parabolic fletching (round back), shield-cut (a chopped back end) or some magnum style, this is a matter of personal style and is not important for flight.

With fletching, the final word may be that whatever size, style or orientation you choose, make your arrows uniform so you can test and tune for best arrow flight.

ROTATION

At the speed an arrow rotates with correctly positioned fletching (beginning an inch to an inch and a half forward of the base of the shaft), the speed of rotation is from 1,200 to 2,500 revolutions per minute.

Trueflight commissioned a test with typical hunting arrows fletched using feathers in a strongly helical Bitzenburger clamp. After the initial "spin-up" period, the arrow rotated at 2,850 rpm, or about one turn every five feet!

A note about consistency: Not only must arrow shafts be matched to a given bow, but they must also be matched to each other. Small variations in length, diameter, head weight and fletching style can make it impossible to achieve consistent arrow flight and tight groups. Your finished arrows should be identical in weight. Even with identical spine values, arrows with weight variations as small as five grains can have differing impact points at various ranges, especially shooting broadheads. ■

Pressing Your Point Home: Your Broadhead

STAY SHARP!

Floyd "Sonny" Templeton owns a septic tank cleaning business in Lincoln, Montana, a mile-high mountain town of 1,000 residents 14 miles west of the Continental Divide. It is hard work, but the area is stunningly beautiful, rich in big game and he is his own boss.

Templeton sets his own hours and he turns down jobs if they conflict with his hunting. Typically, he begins work as the snow melts sometime in April and, except for emergencies, he is finished for the year by mid-November when the ground begins to freeze again. It is this freedom, this very American self-indulgent entrepreneurial attitude, that nearly got him killed.

On the 22nd of September, 1997, Templeton stared into the cold, impassionate eyes of a man-killer and the experience was one that sends chills up his spine to this very day. That he lived to tell his story is a testament to years of experience in the outdoors, to keeping a cool head under extreme circumstances and to making the perfect shot when the pressure was on.

Ask about Floyd Templeton in Lincoln and people will shake their heads. Everyone knows him as "Sonny," a family man with grown-up kids. He laughs in a congenial and self-conscious manner and says he's "more or less a homebody."

Templeton may seem average, but get him on the subject of bowhunting and this homebody demonstrates a superior grasp of environmental concepts, biological issues and hunting tactics. Templeton truly "lives to hunt."

Templeton's brothers-in-law taught him to hunt "back east" in Bucks County, Pennsylvania. By 1968, though, he had gotten tired of the "rat race" and so moved his family to Montana. He says they would never, ever consider moving "back east."

Despite his laid-back attitude toward business, Templeton is not a sleepy, stay-at-home guy. He is thoughtful and well-traveled, an instructor for the International Bowhunter Education Program and a former Director of the Montana Bowhunter's Association. Bowhunting since he was 15 years old, the 50-ish outdoorsman has 17 animals listed in the Pope & Young record book: whitetails, pronghorns, elk and mountain lions.

"I haven't hunted with a gun in years, now," he says.

Standing five-feet-ten-inches tall, with a salt-and-pepper beard and a

Sonny Templeton is an informed and dedicated bowhunter who understands environmental issues and is involved in the rough-and-tumble politics needed to ensure a future for those who want to hunt in a state with such rich and diverse resources as Montana. Sonny is proud of a string of bowhunting trophies that include his 70 6/8 P&Y antelope.

wide-open, Big Sky kind of smile, he's every inch a friendly, robust mountain man. When he fits an arrow on the string of his compound bow, however, he is anything but laid back. "Concentrated" comes to mind, for Templeton shoots instinctively, without sights. He "looks" his arrow into its target, a difficult shooting technique to master.

On Templeton's special day that September in 1997, he was elk hunting alone, even though it is not elk but whitetails that are his particular passion. Long, cool shadows were flooding down the slopes and reaching out across the floor of the high mountain meadows.

His enthusiasm to hunt, which he admits is boundless some days, overwhelmed the practicalities of his situation. He could hunt. Therefore, he did.

Templeton did not give a lot of thought to what he would he do if he actually killed an elk. How would he manage, faced with the deep, starry darkness of the high Rockies, the certain possibility of predators, including grizzlies, a long hike to his pick-up truck and 800 pounds of meat and antlers on the forest floor? Knowing Templeton, he would have managed . . . somehow.

On the 22nd, Templeton was hunting at almost two miles above sea level. Elk were visible in a distant meadow and it stood to reason that he would find a good bull or perhaps two, shadowing the herd of cows, calves and immature males. He made his way in their direction and bugled loudly. It was a melodious and echoing, multi-note screech that ended in a diminishing series of grunts and chuckles. Perfect.

Laying his bow at his feet, the right hander next chirped vigorously, making the high-pitched twittering sound of a cow talking to her calf. The elk were relaxed, as if they had never been stalked by man or beast.

Templeton had not passed another truck for miles on the rugged, unpaved US Forest Service logging road. He was very much alone and he liked his hunting that way: silent, lonely, deadly.

"Something," Templeton says, made him turn his head to the right. It could have been a deer or a bear, or even a trophy bull skulking through the timber, searching for the interloper who was squealing challenges down into the mountain basin. A bull with antlers surpassing his most recent trophy would cause his heart to pound with excitement, but any elk up close is exciting.

Templeton was not afraid of hunting alone, except for the possibility of getting lost in the Lewis & Clark Range. That would mean spending the night on a cold mountain and hours of fumbling around until he cut a road. It was not Montana's most difficult real estate, but it was tough enough if one became disoriented without a map or compass.

Templeton had seen occasional lions and bears, and his stepson, Chris, had an uncomfortably close encounter with a lion once. Other hunters told stories about the rangy, quarrelsome cats . . . predators which rely primarily

Sonny Templeton was already an experienced bowhunter when the mountain lion stalked him in September 1997. A few years earlier, in December 1993, he took a lion that weighed 170 pounds and scored 14 11/16 P&Y.

on sight and sound rather than smell . . . walking right under their treestands, unaware of the human competitor. Had the lions detected them, the hunters would have known immediately, because cats are inquisitive, superb climbers and very fast.

"Doggone that elk scent!"

The bowhunter had, in fact, killed a big "book lion" just four years earlier. It weighed 170 pounds and lived on as a crouching, snarling wall mount to remind Templeton of his high altitude chase through the snow.

Templeton was not concerned about lions. He figured he knew lions. He had killed a big one already.

Or perhaps Templeton just thought he knew lions, because the rustling in the willows nearby was not a deer or a squirrel; it was a stalking lion and it was well aware of Templeton's presence. The hunter had become the hunted.

Templeton's first emotion was irritation. His sublime, human cocoon of superiority was not immediately threatened. He might have to yell at it to scare it away and there would go a perfectly good elk set up.

Templeton's time had come. Too bad about the elk hunt. He hollered at the lion, which slipped out of the brush a scant 15 yards away. The lion dropped into a crouch and crept toward him, legs tensed, ears laid back. Perfectly silent on four splayed, padded paws.

Templeton yelled again and still, "It just kept coming."

Adopting a tactic that wildlife management professionals suggest may work in some situations, Templeton opened his camo jacket as wide as possible to appear larger than life. All the while, he kept yelling.

In its totality, the incident only lasted a minute, but to Templeton it seems, in the recounting, to have taken far longer.

Templeton and the cat never took their eyes off each other. Each sized up the other for a weakness. Templeton was mystified by the unrelenting gaze of the carnivore, the glassy-eyed stare of the cat's oversize watery pupils.

The lion was telling him, "Don't take offense. This isn't personal." Templeton, of course, knew otherwise. It was rapidly becoming very personal.

The big cat crept closer and finally, in exasperation, Templeton did what any hiker or hunter would do: He reached down and picked up several rocks. Throwing them at the stalking lion, Templeton believes he would have done anything to break the cat's concentration.

Templeton's first throw missed high, but the second whacked the animal squarely on the shoulder. Hard. The cat was undeterred. Less than ten yards away, its long tail twitched and its belly scraped the ground. Crouched. Tense.

In a single leap, big cats can cover 40 feet, six times their body length. Had it chosen to spring, it would have been on top of the bowhunter in an instant. But this cat just stared and bared its yellow teeth as it advanced, perhaps allowing the hot closeness of the hunter's anxious scent to center it mentally for one death-dealing charge.

"After the rock hit and it didn't run away, I thought, 'I'm in trouble.' I don't know why it didn't occur to me earlier, but at that point I began to get scared." At that point, Templeton decided his only salvation lay in self-defense.

He knew that if he ran, the lion would kill him. His death would be swift, a few seconds. Compared to a healthy, middle-aged man, a lion is far stronger and lightning fast. A killing machine, its teeth and hinged jaw are designed for separating vertebrae and crushing the victim's windpipe while its two-inch claws slash deep for a bloody hold as its victim staggers in terror.

Unlike the old saying, Templeton would know what hit him. Even though it would be over quickly, the last moments of his life would not be pleasant. Roughly equal in size, there was a chance that he could have fought off the attack . . . an outside chance.

Templeton's bow lay at his feet. Without taking his eyes off the advancing cat, he picked it up and nocked an arrow. The lion edged closer, never blinking, never stopping.

Compared to his 170-pound trophy, this animal seemed huge, but on that earlier day in 1993, Templeton had been the hunter, not the quarry. This lion moved toward him in absolute silence, never once blinking. As its soft paws filed inexorably forward, the beauty of great strength showed in the thick muscles of its back and shoulders, sending a shiver up Templeton's spine.

Literally in the lion's face, the bowhunter was out of time. He did not want to think about his training, especially how the bow is an effective killing instrument, but not a "stopper." A 165-grain ballistic tip bullet from a high-power rifle traveling 2,800 feet per second with a force of 2,873 foot pounds of kinetic energy . . . now that's a stopper. But a 60- or 70-foot pound bow was all Templeton had.

Ears laid back, head up, the lion was a mere eight yards away now. Its long, tawny body hung low to the ground, tail twitching from side to side, when Templeton drew, sighted instinctively and released his arrow. One shot. It had to be good. At this close range, it had to stop the big carnivore. Templeton's life depended on it.

Traveling at 200 miles per hour, the 600-grain broadhead-tipped arrow slammed into the lion's skull just beneath its left eye. With the cat making directly for him, there was no option other than a head-on shot.

If Templeton missed or only slightly wounded it, the cat could still have caught and killed him, sinking its narrow, wickedly curving canines deep between two neck vertebrae or disemboweling him with powerful claws on whirling, muscular rear legs.

But this day, Templeton did not miss. The stunned animal screamed in surprise and whirled, writhing in pain as it tore at the aluminum shaft. With supreme presence of mind, Templeton shot again, this time taking the lion squarely through its chest.

The scrambling, eerily whining cat disappeared; it was dead or dying. Templeton was certain the second arrow had delivered the fatal blow.

He was angry that this encounter had taken place. It seemed to be a terrible waste. As Templeton wrestled with adrenaline-tremors, the anger for having his day's hunt ruined ebbed. He had lived an adventure, one he would tell his kids about. Perhaps his grand-kids, too, but he hated to shoot the lion. He wished it had run away when he hit it

In September 1997, bowhunter Sonny Templeton of Lincoln, Montana, remained cool under extreme pressure and buried his three-blade broadhead in the skull of a mountain lion at about six to eight yards as it methodically stalked him.

with the rock. It was a beautiful creature and the mountains belonged to it and its prey. Templeton knew he had just been in the wrong place at the wrong time, so he headed toward his pick-up.

Overarched by looming pines and shrouded by dark green firs, the dirt road gradually disappeared beneath his feet. The lion was nowhere to be seen or heard. That could be a good thing or it could be bad, depending. The elk, of course, were long gone.

It was eerily quiet now and Templeton was suddenly conscious of being alone. His footsteps echoed in his ears as he listened to night sounds and the swishing throb of blood in his ears. A scurry in the bushes. A hooting owl. The distant, yipping howl of a coyote. But there was no soft pant or moonlight glint off yellow fangs.

The hike out took forever. When Templeton's body fully responded with a burst of chemical emotion, he shook with anger at the waste of the cat's life and, at last, the fear of "what could have been," as well. The shaking left him with a touch of nausea and the classic self-doubt of adrenaline withdrawal.

Still, his outdoor training and a cool head guided him, because as he walked he hung blaze-orange ribbons to guide him and Montana game warden Jeff Campbell back to the spot of the encounter the next day. Never once did Templeton stop moving, though, not to tie a boot lace or pee in the bush or drink from his canteen.

When he reached the safety of his truck, Templeton rolled up the windows, locked the doors and turned on the lights. Then he made the decision that separates him from many others. He decided to notify the game warden.

"I was afraid they wouldn't believe me and that they would fine me or I would lose my hunting license," Templeton says, but he called Campbell anyway. He could as easily have remained silent and no one, barring some freak happenstance, would ever have been the wiser.

Returning to the mountain the next day, Templeton and the warden found the lion just 25 yards from the spot Templeton was standing when it first approached. It had died within a minute of the second shot. The first arrow split the bone at the base of the left eye and would eventually have killed it, but the arrow through the chest spelled the cat's doom.

Examining the scuff marks and the dried blood, the game warden determined that Templeton waited to shoot until the lion was only six yards away. Campbell agreed that Templeton shot in self-defense. Laboratory analysis found no evidence that the lion was diseased, injured in any way or somehow pathologically predisposed to attack.

"He told me I did everything right," Templeton says. "He said he wouldn't have let it get that close! One leap and it would have been on top of me."

Today, Templeton thinks of his lion encounter as an isolated incident. "In the back of my mind, though, it's always there," he reflects. "I carry pepper spray now, but you know, until that happened with that lion, I never hesitated a minute about going off to hunt. I'd just go. I'm much more careful about that . . ."

THE CUTTING EDGE

No arrow is complete without a specialized point. Shooting an arrow without a proper point at any target is a sure way to destroy the arrow and miss

The original Judo Point (second from left) and some of the more recent imitations. Judo-style blunt heads retard penetration because the wire arms make the flying arrow flip upward rather than bury itself under the grass, so your arrow is easier to find after a shot on the range or in the field. Combined with a field point, springy-arms are extremely effective on small game and, with a broadhead, the sturdier Adder (second from right) or a set of Muzzy Grasshoppers (to the right) is great for preventing pass-through shots on wild turkeys.

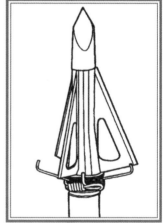

the target, as well. Without a sharp, sturdy broadhead on his arrow, Templeton would certainly have died on the mountain that day in 1997.

There are four categories of arrow point, depending on how you intend to use them. For practice or recreational shooting, you might choose field, bullet or blunt points. For bowfishing, heads are designed with barbs to stab and hold fish. For elite national and international competition, there are points manufactured to precision tolerances that the average bowhunter will never use or need. Finally, and most important to the 3,000,000 bowhunters in the US and Canada, there is a wide variety of hunting broadheads.

GET THE RIGHT PRACTICE

The average bowhunter purchases a handful of field or bullet points when they buy a new bow or even new arrows. A couple will go in their pocket, a few in the fanny pack, several in the archery tackle box and not less than a couple will end up rattling around on the floor of the pick-up or in the glove compartment. You never know when you might need to warm up.

For bowhunters, practice points help you perform the initial zeroing before you begin practice with broadheads. Whether you choose bullet points or field points or a hybrid head, the styling of these practice points makes them fly precisely and pull relatively easily out of any type target–foam, layered fiber or compressed hay bales.

The standard for hunting accuracy for many years has been hitting an eight-inch paper plate consistently at 20 yards. That general size approximates the vital area of a big-game animal. Public shooting ranges are littered with shredded paper plates that have been fastened to hay bales with twisted sections of coat hanger.

Before our 21st century "accuracy environment," however, such technicalities as matching the grain weight of your practice points to the grain weight of your broadhead were not considered to be important, given all of the other factors involved in making a clean shot. Even the engineers at some archery companies said that matching the weight of practice points with actual hunting heads was frivolous and unnecessary. Usually, however, they were not bowhunters.

Today, the bar of accuracy is raised. Even novice bowhunters understand the need to shoot tight groups. Practice points are now available in multiple sizes to match the weight of your hunting head and to help you understand the flight characteristics and impact points possible to your draw weight and arrow spine with differing weight heads.

Practice points are measured in two ways: diameter in .064-thousandths inch (to match the diameter of your arrow shaft) and weight in grains. Typically, these machined steel points screw into a lightweight, threaded aluminum or plastic adapter. If you shoot a traditional set-up, glue-on field points are available for practice with wooden shafts.

One very popular style of practice head that can also be used successfully for small-game hunting or a warm-up during the day (called "stump shooting") is the "Judo Point." Practice outdoors has usually meant that arrows with bullet or field points that miss their target or shoot through it would slide under the grass and then be hard to locate, especially with camouflaged shafts. If you were shooting a broadhead, this can be very dangerous as a vertical blade can cause serious injury if stepped on.

The Judo Point was designed with a blunt tip and extended, springy

Although he is pictured at full draw, as a mature archer Fred Bear developed a type of target panic that caused him to release the bowstring before he reached his anchor point. He called it "snap shooting." Although he was remarkably accurate with a recurve, his shooting style did not adapt to the compound bow.

Archery, bowhunting, and equipment experts like John and Jean Davis of Arrowhead Archery in Seffner, Florida, offer a variety of gear that you can hold in your hands, study at length, and even attach to your bow for a trial on their shooting lanes.

Eddie Claypool enjoys bowhunting for Coues deer in the southwest. "Coues bucks are darn hard to find," he says, "and hard to get close to when you do find them." Nevertheless, his January 1997 typical buck from New Mexico scored 108 0/8 P&Y, well above the minimum score of 65 0/8 required for record-book status.

Many outdoor innovators are successful traditional archers. John Musacchia developed the Muzzy line of high-tech, trocar-tipped broadheads, but was an avid recurve shooter. Keith Shannon (pictured), who developed the unique Bug Tamer insect protection garment, believes in the longbow and hunts P&Y whitetail deer across America.

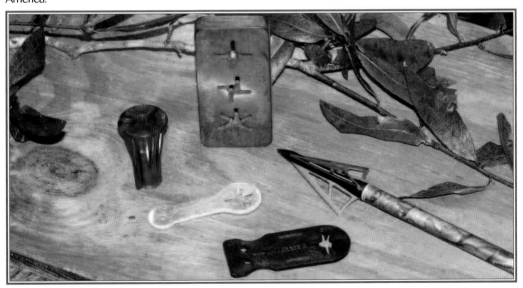

We may not have mentioned the broadhead wrench in the discussion of hunting heads, but using one to tighten or loosen the sharp cutting blades of replaceable—and fixed-blade heads is imperative. Most experienced archers will testify that, at some point in their bowhunting career, they have carelessly and needlessly shed their own blood because they failed to use a broadhead wrench. Lightweight. Cheap. Small. A wrench easily fits in your pocket, and there is often one included with new broadheads.

Diane Brochu works and hunts alongside her husband, Brian. Together, the archery and bowhunting specialists own Brian's Archery in Rochester, New Hampshire.

Twenty-five years ago, putting your arrows within an eight-inch circle from twenty yards was considered accurate, good enough to go hunting. That standard has changed, as bowhunters have demanded faster, quieter arrows.

The best time to teach people about good shooting mechanics is when they are young. With pre-teens, however, teaching them to enjoy shooting and showing them how to have fun with the bow and arrow is much more important than drilling them with the basics of proper form and ethics, or trying to instill any love of antlers or trophy hunting.

Entire books are written about difficulties encountered taking a wild gobbler with a bow, but Tracy Ledgerwood's fine bird testifies that patience, accurate shooting, and good calling techniques will work just fine, thank you very much! To bowhunt turkeys, consider a string tracker or, to inhibit their ability to fly after being shot, consider adding a spring clip or even a large washer behind your broadhead, as this will prevent complete pass-through.

Sonny Templeton is an informed and dedicated bowhunter who understands environmental issues and is involved in the rough-and-tumble politics needed to insure a future for those who want to hunt in a state with such rich and diverse resources as Montana. Sonny is proud of a string of bowhunting trophies that include several that qualify for the Pope & Young record book.

So much discussion of compounds, recurves, and longbows has neglected the crossbow-shooting opportunity. Because it is hefted to the shoulder in the same manner as a firearm, some traditional bowhunters have suggested that the crossbow should not be included in the archery seasons for big-game hunting. A compound crossbow has a slight edge over a "conventional bow" in energy delivery and effective range. Still, there is no reliable evidence to indicate that it is anything other than another type of bow.

Installing a D-Loop behind your arrow can prevent a number of shooting and arrow flight problems. If you are shooting with a release aid, a served-in D-Loop is highly recommended.

Custom built bows have been available for traditional archers for some time, at a price, but for compound-bow shooters, this is something of a novelty and is driven by an economy which allows us to choose not just a cup of coffee, but a "decaf, low-fat, shade-grown latte with cinnamon and artificial sugar."

wires to slow down the arrow's forward momentum and catch or hang-up in grass and weeds. Zwickey advertises it as the "unloseable miracle point."

Similar points or variations on the classic Judo concept are available from several manufacturers. Each is designed to hit with a powerful punch and then snag with their exposed wire arms. Every bowhunter will want to have a few Judo Points or similar wire-arm-equipped arrowheads in their fanny pack for a practice shot or some opportunistic shot at small game.

An acceptable option for small-game hunting is a rubber blunt, because you should not shoot at small game with bare field points. Field points will certainly kill squirrels and rabbits, but their tendency is to pass completely through and continue flying. A small animal would certainly die from the hit, but it may climb a tree or run into a hole before it expires and your arrow could fly 100 dangerous yards from its original point of impact.

MEET YOUR BROADHEAD

If there is one item every bowhunter is opinionated about, it is his broadhead. Bowhunters will argue the pros and cons of broadheads even when they cannot recall the model bow they are using. When they have to study the fabric for a camo name, they will know the width of their broadhead's blades. Fortunately, there are practically as many broadhead brands, styles and weights as there are bowhunters, so there is much to choose from . . . and to argue endlessly about!

Arrowheads for hunting and warfare may date back 30,000 years or even more, well into the Paleolithic or "Stone Age," and before the art of metalworking was widely understood. Once metal became available as refined copper and bronze, it quickly supplanted stone as the material of choice for arrowheads. Frontier reports exist of Native American warriors taking the iron rims off wagon wheels and wooden barrels, then hammering and cutting that supremely tough metal into arrowheads.

Metal supplanted stone because it could be mass-produced to specifications for an army of warriors, not necessarily because it was individually a better killing head. In the beginning, copper and bronze were not harder or necessarily more durable than a finely flaked stone head. With some touch-up to the edges, though, metal heads could be used repeatedly, just like stone.

It is true that stone heads, especially those made of superbly fine-grained materials like obsidian (a rare volcanic glass), could be made as surgically sharp as any metal head–many would argue, sharper. But they were brittle, and delicate stone heads could eat up daylight, manufacturing them one at a time. Whether metal was superior to stone for an arrowhead may ultimately have been more a question of the availability of finely layered materials, such as high-grade flint, that lent themselves to "napping" or flaking to create small pointed heads. In a world of truly infinite possibilities, it could simply have been a matter of fashion, too; the bowhunter's endless argument about the best broadhead.

Regarding broadheads, practical and philosophical arguments abound. Now, with the rise in popularity of mechanical or open-on-impact heads and super-fast arrows, those arguments have intensified.

There are three rules to keep in mind when you are making a broadhead selection. First, the more blades and the thicker the point and ferrule, the more difficult it becomes for the broadhead to achieve maximum potential speed, penetrate deeply and punch entirely through a thick-bodied big-game animal. Second, the more streamlined a broadhead is, the fewer and smaller its blades, the less friction it generates during flight and the more penetration it can achieve at distance. Third, because live, water-saturated flesh does not react like dry, rigid foam, the size of an arrow shaft behind your broadhead affects resistance in flight, but has little or no effect on penetration.

The Nitron by New Archery Products is a good example of styling in replaceable-blade broadheads. The three-blade, 100-gr. broadhead has a 1 1/16-inch cutting diameter. Its ferrule and point are a single-piece, made from steel and nickel-plated. Short and tough, the broadhead comes fully assembled. Each blade is held in place in slots in the ferrule with small screws.

REPLACEABLE-BLADE BROADHEAD

Dozens of companies make replaceable-blade broadheads. Most of them are excellent. This style hunting head essentially became the bowhunting standard in the late '70s. A quality, slim-line replaceable-blade head will fly true, cut easily and penetrate rapidly. Blades lock securely in slots machined in the central shaft, called a "ferrule," which is usually structural aluminum, although various composite materials are also used. You must have a head that will not lose its blades if it hits heavy bone in elk, or even in deer. (There are many stories about bowhunters unexpectedly finding a loose or broken blade with a bare hand, usually from their own arrow, while field dressing a downed game animal. The result can be deadly from bleeding or infection.)

Replaceable blade heads come in a three- or four-blade configuration. Blades are commonly vented; that means sections are cut out of their flat surface. Most bowhunters believe the vented design helps minimize wind-planing, and manufacturers claim that heads are designed so that the columnar loss of steel does not weaken a head's integrity or striking power. (On the other hand, some manufacturers of mechanical heads suggest that these vented sections create additional opportunities for wind interference and friction in flight. If it is true, the vents slow down your arrow.)

The number of blades in a broadhead, the thickness of those blades, whether they are vented or not, the shape of the ferrule and the style of tip on the head (chisel, cut-to-tip or conical) are far less important than obtaining good arrow flight and being able to put your broadhead precisely into the vitals of game animals. Nevertheless, a three-blade style is the most common replaceable blade head in the deer woods. A fourth blade on a head–and remember, this is the leading, guiding edge of your arrow–may require that you increase the number or size of the fletching for good stabilization or rotation in flight. A good rule of thumb is to match the number of feathers or vanes to the number of blades you are shooting and as your head size increases, increase the size of the fletching.

When arrow speed became a factor in purchasing equipment in the early 1990s, most bowhunters began experimenting with carbon shafts tipped with smaller, lighter heads with low-profile (narrower) blades from their compound bows. Lighter heads and shorter, lighter arrows helped boost top arrow speeds above 300 fps–about 200 mph when measured within a few feet of the bow–but complete, pass-through penetration became an issue and it remains an issue to this day.

Speed, in itself, did nothing to promote desirable arrow flight or accuracy. A fast, inaccurate or uncontrollable arrow was worse than a total miss. With fast arrows, it was not possible to assume that broadheads were mounted correctly if they simply remained intact on the ferrule after a shot.

Properly mounting a broadhead of any kind means its tip is in line with the center of the arrow shaft. Upon release, your bowstring thrusts the arrow forward. You want that thrust to load the column of the arrow, thereby delivering the bow's stored energy to your shaft without angled force vectors to torque the arrow in any direction.

After you have grouped arrows using field points, you have to shoot broadheads. Broadhead practice is "a must" before you shoot at live game.

The recommended target is one of the several varieties of durable foam or layered material sold through sporting goods stores. With care, broadheads pull out relatively easily and the design of many foam targets replicates the size and appearance of big game. (Shooting broadheads into these targets will eventually destroy them, but repair kits and replaceable "kill zones" are available from many manufacturers.)

The only certain way to fine-tune arrow flight for accuracy and consistency is to practice with the arrows and broadheads you will use for hunting. If you cannot shoot tight groups with your preferred broadhead, or if it comes apart or the tip bends after shooting, you should immediately try another brand or style. It is much less expensive to experiment with a number of broadheads than it is to miss or wound a game animal.

MECHANICAL BROADHEADS

Blades that open when a head hits its target define a class of broadheads collectively referred to as expandable, mechanical or open-on-impact. Theoretically, these heads fly like a practice point, penetrate like a fixed-blade head and cut like a sharp replaceable-blade head. Open-on-impact is a wonderful idea. For a generation, bowhunters have worked seriously on the design, studying concepts such as "rotational momentum" and "gyroscopic stabilization" that mean little to the average hunter.

Regardless of their engineering and design, mechanical broadheads remained somewhat controversial until recently. Now, many of the practical difficulties have been engineered almost to perfection. In theory, they are wonderful, but the practical difficulties are great.

These are the bowhunting benefits of open-on-impact heads:

They fly like field points. This means your practice and set-up time is shorter because the time needed to tune your heads for excellent flight declines. In a mordantly time-conscious society, this is an important advantage.

Because they offer less resistance to the wind, arrows tipped with expandable heads wind-plane less than any other type head. This means if you shoot inside your effective range, you will have fewer misses, less wounded game.

Tipped with expandable broadheads on arrows that fly straighter to their target, hit with greater efficiency and penetrate as well as any other fine head, bowhunters are making the most sensible and best ethical decision when they shoot mechanicals.

The arguments against mechanicals are that bowhunting is a privilege that requires practice, patience, and dedication. While they may fly like field points, unless they hit and deliver their energy in the perpendicular plane, they may or may not penetrate and cut through as advertised.

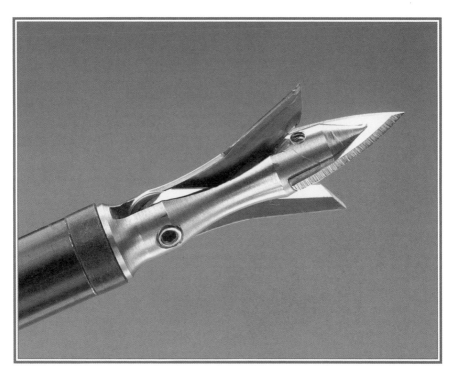

Call them expandable, mechanical or open-on-impact broadheads, but this new generation of hunting heads is designed to fly like a dart and cut like a machete. The 100-gr. Ironhead XP, for example, came pre-assembled and features a one-piece stainless steel body and two .030-inch stainless blades. Wide open, the Ironhead XP has a 1 1/8-inch cutting diameter. This head features relatively new expandable styling, with very small, resharpenable or replaceable cut-on-contact blades set at a 90-degree angle to the main blades, and positioned at the tip of the ferrule.

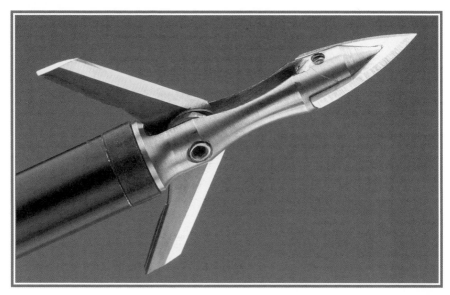

Bowhunters who do not like expandable heads claim they occasionally fail to work properly and that they are responsible for more wounded and un-recovered game animals than non-mechanical heads. They argue that bowhunters shooting open-on-impact heads should consider drawing heavier weight bows to insure that impact energy and penetration are adequate.

Although it cannot be proven, anti-mechanical hunters say that because open-on-impact heads fly like field points, bowhunters are tempted to shoot beyond their limitations. Individuals who are comfortable shooting inside 30 yards will try 40- or 50-yard shots. At those ranges, the arrow has less energy for penetration and the margin of error is greater.

The argument that mechanical heads do not cause a significant blood trail because they usually fail to cut completely through a game animal is questionable, because many thousands of the largest big game have been taken with open-on-impact heads. Most mechanicals are designed to cut big holes on impact and when they are fully deployed inside an animal, but an exit hole is definitely desirable. Otherwise, blood will only seep out of the entry hole, which is higher on the body than the exit hole and tracking is harder. Probably, the energy required to push a mechanical completely through big game needs to be greater than with other heads, as the blades are often much wider than fixed-blade or one-piece heads.

What worries many bowhunters is that if expandable heads fly like field points, and set-up and tuning is fast compared to conventional heads, bowhunters will not be spending enough time practicing and becoming familiar with their gear. In this scenario, the short-term benefits are outweighed by the lack of long-term interest and understanding.

Whether any of the above objections are credible across-the-board is uncertain; probably not. What is certainly true is that bowhunters have embraced open-on-impact heads. Estimates vary, but one hears that as many as half or more of all bowhunters now shoot mechanicals. Some established companies refuse to manufacture any expandable head, but others have accepted the open-on-impact concept and placed their faith in superior engineering.

Nevertheless, common-sense archery rules apply. If you choose to shoot an open-on-impact head, you must experiment before taking them to the field. Shoot into foam targets to test the type and weight head that works best from your set-up. Wait for quality broadside shots. Shoot within your effective range. Think of the animal at all times and remember that the objective is always a quick, clean kill.

Measure open-on-impact broadheads with the same qualities as traditional heads: size, weight, cutting diameter, number of blades, width and thickness of blades, type of point (cut-on-contact or punch-cut) and locking style. In addition, however, these heads have significant mechanical characteristics, such as how the blades are attached to the ferrule; how they swing or spring open; and even whether the blades swing forward or backward on impact.

If you choose an expandable blade head, you will want to be sure the Kinetic Energy (foot-pounds) delivered by your arrow will be sufficient to penetrate, fully deploy the head and then cut a long, wide blood channel. Archery engineers who are also bowhunters recommend shooting no less than 50 ft-lbs for moderate game like deer, and up to 65 ft-lbs or even more for larger game, such as elk.

The most fashionable trend in broadheads is developing a mechanical head with a small, fixed head forward, thereby allowing the cut-on-contact front tip to open an immediate wound channel for the opening mechanical blades. Properly developed, this is a terrific combination of technologies that indeed combines the best worlds of penetration and low-resistance arrow flight.

FIXED-BLADE BROADHEADS

What could be easier than gluing a broadhead on your wood arrow shaft or screwing one into an adapter in your shaft? If it becomes dull, you sharpen it with a file, a ceramic stick or a sheet of fine-grit sandpaper. If the tip hits a rock and the blade bends, you straighten it or throw it away. The only tricky part is your responsibility to keep these heads sharp and flying true, because no head less than surgically sharp should be shot at a game animal.

Single-piece heads are simple, nothing-can-go-wrong arrowheads. Nothing moves, and there is nothing to replace. In practically any thickness–.040 inches is standard for the main blade while the insert or "bleeder blade," if any, may measure only .015 inches–they are suitable for taking any big-game animal. With a heavy bow and arrow combination, this judgment includes elephant and Cape buffalo, as Howard Hill, Fred Bear and Bob Swinehart proved hunting Africa in the 1950s and 1960s with fixed, single-piece heads. Nevertheless, these days a minority of bowhunters uses single-piece broadheads.

Those who shoot traditionally with recurves and longbows gravitate to single-piece broadheads. Traditional bowhunters shooting recurves and longbows derive much of their enjoyment from simplifying their gear and even their methods of shooting and hunting. Single-piece, fixed-blade heads with or without inserts represent less than 10 percent of the total broadhead market.

"Traditional archers shoot more than people using compounds because they have more fun," says Bob Mayo, who manufactures Ace broadheads. "Since we traditional-style hunters usually glue heads onto wood arrow shafts, when we can find good wood shafts, we use one-piece heads because they are tougher and last longer. We don't lose blades or tips when we

The Whiffen Bodkin is an old-style fixed-blade broadhead. The Bodkin was designed by Milwaukee's Larry Whiffen, Senior—now a member of the Archery Hall of Fame—in 1946, field tested by Fred Bear and brought to market three years later. Sharpening a Bodkin is easy as the straight blades are made from soft steel.

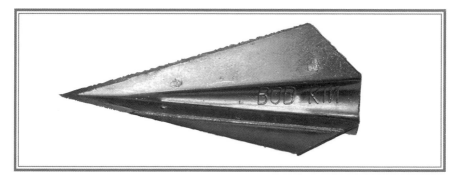

practice shooting into 3-D targets or hay bales."

A fixed-blade head may look simple to bowhunters who are accustomed to complex mechanical heads with moving parts or heads with replaceable blades, the construction of a good traditional head is a precision business.

Traditional heads may be sharpened with sandpaper, a file or on a stone. Mayo glues his 165-gr. Ace Express onto a wood arrow shaft. Then, holding his file stationary, he draws the head toward him, base to tip. When he is using a sharpening stone, he recommends beginning with coarse grit and working toward fine. A few drops of honing oil will increase the effectiveness of this procedure. Finally, he smoothes the cutting edge of his heads with a ceramic stick.

Three-blade Whiffen Bodkins and other styles with edges that lie flat are designed to be sharpened on a sheet of fine-grained sandpaper lying on a tabletop. Use the same butt-to-tip sharpening method Mayo uses with his Arkansas stones. The steel of a Bodkin is soft, so it is easy to sharpen. That also means it quickly loses its edge and must be touched-up often.

The orientation of broadheads on an arrow shaft is a much-debated topic, especially with large, flat heads like the 160-gr., 1 1/2-inch Magnus, the 130-gr. Zwickey Black Diamond Delta or the massive, 210-gr. .048-inch Steel Force Premium from Ballistic Archery. Many bowhunters believe this is irrelevant, but these large blades definitely play a part in steering and stabilizing the arrow in flight.

Mayo says he, like many traditional hunters—and he mentioned famous traditional trick-shot artist Byron Ferguson, for example—mount blades vertically. This is a reasonable accommodation given the normal wallowing of an arrow as it leaves a bowstring released by one's fingers.

Speaking of proper blade orientation, several popular styles are designed with offset blades so that they will spin or rotate independent of the arrow shaft. The 100-gr. Razorbak 100 from New Archery Products, for example, features a .039-inch thick cut-on-contact main blade, a .020-inch bleeder blade and a 1 1/8-inch cutting diameter. Set in a tough composite sleeve, this sleeve with its vented blades actually rotates around the ferrule during flight.

Traditional heads are larger in both size and weight than replaceable-blade or mechanical heads. The super-heavyweight 200-grain Ace Super Express is one of the largest ever produced and sold commercially. Mayo says, "At the distances we traditional archers take game animals, 25-yards or less, these heavy heads don't substantially affect arrow flight, and heavier arrows at short range definitely penetrate better."

FORWARD-OF-CENTER

A technical question about arrow balance with a mounted broadhead has generated considerable discussion. Most bowhunters shooting within their comfort zone can ignore this controversy, but anyone who is obsessed with pinpoint shooting or is experiencing erratic or unbalanced arrow flight should study "forward-of-center."

Forward-of-center or FOC balancing is one of many things that affect arrow flight. It can be critical for speed bows with high let-off and high draw weight. Unlike many technical issues, FOC is easy to determine. First, measure your arrow from the throat of the nock to the tip of your installed broadhead. Next, mark the arrow at the center or halfway point. Place the arrow on the side of your finger or on some other thin balancing point, and also mark that point. Finally, measure the distance from the center of your arrow to the balance mark and divide that number by the total length of the arrow.

For example, the center or halfway point of a 28-inch shaft with nock and head is 14 inches. It will balance forward-of-center because the broadhead is heavier than the fletching and nock on the rear. If the arrow balances three inches forward of the shaft's halfway point, you determine FOC as three divided by 28, or 10.7 percent.

Archery technicians suggest that an FOC of 10 to 12 percent is about right for balanced, accurate arrow flight. Some even recommend a higher FOC, 12 to 15 percent, for carbon shafts and lower FOC, 8 to 10 percent, for aluminum shafts.

In the same example, if you shoot a heavy head and the balance point was four inches forward of the halfway point, the FOC would be 14.28 percent and you could predict marginal arrow flight. To stabilize the flight of your arrow, you would want to try some combination of a lighter broadhead

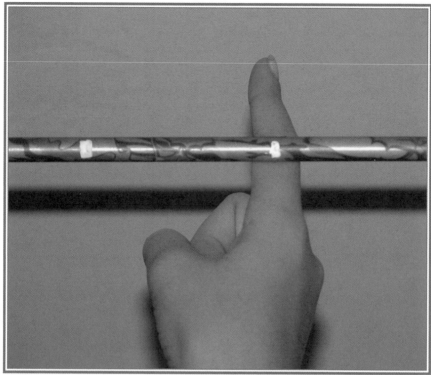

With a nock and broadhead, the author's arrow measured 35 1/4-inches long. The center of the arrow was therefore 17 5/8-inches from either end. The forward-of-center balance was 2 5/8-inches forward and FOC was 7.45 percent. This would be considered low for a carbon shaft and possibly require a heavier broadhead. For the Easton XX75 2213 Superlight aluminum pictured, however, realizing that the author shoots with fingers and that his arrows fly at only moderate speeds (around 240 fps), this is not too low for consistency.

or heavier fletching or even a longer arrow.

Nevertheless, FOC is only one of many indicators that help us shoot a fast, accurate arrow that delivers all of its energy in-line through its tip when it hits.

ALL ABOUT GRAIN WEIGHT

Broadheads are sold at specific grain weights. Bowhunters need to understand that advertised grain weights are only approximations. If you weigh any given broadhead on a digital scale, you will probably find that it varies from five to ten percent heavier or lighter than advertised. Although competition archers fret about matching total shaft weights precisely, this amount of variation is not significant for bowhunting. On the other hand, if you can alter your heads or forward balance to make all heads weigh precisely the same without changing flight dynamics, why not do so.

Although we are not too familiar with weights expressed in grains outside our broadheads and bullets, the "grain" is the basic British unit of weight and hence our inherited system. This system evolved over more than 3,000 years. Historically, the grain was based on the weight of one grain of English barley.

Today, the "pound avoirdupois" is what we typically refer to as a pound when we check a bow's draw weight. Our pound equals 7,000 grains, abbreviated gr. An ounce, therefore–and there are 16 ounces in one pound avoirdupois–equals 437.5 gr.

Why do we still measure broadheads with such an old-fashioned weight as grains? The development of mass-produced, commercially available broadheads may be a 20th-century phenomenon, but bullets were manufactured and sold by grain weight in the 19th century. Ours may be a compact phenomenon, but what are the options? You could measure heads in tenths or hundredths of an ounce, but with 16, not 10, ounces in a pound, this may be really confusing. Or we could switch, with the rest of the world, to the metric scale, and that move is probably on the horizon as more and more packaging contains grams and millimeters and other detritus of that number-ten-based system.

BROADHEAD COLLECTING

There is a serious collector's interest in broadheads. Greg Schwehr, membership chairman of the American Broadhead Collectors Club (ABCC), says the group is a worldwide organization of men and women who enjoy collecting archery and bowhunting memorabilia, including gear catalogs, books, leather goods, bows, equipment, autographed arrows and, of course, broadheads. All of these can be traded for in the club.

In their quarterly newsletter, Broadhead, Schwehr says members find information about old and new broadheads and the manufacturers. One primary function of the club and publication is for members to trade heads. At an annual meeting each summer, usually at one of the large archery shoots in the Midwest, collectors get together to do "some serious trading."

The ABCC has published five books on identifying broadheads: four volumes of Best of Broadhead and one volume of old broadhead advertisements. A list of members is available for trading and networking. A master list of broadheads has been compiled during the past quarter century, listing every head known to have been manufactured and sold, including sizes, weights, date and manufacturer information.

Schwehr says the club designates a member to buy a small number of all new heads. "This individual then makes heads available to other members at a low cost, eliminating the need for every collector to buy complete packages."

Collecting old archery memorabilia is a lifetime sport in its own right, and thousands of archers and collectors participate. The items most in demand are uncommon recurves, longbows and broadheads: The designs are curious, each has an interesting history and many of them are exceptionally rare. A 12-pack (only six show) of 1960-vintage, glue-on Fred Bear Razorheads in their original packaging cost $4.95 in the mid-'50s. Today, this pack could sell for more than $100.

ABCC membership is $20 for one year. If you are interested, please contact: American Broadhead Collectors Club, Greg Schwehr, Membership Chairman, 9717 W. Reichert Place, Milwaukee, WI 53225.

CHAPTER FIVE

Bowhunting Accessories

SETTLING ONLY FOR PERFECTION

Some bowhunters just do not care whether they can hit a pie plate at 20 yards. After all, the emphasis on speed in the 1990s and on silencing their shot in the 2000s has quietly submerged the emphasis on accuracy. Or has it?

Massimillo is one of those bowhunters who could not give a rip about an eight-inch pie plate at 20 yards. That level of accuracy does not interest him for hunting or for practice. Or does it?

Massimillo is one of those rare bowhunters with a target pedigree. Competing in National Field Archery Association outdoor events, he has won 16 Florida State Championships, four Southeast Region Championships and has, in different years, placed #2, #3 and #4 in NFAA World Championships. In the 1980s, he won titles shooting with fingers, but in the 1990s, he switched to a back-tension release aid.

As if he needed to put to rest, finally, the old adage that dot shooters could not hit hair, Massimillo has taken elk, black bears, feral hogs, exotic animals and deer, lots of deer. Indeed, he has a dozen P&Y-size deer to his credit, the largest scoring a whopping 186 6/8 and his second largest a mere 183 0/8! When he hunts and wherever he hunts–except at home–Buckmasters sends a cameraman.

Massimillo is one dot shooter who thrives on hair . . . although he is quick to laugh about his own noticeably thinning head cover. As Dan has matured in archery and bowhunting, he has defied the stereotype that the hunting passion cools in men's 40s. If anything, he is more avid about chasing big deer than ever, but that is only one of the ways Dan defies conventional stereotypes.

GREAT PLAINS BUCK

One of the most coveted trophies in bowhunting is not a record-book animal, but a non-resident tag to hunt deer in Kansas. In 2001, the Gods of the Hunt favored Massimillo's application, and just two months after the terrible events of 9/11, he was on station with his friend Dale Larson, owner of Bruiser Whitetails guide service, two and one-half hours west of Kansas City. Larson's specialty is big whitetails; bucks with tall, spreading antlers and stunning drop tines. Both he and his clients regularly skewer enormous deer.

To Massimillo, a big-woods bowhunter from Florida, where 20 yards is sometimes a long shot, the high plains and narrow, twisting draws and

Florida bowhunter Dan Massimillo does not take his success for granted. He practices regularly at distances from 10 to 70 yards. One of the 10 percent of left-handers in archery, he defies other conventions also: Instead of a trigger-finger mechanical release aid with a wrist-strap, he shoots with a back-tension release. He is also an NFAA champion. Who says dot shooters cannot hit hair!

ravines of central Kansas were a wonder. By November, with the corn and beans picked, deer were bedding in the sheltered draws where there was plenty of cover: brush, trees and abundant relief.

These Great Plains, where the deer browsed at night or occasionally loafed during the day, were either harvested and lying fallow, or growing tall prairie grass with little other cover for miles. Good territory for a riflemen; tough for a bowhunter.

Larsen recommended a treestand about half-way down a draw. From the stand, Massimillo could still see onto the open plains, but the weather was cold and deer were moving through the draw. Bucks were tending estrous does. He might see deer at any time.

On an expedition like this one to Kansas, Massimillo would hunt every possible minute to get a shot at a big deer. So on Monday, when he crawled down from the tree at noon to meet Larson, who was as much his friend as his hunting guide, he both looked forward to the break and regretted leaving the stand. As he lowered his bow, a deer stood up on the prairie. It was a big deer, too, a buck with a drop tine. Massimillo quickly sat back down, but the buck did not budge from the spot, which was perhaps a quarter mile away.

Massimillo climbed down only to find that his guide had also discovered the buck. Larson had, in fact, spent most of the morning studying it through a spotting scope. The buck had not moved because a doe was bedded in the grass nearby and from his hilltop elevation, Larson could see this.

"It will score in the 190s, I think," Larson said, pointing to the enormous deer in the distance.

Skipping lunch, the two bowhunters watched the deer for another hour and, when they could no longer wait, planned a stalk. Two crack-shot bowhunters stalking silently toward a deer doubles the effective coverage, but also increases the chance that a stray wisp of wind will alert the game.

As they were positioning for their final approach, the doe stood up and walked toward the draw Massimillo had only recently vacated. Nose to tail, the buck dutifully followed her. After lying in one place for hours, as the moment of their greatest danger approached, the deer simply faded into the trees of the draw.

The bowhunters were disappointed, but when you must be so close to your prey that you can hear it breathe before you can take it, most stalks are going to end in failure. In the positive column, the bowhunters were now focused on a single buck. They knew its size and the shape of its antlers; they recognized its twin drop tines and, because it was tending a doe, it was careless enough to venture into the open in the middle of the day.

Skipping lunch, Massimillo slipped back into his treestand. That afternoon, a 140-class buck wandered by well within his effective shooting distance. Most bowhunters would have jumped at the chance to take the even-tined ten-pointer, but Massimillo now knew exactly what he wanted, and so he let the buck walk.

That evening, a warm front swept through Kansas and deer movement shut down. Tuesday. Wednesday. Thursday.

Massimillo is an experienced bowhunter. He understands that he can fly thousands of miles, leave his family for a week and spend thousands of dollars as well, only to be skunked. While it does not often happen, it does happen.

"Be patient," Larson advised. "A cold front is coming through on Friday and the deer will begin moving again."

He was right. On Friday, practically every deer in the Midwest moved within a few hundred yards of Massimillo's stand. Friday was a veritable deer parade. Every deer . . . except the very one he wanted. One deer tempted him. A buck in the 150s. Heavy. Wide, beautiful rack. Just not The One.

Then, over a quick sandwich on Friday, he was introduced to temptation as slyly as a thirsty man in the desert crawls up on a salty puddle.

"Why not stay just one more day," Larson suggested, and it was not actually a question. "The bucks really are just beginning to move again."

No. An extra day was impossible. On the other hand, maybe he could delay his flight a little and squeeze out a few hours . . . and so he did. The delay meant that he could hunt a total of three extra hours. On Saturday

"The same techniques that will let you take a trophy deer will let you take a trophy elk," Dan Massimillo says of his first bull elk. "Draw enough weight to do the job, but do not be 'over-bowed.' Keep the wind in your favor. Determine your effective range, practice throughout that range and believe in yourself."

morning, Massimillo would have to be out of his stand precisely at 9:00. He would have to pack quickly, and then avoid Kansas state troopers during the 2 1/2-hour sprint to the airport in Kansas City to arrive at the gate an hour before his flight. On Friday, it felt like a lot of work for three measly hours.

The next morning, Massimillo was on stand shivering in the cold long before daylight. At 7:00, a 150-class deer tempted him. It was, after all, the last hours of his hunt and this was a wonderful deer. He drew, hesitated . . . and let it pass. He had several 150-class deer mounted on the trophy wall already.

At 8:05, with less than an hour remaining in his dream hunt, Massimillo noticed another deer skulking up the draw. It paused at a scrape the bowhunter had measured at 61 yards. This was a very big deer and it was broadside. Massimillo raised his bow, and the moment the buck stepped away from the scrape, the Floridian drew and grunted.

"His head swung around and he walked toward me for about ten yards and then stopped," Massimillo recalls. "Now, I'm at full draw, but couldn't shoot because it was a terrible angle from my stand."

Finally lowering its head, the buck turned back up the draw. Massimillo already had a spot selected and knew the range exactly. When the buck walked through the opening, he sent a carbon arrow to meet it. The spot was 50 yards from his treestand and the 183 0/8 buck ran less than 60 yards before dropping dead. It was not The Buck, but it was a magnificent and mature animal.

Massimillo checked his watch. 8:12. By the time he took a picture, raced through the field dressing, and dragged the deer up the draw, he would have to rely on Larsen to get it to a butcher and send him the cape, antlers, and meat. "Well, if you cannot use your friends," Massimillo often says, "who can you use?"

The morning was too rushed; the sky too beautiful, the deer altogether too proud for such a hurried exit, but Massimillo had no choice. When he stepped on the plane in Kansas City, they closed the door behind him and began backing away from the gate before he could buckle his seat belt. It was that close, but the deer and the experience were worth any effort.

LESSONS: RIGHT AND WRONG, BUT NEVER INDIFFERENT

There are plenty of stereotypes about bowhunters, and they are probably right on target for a lot of people:

- By age 50, most bowhunters are no longer interested in chasing deer around the woods.
- Most great bowhunters are right-handed and right-eye dominant.
- Bowhunters who shoot release aids and peep sights do not come to a solid anchor point.

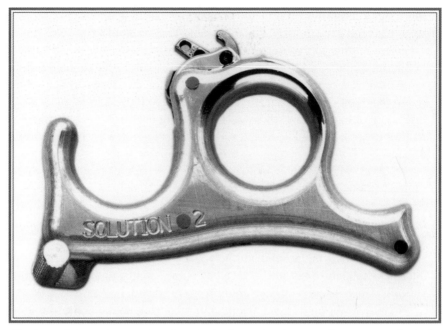

The Carter Solution 2—recently replaced in the Carter line—is an excellent example of a back-tension release designed for competition but, as Dan Massimillo demonstrates, it can be equally appropriate as a hunting release. The adjustable Solution 2 allows you to begin your rotation from any point once the safety is disengaged. Because it is very short from fingers to hook, it does not shorten your draw length. The Solution 2.5 adds a longer body for the pinkie finger and the Solution 3 eliminates the middle finger loop but incorporates the ability to switch back and forth from back-tension shooting to a thumb-trigger release.

- Like gun hunters, bowhunters prefer wrist-straps on their releases and index-finger triggers.
- Shooting beyond 20 or 30 yards is unethical and dangerous for a bowhunter.

At almost every turn, Dan Massimillo defies the stereotype. At the half-century mark, he says he is just getting warmed up. His son and his wife are archers, too, and besides, their log cabin home still has a few spots for trophies.

The rest of us would do well to emulate this attitude. There are children who need outdoor mentors, spouses who are slowing down in their careers and therefore have more free time, and a huge public that needs to be positively influenced to preserve our hunting and shooting heritage.

Massimillo is almost fanatic about his equipment, perhaps more so now that he has hit the five-zero mark. He crests his small carbon shafts, builds multi-color shield-cut feathers, tinkers endlessly with fine-tuning his set-up, and he practices, shooting a few arrows every day.

Massimillo is one of the very few bowhunters who hunts with a hand- or finger-held, back-tension release aid. His strapless Carter Insatiable is perhaps the greatest surprise in his equipment ensemble, though.

"Because I used to shoot competitively in NFAA tournaments," he says, "I know that back-tension shooting gives you the most accurate arrow. It's a tricky way to shoot and can be tedious to learn. Once you do learn shoot with back tension though, the results will convince you that you never want to shoot in any other manner."

When Massimillo comes to full draw, he anchors, palm out, below his ear at the point of his jaw. The closed jaw of the release hooks securely around the D-Loop on his bowstring. His thumb touches and stays tightly planted against his forefinger. When a big game animal is at the right spot, he has trained the muscles of his back to draw inward or together. His left arm then begins a slight movement to the rear, and this causes his hand to rotate around the barrel trigger of the release, which snaps over the sear.

"It surprises me when it goes off," he says.

There is no active punching, pushing or conscious triggering. In this manner, he shoots more accurately, more consistently and avoids target panic in all of its forms.

As NFAA Master Coach Bernie Pellerite says in the preface to his book, Idiot Proof Archery, "You're not weird if you have target panic . . . you're weird if you don't."

Pellerite has worked with hundreds of bowhunters who, at some point in their shooting career, find that they can no longer hit what they are aiming at: Ted Nugent and Myles Keller among them. His teaching usually begins with a review of good shooting form, then mental adjustments, and proceeds to back tension. Within a few months, he says, careful practice helps most bowhunters overcome their shooting inabilities and they end up shooting better than ever.

The trouble is that we value being pro-active people. We learn early to be problem solvers, to "take the bull by the horns," to trigger our shots. Using a back-tension release works behind that philosophy. Massimillo Massimillo, because of his years as a competitive shooter, understands this and, going against the grain, uses a small, silver back-tension release that he holds in his hand or rather, in his fingers. (Pellerite's own Can't Punch back-tension release, however, does work with a full wrist strap.)

Another point of Massimillo's shooting that will strike the reader as peculiar is that he admits taking a 50-yard shot at a trophy buck. Our standard, 20-yard caution is based on reasonable experience, but it is a holdover from an earlier era, a time when bowhunters had no choice but to shoot recurves. In those days, a 30-yard shot under hunting conditions was truly reaching out.

Equipment has evolved tremendously in the past 25 years, however. The author began hunting in 1979 with a used Bear '76er Take-Down recurve that drew 45 pounds and, when I at last chronographed one of my aluminum arrows, discovered that it was achieving every bit of 165 fps! Massimillo's Jennings CK3.4R one-cam compound bow is a 280 fps rocket, which he draws to an astonishing—at least to the author—80 pounds.

When Massimillo committed to the 50-yard shot, he released with confidence because he regularly practices shooting that distance. "If you even think about taking a shot that far," he says, "you have to practice it with broadheads and then you have to feel good about it. I do."

Outside the city of Gainesville, Florida, where he lives, Massimillo shoots 3-D deer and Block targets from the ground and from an elevated practice stand at distances he might shoot when hunting. Holding the thumbs and forefingers of opposite hands together, he indicates groups he shoots with 100-grain fixed-blade heads at 50 yards as "three to five inches on most days." Thus, in a condition of no wind and with no interference between his stand and the buck that he had stopped with a simple grunt, he pulled off the perfect shot.

"In Florida, most of my shots are 20 to 30 yards," he says. "Out west where country is truly big, and on the high plains where there are no trees except down in the draws and wash-outs, visiting bowhunters need to understand that the shot they get on a trophy is probably not going to be the distance they will see back east. Therefore, they need to focus on preparation and practice with broadheads at what seems extended range. Then, if they still can't make a longer shot than 30 yards with confidence, they shouldn't take it."

The lesson, says the left-hand, left-eye dominant bowhunter, is to hunt outside your confidence range, but shoot within it. Two sides of his personality make Massimillo a superior archer and bowhunter. First, he is a master of detail. He blouses his camo trousers meticulously into his boots. No string tip is left hanging as much as an eighth of an inch after he serves a peep. His approach to the game is entirely self-conscious and this pays off on a hunt.

Second, he is not at all afraid to experiment with his shooting style or his equipment. Relatively late in his shooting career, for instance, he switched from fingers to a release. This required that he reexamine his arrow rest, style broadhead and arrow grain weight.

Massimillo would be the first to admit that anyone can use a focused approach to build the perfect bowhunting set-up. Fortunately, in the world of bowhunting today, there are accessories for every shooting style and need.

ARROW RESTS

Other than your arrow, the most important accessory you will buy is an arrow rest. Not sights. Not silencers. A good argument could be made for a release, but the arrow rest is the final point of contact with your message as it speeds off the string and down range toward the trophy deer that is your quarry. Your arrow rest needs to be chosen with care and set up perfectly.

Bowhunters use two string release techniques, with fingers or with a mechanical release, and three arrow rests are designed to serve them. The shoot-through style is best thought of as a release shooter's rest, although a good finger shooter can use it with great satisfaction. A shoot-around style is preferred by finger shooters. A drop-away or fall-away rest is the current best-selling favorite of release shooters, but a careful finger shooter can handle it to good effect also.

At any one time, several hundred rests will be commercially available. Their cost ranges from as little as $5 for a simple rubber stick-on like the Bear Weatherest to nearly $200 for a micro-adjustable shoot-through like the Golden Key Infinity or $150 for a quality drop-away rest like the much-imitated UltraRest from Quality Archery Designs. Of course, you get what you pay for, but there are many superior, highly adjustable rests in the $50 to $90 price range.

Remember. Your arrow is only in contact with your bow at two places, the string and the rest. Wherever else you economize, it is never a good idea to buy a rest in which you do not have utmost confidence.

DROP-AWAY RESTS

The "drop-away" or "fall-away" rest holds your arrow until the nock is released by the bow-string. At that point, the arrow has moved

When you release, the drop-away arrow rest holds your arrow for a fraction of a second, until the cord tied to your cable begins to relax as the cable moves forward. During this split second, your arrow is charged with energy and is already accelerating away from you. This style rest and others similar to it, use a cord to draw the rest into position and then release it to fall away to prevent any hint of arrow-fletching interference.

from zero mph to maximum velocity, and it has absorbed all of the kinetic energy the bow can give it. When the bowstring exits the nock, your arrow rest is forced downward by the vertically porpoising arrow and drops out of the way of the approaching fletching. Because you can shoot any fletching orientation with a drop-away rest, your bow tunes faster and easier. By the time your fletching reaches the rest, it is gone.

The downside to drop-away rests is that they usually have more moving parts than conventional rests. This is never a good thing on a bowhunting trip, where anything that can go wrong frequently does.

Drop-away rests are excellent for bowhunters who shoot with release aids, which propel the arrow directly from behind. This, of course, minimizes any side-to-side swing of the bowstring. Drop-away rests are not considered especially desirable for finger shooters, though, because they generally need some stabilizing pressure such as a cushion plunger on the bow riser side, especially for the first, large bend of the arrow.

Of course, there is no reason you cannot install a pressure button except that there is a space issue on your bow riser. A 2- to 2 1/4-inch Berger button screwed into your riser can interfere with mounting a rest, sight and quiver. Before you make equipment commitments, you have to be sure your set-up will physically handle them, and an archery pro shop is the best place to do this.

An occasional problem when tuning a one-cam bow is discovering that your bow pushes arrows to the right. There are a few cam designs with which a drop-away rest just does not work well. In these rare cases, a shoot-through rest with some additional side pressure may be necessary.

To solve a problem like this with a two-cam bow, you can tinker with cam roll-over timing, but a one-cam bow eliminates timing problems. So it is a case of solving one problem only to discover something else to worry about.

Keith Barner may have developed the first working drop-away arrow rest. A magnet held up the arrow supports of his early 1980s model. In the early '80s, bowhunters were just discovering they could shoot faster than 200 fps, though, and drop-away rests never caught on.

A dozen years later, we understood that drop-away rests could solve some of the problems associated with fast, short axle-to-axle bows and critical shooting around 300 fps. Suddenly, drop-away rests began appearing in every hunting camp.

Muzzy's X-Celerator is a springless, cable slide-driven drop-away rest. When you draw, the cables move a slide coupled by an adjustable linkage to a plastic hook that grabs and lifts your arrow into firing position. When you release, the X-Celerator guides the arrow for only a few inches before being driven downward by the synchronous movement of your bow's cables. This movement eliminates contact between the rest and the rear three-quarters of the arrow where most of the flexing occurs.

Like most drop-aways, the X-Celerator is not sensitive to arrow diameter or nock-to-fletching-to-string orientation. Because the rest is not in contact with your arrow when most bow torquing occurs, torque-related problems (left-right arrows) are reduced.

A plastic hook on the X-Celerator lifts your arrow off the bow shelf and into firing position as you draw. An adjustable "V-groove" in the hook positions your arrow quickly for centershot and the wide hook itself ensures that no arrow will fall off or through the rest, no matter its size, its fletching nor the type or weight arrow head you shoot.

Drop-away rests do not interfere with arrow speed. In fact, they ensure that you realize maximum arrow velocity.

Your arrow's fletching provides essential flight control and stabilization of a shaft in flight, and a drop-away lets you experiment with fletching types. Because the arrow rest will not be in the way of the fletching, you are free to shoot a high degree of helical offset, typically thought of as the fletching style that provides the best in-flight stabilization. With a properly functioning drop-away, you do not have to worry about whether the cock feather is up or down, either. It will not matter.

Trophy Taker has fall-away rests that are simple, but effective. They give you the opportunity to shoot large, helical vanes, yielding superior down-range stabilization, without worrying about clearance. This is a benefit for people who want to shoot a large, fixed-blade broadhead such as Simmons Sharks. Trophy Taker says a drop-away rest helps reduce the effects of post-release shooting-form errors, such as torquing the riser, since the arrow only connects with the rest for the earliest moment of the shot.

The Trophy Taker is a big "Y" attached between your riser and your cables. As you draw, a cord pulls it upward, lifting your arrow. Adjust this rest's timing by changing the length of the cord tied on your cable.

Trophy Taker's oddly named Shaky Hunter drop-away has few moving parts and its adjustable stainless steel spring is fully enclosed for protection and snag-free operation. The wide-mount, one-piece stainless-steel launcher is anchored in a machined-aluminum bar that rises and falls via a durable cord connecting to your cable or cable slide.

The adjustable Free Fall drop-away is a Golden Key design. The Colorado company says some arrows need guidance before the rest drops completely away, and that this relates to nock travel. If your arrow rests against the nock-point locator, that little brass button on the bowstring influences arrow flight for a microsecond or until the arrow has left the string. If the rest drops immediately after you shoot, your arrow is naturally going to drop, too.

Golden Key advises setting the length of the tubing provided for the Free Fall so that the rest reaches its final "up position" when the string is short of full draw by five to eight inches. This way, the rest falls more gradually and offers plenty of guidance to smooth out potential nock travel problems.

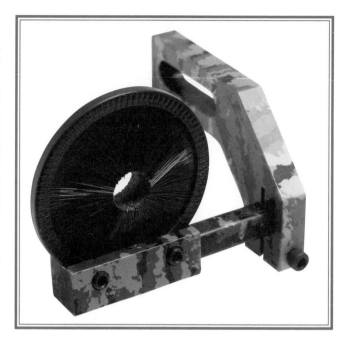

The Whisker Biscuit has been a popular arrow rest for several years. Easy to set up, its universal arrow alignment and large "sweet spot," shooting through the ring of bristles, allows you to quit worrying about fletching alignment. Several styles of this popular rest are now available, all operating on the same principle—smooth, easy, minimal interference.

Copper John uses machined-aluminum brackets in its CAT adjustable drop-away series. CAT rests rotate around a central point on a stationary horizontal arm. Copper John shrink-wraps the launchers or rest troughs with a Teflon-coated polymer to eliminate noise. Because the arrow rises away from the rest during the shot rather than the rest falling out of the way, these may not be thought of as true drop-away rests. The high-end TomCat features a unique CatTail spring-loaded arrow holder that automatically flips out of the way when you draw.

SHOOT-THROUGH RESTS

Shoot-throughs typically support your arrow on two prongs or fins, which actually touch your shaft between two of its feathers or vanes. These rests became super-popular when bowhunters almost en masse began shooting mechanical releases.

Because the string and arrow respond to different force vectors when shot by a release than when shot by fingers, a different style rest was needed than the older "shoot-around" variety. Leaving a mechanical release, columnar loading–the force applied directly to the base of the arrow shaft–causes your arrow to "porpoise" or flex in the vertical plane. Finger-released arrows tend to "wallow" or flex horizontally. In addition, the bending is significantly less from a release than from fingers. Although it remains in contact with your arrow longer than a shoot-around finger rest or a drop-away rest, a shoot-through rest whose arrow-support fins are adjusted with spring tension will rock down and out of the way of the arrow and fletching.

What makes a shoot-through rest like Golden Key's Infiniti work is the in-line energy delivery of a release aid to your arrow, and the orientation of your arrow's fletching so that the springy launcher arms of the rest will not interfere with them as the arrow passes in flight. Your cock vane can be shot straight down to pass through the middle of the rest launchers or even straight up with the other two vanes (assuming that most archers shoot three-fletch feathers or vanes) spread to about the four o'clock and eight o'clock positions. For this rest to work properly, the vanes must clear the rest launchers.

The Infiniti has a black mounting bar and spring housing made from machined aluminum and they are accented with polished aluminum and brass. There is one-half inch of adjustability in the vertical (for tuning and clearance) and horizontal (for centershot) planes on the self-locking Micro Adjustment. Tuning gradients are marked in white. Ultra-fine spring adjustment is accomplished with 12 tension-setting positions, with a separate increment gauge. Stainless steel launchers are independently adjustable with their own set screws and may be replaced with one of Golden Key's many launcher styles (four sets are included) or covered with shrink tubing or Teflon silencing film.

The Infiniti has a Tuning Gauge that is supposed to indicate when your settings are incorrect: bad arrows, nocking-point alignment, downward deflection, vane deflection, arrow condition, arrow-spine problems, arrow-nock installation, centershot, spring tension and wheel timing. The gauge has red, yellow and green areas to indicate problems, a marginal situation and "well-tuned." That is a lot to ask from a simple spring.

The beauty of the Infiniti rest is its independently adjustable elements, but its drawback for bowhunters who need rugged gear is that it may be too delicate for field use. Besides, asking your arrow rest for an opinion about your bow-tuning set-up is either criminally bizarre or utter genius.

A popular arrow rest is the Whisker Biscuit, now part of the EBSCO or Bear Archery group. The Biscuit is a round, fully enclosed rest that supports your arrow in a 360-degree ring of synthetic bristles. Using a Biscuit, you can launch arrows quietly while shooting from any position; your arrow will not fall off or out of this rest. Whisker Biscuits are manually adjustable. By moving the axle from one side of the rest to the other, the same rest will work for left- and right-handers.

The advantage of this rest is its simplicity. After set-up, it holds your arrow effortlessly in position and it can be used with any orientation or number of fletching. Bear recommends short, straight fletching and says a loss of one to two fps can be expected with four-inch straight fletch and a greater loss, up to

15 fps, with helical fletch. An archer should weigh the benefits of this unique rest against the loss of arrow speed and stabilization before committing to it.

Bodoodle's machined-aluminum rests are designed to modulate the initial bending of your arrow and thereby stabilize your arrow rapidly. A Pro-Lite's twin stainless-steel launcher arms attach to an adjustable pivoting yoke that supports your arrow with a minimum of force. Bodoodle rests are built to accomplish the same purpose, and rely on an adjustable (but unprotected) spring for launch support.

The Zapper uses multiple launcher arms to encircle an arrow. Therefore, because the arrow will not fall off the rest, shooting downward or at odd angles is easier. Nevertheless, this simple rest requires that you pay attention to fletching orientation. The noise of an arrow passing over the steel launchers can be dampened with the application of Bodoodle's Teflon-coated "Smoke Quiet" taped to their tips.

The unique APA Ultimate rest cradles your arrow from the overhead position, and your arrow will have to work to fall off or out of this rest. It will accommodate any size or style arrow. Apply its cam fleece (included) on the wire arms and this rest should be excellent for bowhunting because a broadhead can never threaten your hand and arm at full draw. The Ultimate should shoot very quietly. (For finger shooters, a wider wire armature is available for the left-right flexing of the arrow.)

SHOOT-AROUND RESTS

Shoot-arounds are just right for finger shooters, but does any bowhunter shoot with fingers these days? Well, yes. Some. Perhaps 10 to 20

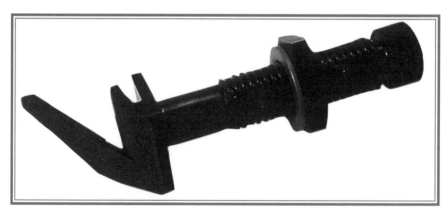

The shoot-around CenterRest is an inexpensive starter rest for finger shooters. It is essentially an interchangeable head mounted on a screw-in cushion plunger. The CenterRest Flipper replaces the plastic head with a springy-wire arrow support that is covered with a Teflon sleeve. For novices and some recurve set-ups, this simple rest is just right. This rest is easy to adjust for centershot.

percent and most beginners.

Released by your fingers, a bowstring rolls off the fingertips in a semi-circular motion, and this causes the arrow to flex sideways or "wallow" in the horizontal plane in a left-right pattern. The middle of the arrow bends in the opposite direction as the nock and head and, for a few microseconds, the rear of the arrow move in a different pattern than the front of the arrow. Half-way through the power stroke, as the arrow leaves the string, the nock then swings in the opposite direction. Even after all of this horizontal movement, a properly spined arrow–amazingly–stabilizes within a few yards. High-speed photography verifies that only about a quarter of your arrow is actually in contact with the rest, as little as six to eight inches of shaft. Typically used in conjunction with a spring-adjustable, Teflon-tip Berger Button for cushioned side pressure, a shoot-around rest allows your arrow to move naturally into its natural flexing cycle, called "archer's paradox."

Shoot-around rests are out of fashion, primarily because the percentage of bowhunters shooting releases from shoot-through rests has skyrocketed and drop-away rests have come on strong. A release shooter was rare just 20 years ago.

New Archery Products' Centerest Flipper combines a rest arm and cushion plunger in one unit. It is easy to install and adjust. The shaft screws through the arrow rest hole and the head of the rest can then be snapped in place. The head consists of a wire flipper arm with a silencing Teflon sleeve and a cushioned cut-out that acts as a set-off to help control the flexing arrow as it passes.

NAP notes that for accurate shooting, archers need to be conscious of nock-point placement when they use a shoot-around rest. Typically, you should begin tuning with your nock a little high, as a low nock will not work.

There are several styles of shoot-around rest. The Cavalier SuperFlyte mounts on the side of the bow. Adjust it vertically by levering it up and down with your finger as you tighten the cap screw. Adjust it horizontally with the long hex rod. The built-in, stainless-steel side pressure plate acts as a cushion plunger. This steel plate may be removed to use the SuperFlyte with a cushion plunger. The wire, arrow support arm has a smooth Teflon sleeve for quiet shooting.

SHOOTING TRADITIONAL BOWS

This topic may require a book of its own, but most recurves and longbows are shot with fingers right off the built-in arrow shelf. Indeed, the classic rest for traditional shooting is the shelf itself. Recurves typically have a wide shelf. Frequently, it is crowned in the center and bowhunters cover it with a piece of low-pile carpet or even a leather patch. In humid conditions, this carpet will soak up water, but if it is synthetic and the carpet pile is low, you can minimize any serious problem.

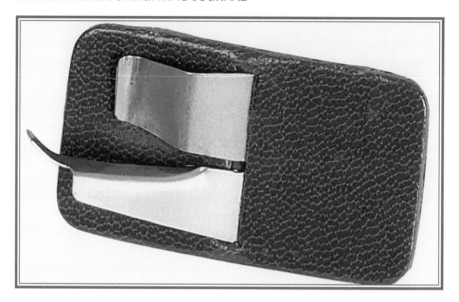

A stick-on, shoot-around arrow rest is fine for low-weight starter bows or for recurves. The pressure plate and arrow-retaining finger are lightweight, stainless steel.

The Bear Hair is a traditional-style rest that comes in two pieces. The shelf cover is a lightweight, synthetic carpet that you can cut to fit your bow shelf. The leather side plate keeps the arrow away from the wood or metal riser.

Any cheap stick-on plastic rest will work, although they are only used on beginner bows. Shoot-around rests like Cavalier's Super T-300 will also fit traditional bows. The Super T has a stainless-steel spine and Teflon-coated arrow support arm. The older style Flipper II from New Archery Products, with adhesive backing, also has a Teflon-coated stainless-steel flipper arm and a nylon button for some offset from the riser.

Plastic vanes do not typically fly well when shot from a traditional bow because you will not have vane clearance when you shoot off the shelf or with a stick-on rest. As the arrow flies by, the plastic vanes will almost certainly hit the bow shelf and/or the rest, and this will cause erratic flight.

A cushion plunger is recommended for high-quality shooting with fingers. Used with a shoot-around arrow rest, it helps control arrow flight so that with good form, a smooth release and follow-through, finger shooters can achieve superb hunting accuracy at a reasonable distance. Depending on the set-up, a cushion plunger can occasionally be used to good effect by a release shooter with a shoot-through rest.

Cushion plungers screw through the arrow-rest hole in the riser. They are typically locked in place by a couple of hex nuts and set screws. The plunger itself is a hollow, threaded brass or aluminum sleeve with a spring inside. The end in contact with your arrow wears a nylon tip, which allows arrows to slide against it with little friction. On some models, an internal Teflon sleeve smoothes out spring movement. As an arrow slides against it, the plunger tip compresses against the spring in the sleeve. This cushions an arrow's flight around the riser and moderates the initial left-right flex typical of a finger shooter's arrow.

Plunger barrels from Cavalier are stainless steel and have an internal Teflon sleeve and a white nylon tip. Expect to pay $40 to $50 for their adjustable (for spring tension and length) Master Plunger. Golden Key makes an economy plunger with a brass sleeve and black nylon tip for about $20.

SHOOTING AN OVERDRAW

Today, many bowhunters shoot overdraws without realizing it. Flinging arrows from an overdraw means you are drawing your broadhead back into or even behind your riser. This technique lets you shoot a very short arrow, much shorter than you would shoot if your launcher tips were in line with the arrow-rest hole in the riser and the broadhead insert in front of the bow rather than behind it! Using an overdraw, you can trim your 30-inch arrow to perhaps 28 inches or even less.

A shorter arrow saves weight. Saving weight increases speed. Increasing speed flattens trajectory. A flatter trajectory makes distance

An overdraw allows you to place your arrow rest behind the bow riser. The theory is that you can then shoot a shorter, lighter, and much faster arrow. In the late 1990s, overdraws extended so far back that they interfered with the natural oscillation of the bowstring and the movement of the cables. Many newer overdraws are generally shorter than this set up, which allows you up to about three inches of adjustability.

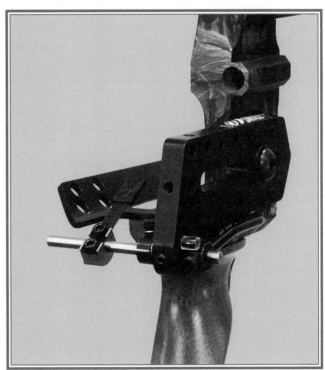

judging slightly less critical. Now, how flat your trajectory will become and how much speed you can pick up and how much distance error is "slightly less" depends on your set-up and your abilities. You can sometimes achieve an additional 20 fps, however.

There are many issues with overdraws, though, and the first is the arrow itself. Archers with short draws have a greater shaft selection than those with longer draws. When you have a long draw, arrow charts prefer large, stiff, heavy shafts. About length, the charts are not very forgiving. So cutting a couple inches off your shaft length opens up the arrow-spine chart for shorter, lighter arrows.

Few pro shops will recommend an overdraw to a bowhunter, though, unless they shoot frequently and have good, consistent form. Otherwise, an overdraw will magnify errors in shooting form and make your bow less manageable. Overdraws were popular before carbon arrows opened up additional size and weight opportunities, but these days, it is rare to see one of the old-fashioned, black shelf overdraws in the field.

If you have an overdraw, however, do not throw it away. Although they are a thing of the past, like Confederate dollars, they may one day return.

Another problem with the overdraw is that there is little distance between the cables and the back of the overdraw shelf, especially with low brace height bows. During the overdraw craze in the early '90s, archers installed overdraws as long as four inches. They soon discovered that their cables hit the back of the shelf, which caused extreme difficulties with wear, noise and arrow flight. The first answer was to pad the back of the overdraw, but bowhunters quickly found that with the increasingly popular short axle-to-axle bows, a quite-short overdraw gave them maximum speed, increased versatility to choose arrow shafts and maximum control. Today, we know that a minimum of two inches should be available between any overdraw and the moving cables.

Of course, for every rule there are exceptions, but overdraws cannot be shot effectively with fingers. Short arrows shot from high-energy bows mean that your release is critical. With reduced space between the cables and the back of the rest, finger-released arrows are still in the middle of the initial bend as they cross the back of the overdraw and this may cause interference.

The most serious consideration when shooting an overdraw is safety. Because overdraws allow you to pull your arrow behind your hand or wrist, they must be equipped with significant arrow-catcher trays. The wind, a slight twist of the bow, bumping a limb against your stand or jerking the release may cause the arrow to fall off a shoot-through rest. Releasing with the arrow improperly centered on your rest means you will miss your target, may damage your bow and may hurt yourself seriously with a splintered shaft.

BOW SIGHTS

Should you use a sight to aim and shoot? If your goal is to hit what you are aiming at, you are more likely to do that with a sight than without one. There should only be one goal for a bowhunter and that is to place an arrow precisely in the vitals of a game animal to ensure a quick, clean kill.

While many traditional shooters refuse to use sights, releases or even rests, you could argue that this is inherently unethical when high-quality gear is available. However, although there are no scientific data to substantiate their claim, traditional archers shooting instinctively say that they practice more and become more proficient with their gear than bowhunters shooting compounds. I, for one, believe that this claim is probably true and, indeed, if they are going to accomplish the bowhunter's primary goal, they must do so.

Instinctive shooting requires a bowhunter to swing into his target, estimating range, wind speed and direction, angle of the shot and the movement of game without pausing to select a specific pin. A good instinctive shot is a thing of beauty, but it takes a great deal of practice to perform |consistently and well. An instinctive shooter must understand personal limitations, exercise patience selecting their shot, and possess some indefinable but very real shooting-sense to pull it off cleanly.

A bow sight is a ready reference, a way of remaining steady when buck fever makes us shake. Like good instinctive shooting, using sights gives us a mental checklist and a physical routine. When we are under pressure, routine is a good thing. Sights give us an extra second to check our mental data, analyze our shooting form and verify our intentions! They increase our ability to make good, repeatable shots.

There are a myriad of sight styles available and they seem to change every few days: pin sights, pendulum sights, scopes and hybrids, such as fingertip-adjustable scopes with pins.

The dominant factor in choosing a bow sight is the task you need it to perform. Cost should not be a factor because sights range from $5 to $150 and after you assemble all of your other gear, do your year-round scouting and raise your bowhunting expectations, whatever you spend will be small in comparison to the total. Use the best sight you are comfortable with, because you may get only one shot . . . and is the trophy on the opposite side of your pins of value to you? Of course it is, but would you measure that best in money or in Winston Churchill's famous "blood, sweat and tears" analogy?

PIN SIGHTS

In the early 1980s, you might have glued or taped a sight to the face or back of your recurve bow's wood riser. Around 2005, on every commercially made

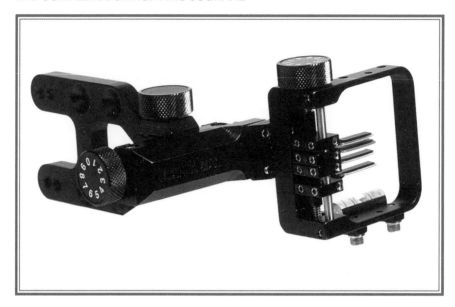

This direct-mount sight using four fiber optic pins is micro-adjustable in all directions and the level may be mounted on either side of the pin frame. Two sight bar extension lengths—3- and 6-inch—are available. The influence of the 3-D shooting movement, which peaked in the late 1990s, caused bowhunters —who previously sneered at such an effete target-shooting element—to accept levels as a   beneficial accessory.

compound and recurve bow, sights mount with two standardized screws above and on the opposite side of the riser from the arrow shelf. Holes are drilled and tapped into metal risers to accept standardized accessories and wood risers come with threaded brass inserts. A sight is commonly stacked between the riser and a quiver, which mounts in the same two holes.

Pin sights come in dozens of shapes and sizes. Except for innovations like fiber optic and tritium pins, pin sights are old technology. They are popular because they are inexpensive, easy to learn to use and effective.

Except for the least expensive, a pin sight consists of four basic elements: pins, bracket (attaches the sight to the riser), pin housing and the pin guard.

In the simplest pin sights, several brass pins slide up and down in vertical slots in a stamped-aluminum body that bolts directly to the side of your bow. The body is not adjustable, so you slide the pins up or down to adjust for elevation. For windage, you lock the pins on either side of their slot with knurled nuts and lock washers, moving it manually in or out for left-right impact adjustment.

A sight like this is simplicity itself. Before long, however, even a novice discovers that making a fine-tuning adjustment is a chore. Changing windage or elevation requires both hands and loosens the pin entirely, so it is difficult to reposition it precisely after you make an adjustment. Move a pin left or right and you will likely alter the vertical alignment. Take this sight off your bow and the pins slip. In addition, shooting this style sight with a high-energy compound causes the nuts to loosen. Eventually, you find the pins far out of alignment.

Stepping up from a beginner's Cobra double-slot sight with wire sight guard is a pin sight such as the Cobra Venom, with a bracket allowing dovetail windage and elevation adjustment. To adjust this sight, loosen the jaws gripping the dovetail and manually move the sight body left or right, or up and down. At this level of sophistication, sight bodies are machined aluminum and pin guards are sturdier, either vented machined aluminum or "high-impact" plastic. The pins will also be upgraded to a single-locking bracket system requiring an Allen wrench for repositioning.

If you are shooting with steel sight pins, dip their tips in fluorescent paint. Bright pin tips stand out in the confusion of a shot out of doors. If your pins are color coded for distance, it makes it easier to avoid this common mistake: "I guess I used the wrong pin."

Many men are color blind in the red-blue spectrum, so experiment with colors that work best for you. One common combination features a white 20-yard pin, red 30-yard pin, lime green 40-yard pin and finally another white-tipped 50-yard pin.

With any big game, this kind of sight gives you all the versatility you need.

You can spend between $100 and $200 at the next level of pin sights. The product offerings are diverse and you are approaching top-of-the-line status. This level involves fiber optics, perhaps even sight pins combining phosphorus with the radioactive element tritium.

Decide just how you will use your sight before you buy. For shooting from a ground blind or from a low treestand, fixed-pin sights are fine. Any higher than shooting from 20 feet up, though, and the shot angle becomes a problem. Then you are shooting the longest side of the triangle, not the distance you paced off from the base of your tree to a pile of corn.

There is a real-world problem with pin sights and treestands. What if you release your arrow from about 25 feet high with a buck standing angled away from you beside the 30-yard (90-foot) stake you set out from the base of the tree. Your shot must cover about 93 1/2 feet or about 31 yards accurately. You are probably going to place your 30-yard pin on the top of the buck's back, but it will surely jump the string a little. So, where do you hold exactly? Low or real low or in between?

How many pins is enough? Slotted sights allow you to add as many pins as you want. Most bowhunters use four and adjust them for 10-yard distance increments, from 20 to 50 yards. If you shoot a fast arrow, 260 fps or faster, though, you may only need one or two pins to mark the shooting range you can effectively cover, setting the highest pin perhaps for 25 yards and holding a touch high for 30 yards and a touch low for 20 yards.

As you study sight systems, check how close the pins can be set. If you use multiple pins, faster bows need very close pins because the trajectory of the arrow is flatter than for slow bows. Look for "zero gap" spacing with fiber optics even though in extreme cases this can obscure your target. If you are comfortable with a slower bow, something in the 220 fps range, you will have plenty of room with almost any pin sight to adjust for shooting performance.

One sight with fiber optics pins is the Micro Matrix from Trophy Ridge. The pin body is lightweight, high-impact plastic and the bracket is machined aluminum. Five independently adjustable pins are extra-long, wrapped, .019-inch diameter fiber optics, micro-adjustable for elevation. These tiny pin dots are set on an equally small pin post. The vertical and horizontal scales are etched in gold on black, a level is included, the aperture is a circle to match most peep apertures and the bracket includes a double, built-in Mathews Harmonic Damping unit. The vertical, in-line fiber-optic sight pins adjust with a gear drive and a cam-lock pin holder.

The number of fiber-optic pin styles is large and there are just as many ways to mount fibers in a sight. The mounting objective is to protect the fragile fiber-optic filament, so they are typically encased in a clear plastic sleeve. Designers also give thought to gathering as much light as possible so you have an aiming point even when light is low, and giving their sight a distinctive look. Fiber-optic strands are delicate, so these days it is not enough to simply offer fiber optics. They must be protected but still have a lot of the fiber showing to collect light.

A drawback, if there is one, to fiber optics is that they are brightest when you need brightness least, at noon, when ambient light fills the air. When you need brightness most, on dark cloudy days, they are relatively dim. Fiber optics channel available light directionally and unless they are supplemented by an artificial light source, they totally depend on ambient or available light. Still, they are better than the alternatives (except perhaps for the fatter tritium/phosphor pins).

The Micro Matrix and other superior pin sights of its genre such as the TruGlo Glo-Brite blend these relatively new elements. Their pin guard is round, like a target sight, not rectangular. Sight pins are "stacked" vertically, front to back, not horizontal. Sight guards and housings are plastic. A level is often included (it is optional in the TruGlo model). The sight body and housing are camouflage. They feature independent and indirect secondary sight pin adjustability.

ADJUSTING YOUR BOW SIGHTS

Adjusting your sights is key to hitting what you are aiming at. The quicker you make your arrows fly accurately, the more you will enjoy shooting.

Pins of any style, steel or tritium, follow or chase the shot. If arrows hit

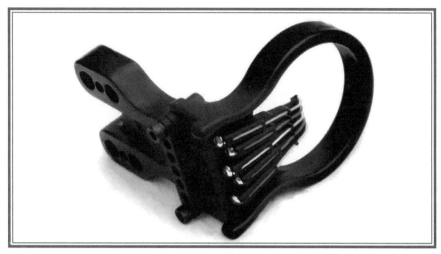

The Barebones pin sight has user-friendly versatility with a Limited Lifetime Warranty and your choice of five fiber-optic pins in .019- or .029-inch diameter, tritium or even steel micro-adjustable pins. This sight mounts either left- or right-handed and the sight block can be moved vertically or horizontally as a unit. A round pin guard is standard and a level is optional.

to the left, move your pins left. If arrows hit to the right, move your pins to the right. The same is true for vertical adjustments. Hit high, move higher. Hit low, move lower. Although it seems counter-intuitive, adjusting sight pins quickly becomes second nature.

UNDERSTANDING FIBER OPTICS

Optical fibers are tiny, transparent rods of glass or plastic that are spun or extruded and then stretched, dyed and bundled together. These fibers become long and flexible and can be made in almost any diameter.

Light travels along a fiber optic rod because the rod has a property called "total internal reflection." That means, it transmits light better than air!

Most of the light in a fiber optic rod is confined inside by a "cladding" or coating, which does not transmit or carry light as readily as the spun threads. A small percentage of light is lost as it travels along the rod, which makes it glow slightly along its length. The remaining light is what you see on the melted tip of your pins–and hence slightly larger in diameter than along the length of the rod.

Although a smaller pin covers less of your target, you may want a supplemental sight light and a large diameter fiber optic if you hunt when you return home from work. If you are also a 3-D shooter, you may want a separate sight with a small diameter fiber optic, because your ultimate target is a circle not much larger than a silver dollar on a 3-D target. (An inch one way or the other in the vitals of a deer may not matter for a quick kill, but an inch will position you out of the money in a 3-D tournament.)

A small sight light, where legal, can outfit your sight bracket with a useful add-on for low-light conditions, but look for one with variable intensity. Typically, sight lights have a red filter, but blue has become increasingly popular.

The size of the block that holds the fiber-optic rod and the size of the rod itself may be different. Manufacturers advertise numerous diameter rods, but the ends are melted so the fibers do not unravel. You usually see an end that is about .015 inch larger than the actual fiber.

CROSSHAIR SIGHTS

Two-season hunters with gun and bow should like the crosshair sight. With a crosshair, their aiming picture will feel correct.

Crosshair sights have some advantages over pin sights. The vertical crosshair helps keep you in the vertical plane, preventing "bow cant," which can be a problem when you are shooting on hillsides or from a treestand. If you shoot a lightweight bow with a quiver full of arrows attached, the bow is heavier on one side. Unconsciously, your attempt to correct this will throw your balance off more. A bubble level can help, but the bubble is slow to stabilize and even slight movements cause a bubble to move. That is distracting, especially if you pay attention to the bubble rather than picking a spot. To shoot successfully with a crosshair sight, align the vertical crosshair with the animal's legs and your bow will be vertical.

Because they divide a game animal–the vertical crosshair behind the front legs and the horizontal dissecting the lower third of the body–crosshairs help you pick a spot. Many find this easier than trying to place a single pin on the side of a deer.

A point stressed by Jim Sherman at Timberline is that bowhunters and 3-D shooters alike believe a small aiming point increases accuracy. A standard fiber optic has a fiber end that is about .062-inch and most pin blocks holding it are about .080-inch. This obscures some of your target. The crosshairs in the Timber-Glo are only .016-inch wide, the smallest aiming point in bowhunting. In addition, the light gathering crosshairs of the Timber-Gloss are easy to see, even in low light.

The HiViz Xcel HD eliminates the need for a peep and incorporates an "X" style crosshair. This unique sight is built on a rugged machined-aluminum frame. The independently adjustable pins are mounted in a sight bracket in front of the riser, while the adjustable X crosshair is in a bracket behind the riser. The two brackets are connected by and mounted in the sight's frame. The Xcel HD utilizes two HiViz pins that have a durable, clear "over-mold" to enable maximum light gathering while providing protection against the knocks bows take in the field.

PENDULUM SIGHTS

These days, pendulum sights are rare. Increasing arrow speed and the development of the drop away rest have virtually eliminated the need for pendulums. Nevertheless, here is the theory and a few of the rests you may still see circulating in archery and bowhunting circles. Pendulum sights help bowhunters shoot at downward angles from treestands. The higher you hunt, the less your chance of being detected by a deer, but hunting higher increases the difficulty of identifying the correct aiming point and making a clean pass-through shot. The idea of the pendulum is that no matter what the distance to your target, at least out to 30 yards, you can sight dead-on the vitals without having to make split-second pin and gap decisions.

Pendulum sights work, but if you are thinking about purchasing one, swing it back and forth to check for noise. It does not take much mechanical sound to spook a trophy buck. Next, ask about its effective shooting distance. Pendulums must provide a free-swinging pendulum, but one that will not jiggle every time your heart beats. The operation must be silent, relatively stable and effective at least to 30 yards.

Keller's black, all-metal Series 2000 is a good example of a quality pendulum sight. It uses a single sight pin floating on an axis, which may help eliminate confusion associated with multi-pin sights. A slot in the bracket

For shooting from treestands, a pendulum sight is typically accurate from zero to 30 yards. If you consider a pendulum, make sure that its operation is quiet and that its cradle does not swing so freely that every breath you take will cause the pendulum to swing erratically. The pendulum sight pictured uses one .040-inch fiber optic. Bowhunters who are competent beyond 30 yards will want to find a pendulum with a second pin.

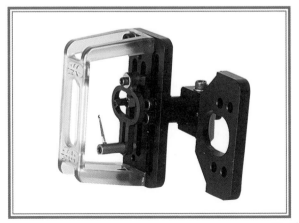

allows the sight swing to slide up or down for sighting. There is no need to guess distance, treestand height or arrow speed, and the effective shooting distance is from practically straight down to 30 yards. The Series 2000 comes with two sight pins for ranges beyond 30 yards. A removable, battery-powered LED can be screwed into the bracket to brighten the pendulum.

Pendulums from Savage Systems are cushioned so that if you move your bow quickly, the floating bracket will not make noise. The up-pin Feather Weight Pendulum offers a variety of pin options: a tritium pin, a fiber-optic rod, a twin fiber optic for extra distance, a FiberGlo pin and a tritium-powered fiber optic.

Tritium is a radioactive isotope of helium that is contained in a sealed glass capsule. Because it glows or emits beta particles continuously and will do so through its "half life" of 10 to 12 years, tritium is an independent light source that can power up a fiber-optic rod. It provides years of illumination and can be used as either a stand-alone pin or to provide illumination to a fiber optic. The FiberGlo pin provides an aiming point for two hours when the power source is charged. It recharges in minutes with ambient or UV light.

Savage recommends sighting-in on the ground at 20 yards. Then you should be set to shoot accurately from almost directly beneath your tree to 30 yards. Faster bows will get a little more distance; slower bows, a little less. Savage pendulums can also be outfitted with a standard bracket and a set of ground pins.

FINGERTIP ADJUSTABLE SIGHTS

SightMaster was the first fingertip-adjustable sight with a modern design. A fingertip-adjustable sight gives bowhunters easy sighting versatility with a single, moveable pin in a round plastic aperture. You move the pin and aperture with your fingertip; on some models, this can be done at full draw. These sights bolt directly onto your riser; with an offset block, your quiver attaches on top of them.

One of the most complex fingertip-adjustable sights is the Savage Quick-Click (QC) Ranger. The QC lets you shoot from 20 to 70 yards and the fingertip-adjustable yardage lever does not need to be screwed down before you shoot. Yardage references are laser engraved so there is no need to mark distances on tape with a pen. You can preset the incremental yardage clicks for one-, five- or ten-yard increments. The unique QC accepts a Savage pendulum cradle, fixed pins or even a round scope.

The key to the QC's performance is setting your arrow speed correctly on the yardage lever arm. Although it is a touch heavy and bulky, once you program in your arrow speed, it is extremely versatile.

The Elite Micro II from SightMaster weighs 8.4 ounces. Fully extended, it is 6.4 by 3.5 inches. It has both a fiber-optic aiming point and black, non-reflective wire crosshairs behind the fiber optic. The scope plate has seven positions for the threaded scope rod, which lets you make large initial adjustments before fine-tuning. The frame is machined aluminum and brass offsets allow you to mount a quiver above it. The yardage arm is locked in place with a brass knob. A bubble level on the clear, polycarbonate scope ring is standard.

Setting yardage is easy with an Elite Micro II. Choose one of the seven scope-plate positions, mark off 20 yards and shoot a group of three shots. The scope arm adjusts to make sure there is no difficulty with clearance between your arrow and the bottom of the polycarbonate scope. You must test hole selection so your shortest and your longest shots will all clear and will have sufficient space on the back of the mounting plate for yardage-reference stickers (provided). If you change arrows or broadheads, or increase draw weight, your peel-and-stick yardage-reference marks may need to be changed.

You first estimate the distance to the point where you want to introduce a game animal to your arrow. Then, move an indicator arm exactly over your pre-determined yardage marker on the back of the sight. When a deer steps onto your chosen spot, you know the distance exactly.

The bowhunting benefit is obvious. With a quick adjustment, you gauge precisely where you want to place the arrow. Because one pin covers every shot from practically zero to 80 yards, it is harder to become confused.

Fingertip-adjustable sights look complicated. Perhaps when a trophy appears, you are just as likely to fumble with the yardage-adjustment lever as to choose the wrong sight. Fiddling with a yardage knob means there is additional movement, albeit small, that a game animal may detect. Finally, today's hot bows need a lot of noise and vibration damping to keep from damaging the rod that holds the sight on the bracket. Rod breakage has been common in the past.

THE PEEP SIGHT

Peep sights preceded the compound bow, but with the increased energy and arrow speeds of a shot today, a secure, well-positioned peep is fundamental for accurate shooting at anything but very close distances.

A peep is a hole in a machined piece of metal or a molded piece of plastic that fits into your bowstring above the nock. It can be round, square or oblong. When you draw, you pull the string to your anchor point and, if everything is set up right, the peep centers its hole in front of your eye, blocking out the area around it. You want to center the proper distance pin or the correct gap in the exact center of your peep.

Experienced bowhunters serve their peep, which means they tie it in place with string above it and below it to make sure it will not move. Once served, a bowstring on a compound bow is so tense that, barring an acci-

This peep sight can be served into your string in several configu-rations, 3- or 4-notch, which is useful depending upon the number of strands in your bowstring. Available options include apertures in .125 and .060 inches. Bowhunters understand that the larger the hole, the better for low-light conditions, but the larger hole is less helpful than the smaller hole for centering your sight pin.

dent, the peep will remain perfectly in place until you remove it or the string is relaxed. When you remove the string or relax a recurve, you must be careful to make sure the peep stays in place.

Former pro-shop manager, bowhunter, and pro-fessional 3-D shooter Jeremy Blackmon says a peep makes the difference between winning and losing. "If you want to consistently hit what you're aiming at, you have to use a peep," he says, and he uses one for hunting and 3-D. "If the average guy who shoots a six-inch group at 40 yards would use a peep, he would cut his groups in half."

A peep sight works like the rear sight on a rifle. Put it in proper alignment with the front sight and you should hit what you are shooting at. On the other hand, if you do not use a peep and your anchor point is not lined up perfectly, it can cause you to miss even if your front sight is dead-on. You can quickly sketch this out on a piece of graph paper to see the difference a peep makes. Finger shooters can vary their impact point by several inches left or right if they only smile!

Essentially, a peep sight serves as a rear anchor and it helps you pick a spot. Recurve shooters understand that anchor point is extremely important. They practice drawing to a consistent spot: index finger at the corner of their mouth, or string touching the tip of their nose, for instance. Today, with fast compounds and release aids, archers talk about a "floating anchor point," or not coming to a precise spot each time they draw. This is wrong. A peep helps solve left-right shot problems resulting from a floating anchor, because it helps you focus your vision in the center of the hole in the peep.

The moment when you have to execute your shot perfectly is the most difficult single second of any hunt. Anyone can stand in the back yard, relax, breathe and shoot a 3-D deer. It is something else entirely when the pressure is on and hair is growing on your target. Things go wrong: you have to hurry before the deer goes behind a tree and out of your shooting lane, for instance. A peep sight helps keep Murphy's Law from becoming a prohibitive factor at your moment of truth.

"I use a non-reflective black, machined-aluminum Fletcher Tru Peep," Backmon says. "A small 1/16-inch aperture is okay for 3-D. I shoot a larger aperture for hunting, though, about one-quarter inch, because you can never tell what the weather will be like. Trophy deer are most often taken when the light is dimmest, so I want the larger hole for bowhunting."

A potential difficulty using a peep is that it will not align when you draw. Release shooters have an easier time with this than finger shooters, who typically twist the string and have to be aware of peep alignment. With a release, the string comes back to your anchor perfectly every time. Finger shooters who twist the string risk staring at the side of the peep and then must twist it at full draw or let down and draw again so the peep aligns with their eye. When a deer is moving into your shooting lane, you do not want that problem, so a self-aligning peep is probably the correct choice for finger shooters.

Another difficulty using a peep is string stretch. Synthetic strings may be stronger than steel, but when they are warmed or continually stressed, they elongate, and when this happens your settings change. It is always a good idea to draw and check peep alignment before you climb onto a treestand.

SELF-ALIGNING PEEPS

The Fine-Line Zero Peep set the standard for self-aligning peep sights. Their peep was molded black plastic with a tiny hood over the hole to eliminate glare. It served directly into the string. A latex tube fit over a post on the rear of the oblong peep; the other end of the tube fit over a post on an adhesive anchor pad that stuck to the inside of the top limb. Today, Fine Line's Pick-A-Peep has a slotted receiver so that you can easily switch different-size apertures. An optional style ties the latex tube on the cables. This highly successful peep, and its imitators, give you an almost perfect view, even if you twist the string slightly.

Several other manufacturers market self-aligning peeps with distinctive features. The Ace Clearview angles through the string so that at full draw you look straight through the opening. Golden Key's Total View Line-O-Peep does not need to be served into the string. A small screw tightens a self-locking clip into place. The hole for this peep is drilled to 1/4-inch diameter and the surgical tubing locks onto the cable.

The only knock on self-aligning peeps is the rubber tubing. Installed improperly, it can slip off the post or even break when you come to full draw. The end can slap you in the eye, causing an injury. High-speed photography shows that when you shoot, the tubing becomes hyper-active and causes slapping noises as it gyrates wildly before the bow's left-over energy dissipates.

Inglewing's self-aligning C-Peep bracket fits through the string, but the peep itself is actually to the side. One open side and three triangular aiming

Depending upon the stage of their physical development and their interest in archery, you may effectively start young people with the simplest bows–no sights and no release aid, shooting with a finger release–or you may want to step them up to a lightweight compound with sights and release. It is important to help them have fun and progress at their own pace. Too many rules, pressure to conform or to excel can quickly turn a young person away from the sport.

posts make this a distinctive looking set-up. The open slot on the side allows more light to enter and thus gives hunters 10 to 15 more minutes of hunting time, Inglewing says. In addition, the molded-plastic peep is angled, and this allows the sight to "square-up" for a clear hole to look through when you draw.

THE INDEPENDENT PEEP

Practically all peep sights are served into your bowstring. Some fit vertically and may be thought of as free-floating. Others fit horizontally, so that when you draw the string the hole presents a clear oval picture; peeps that tie in while the bow is at rest give you a round hole for pin centering.

The Shurz-A-Peep and Pro Hunter Peep have three slots in their horizontal machined sides. You have a lot of flexibility dividing the strings for perfect rotational balance, but this particular style of independent peep gives you an aiming oval that will not hamper vision no matter how the string rolls.

Specialty Archery Products has an "accessorizable" machined aluminum peep sight. Not only is its Specialty Peep offered with five different hole sizes, but it has several tiny Zeiss "clarifier" lenses for magnification. Its Super Peep Kit includes the peep housing, three size apertures and a special aperture wrench. While the use of magnifying lenses so close to your eye can be a terrific assist, lenses attract dust and moisture and can be a problem in the field.

The Nite Hawk Peep is made with a "+" style hole. The theory is that diffused light bending around the edges of a peep aperture is a big reason we miss. Therefore, light coming through the four arms of the peep is diffuse or appears hazy, but the light passing directly through the tiny square center cannot be hazy because the center has no edges. Therefore, the tiny square hole works in any hunting situation. The Night Hawk is available in four sizes, small to extra-large.

MAKE YOUR PEEP WORK

Serious bowhunters say the two archery accessories that make you a finer shot are your peep and a mechanical release aid. Each has its pitfalls though. If you are not attentive to a release, you can trigger it prematurely or torque it and thereby twist the string, even though this is harder than with fingers. A peep sight cannot just be screwed onto the riser like your front sights. It has to be tied or served securely into place in your bowstring. If it slips or is improperly positioned, it can cause you to miss.

After you select a peep, you must insert it into the string and fix it in position. You will see archers try to do this with their fingers, but it is difficult with a high-poundage bow that stretches the string extremely tight. Most manufacturers recommend that you relax your bow weight in a bow press, insert the body of the peep between the strings with strands divided evenly to a side or to the appropriate slots. There may be three or even four on some horizontal peeps.

Using a bow press to relax the strings so you can insert a peep is fine if you have one or there is a pro shop nearby, but most bowhunters do not. When the string is relaxed it is easy, but lacking a bow press, you can carefully spread the strings with an EZ String Separator or dull screwdriver, not a knife! With the strings separated and held apart, you can manually insert the peep into the string and position the string's strands in the appropriate grooves.

Adjust your peep to line up perfectly in front of your eye at full draw. You can do this yourself, but a friend can help position the peep for you quickly. When you draw, make sure it is the way you draw when you are actually shooting. Think of good form and come to your anchor naturally. The test is whether you can naturally look through the peep and see your pins. When you draw, you want the correct pin in the exact center of the peep's hole. Test the peep by closing your eyes and drawing. When you open your eyes, the peep should be perfectly positioned.

Experienced bowhunters make a record of the distance from the top of their nock set along the string to some point on their peep, the bottom or center of the hole. Then, if you have to re-set the peep or want to set up a spare string and do not have a friend to help, you can do it quickly by yourself.

There are bow sights that offer both front and back posts or pins and apertures. The EZ Bow Sight from Muzzy, for instance, uses the same aiming system as a rifle with adjustable front and rear fiber-optic or tritium sights on a lightweight bracket. The EZ eliminates the need for a peep with fluorescent red fiber optics in the rear aperture to horizontally bracket a fluorescent green fiber optic in the front aperture. When aligned at full draw, the rear aperture frames the front aperture. This makes target acquisition faster and reduces torque.

The front and back sight brackets of the X-Cel from Simpson Quality Designs are independently adjustable and a single fiber optic occupies the front sight frame. A fluorescing "X" style crosshair rear sight quickly centers your eye on the front pin bead.

Timberline's No-Peep is an unusual design that helps you achieve a positive and consistent anchor. The No-Peep is an "eye-alignment device," not an additional or rear sight. The 2.2-ounce No-Peep mounts on a rear-facing bracket and has an internal lens with a dot. Behind that lens is a ring. You adjust it so that the dot is inside the ring when at anchor. If you draw while looking at your sight pins, you see the No-Peep in your peripheral vision. The optics of the No-Peep magnify misalignment. The principle works with any type sight: pins, crosshairs, pendulums or wires and beads. Because you can only see the No-Peep with your eye behind the bowstring, you can shoot with both eyes open for increased depth perception.

STABILIZERS

Bowhunters must consider using a stabilizer for two reasons. First, we are in the middle of a "quiet-shooting" revolution and the right stabilizer helps with that. Second, bow design underwent a dramatic change about a dozen years ago. Cams changed from soft to hard, one-cams with idler wheels replaced most twin-cam designs, and hunting bow risers became significantly more reflexed. In spite of their advantages, deflex risers (bending away from the shooter) were identified with novices and inexpensive bows.

Today, stabilizers use aluminum or carbon housings. They are buffered with rubber fittings and filled with springs, oils, gels, powder and even sand. There is good news, too, for bowhunters who cannot give up the "old days." You can still buy a solid-steel stabilizer.

Purchase a stabilizer because you want the perfect bow balance for your shooting form . . . just like the dot shooters. Balancing your bow lets you maintain a loose grip. This minimizes torque on the riser and, hence, on your arrow.

You grip a bow below center, so when you hold it lightly in your shooting hand, the top limb swings back toward your face. The proper weight and length stabilizer will help keep it in a vertical position. After you shoot, a stabilizer helps rock the bow slowly forward. This lets you catch it with your wrist sling rather than having to grab it with your fist. In this manner, a good stabilizer helps with your follow-through, too.

Most bowhunters still do not use a wrist sling. Of course, in spite of years of teaching, most bowhunters still grab and twist their bow. We also tend to over-draw or draw "up the valley," beyond our peak draw weight, and the pressure on our string and shooting hands causes us to twist the riser. Admit it! And we wonder why we miss.

The weight of a stabilizer provides some additional inertia to help keep your shooting consistent. Most fully tricked-out bows weigh eight pounds, as much as a loaded shotgun, so the additional six-to-ten ounces below and forward of the grip are significant.

You also want your stabilizer to help reduce the noise and vibration from a shot. Shock and vibration can have numerous detrimental effects in your shooting system, which includes your hand, wrist and arm. It can cause hand and arm fatigue; contribute to painful joint inflammation; and create enough vibration in the mechanical system to shake loose your accessories. This is straightforward wear and tear and you can prevent it. You probably have a $1,000 or more wrapped up in your bow and accessories, so you have an investment to protect.

Your stabilizer should be part of a balancing, silencing and vibration damping system that makes shooting more comfortable and more accurate.

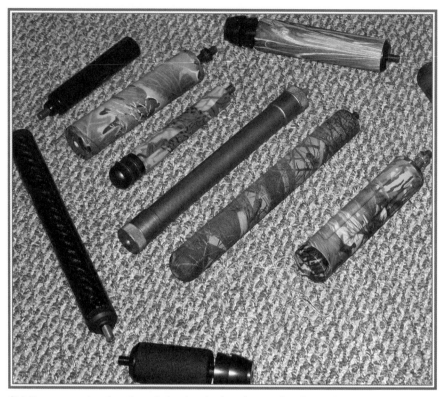

Stabilizers serve two functions, balancing the bow in your hand and absorbing shock. They vary from as little as three to four inches to as much as a yard in length. They are filled with a huge variety of oils, sand, ball bearings, internal baffles, and even game-tracking string. Stabilizers were the first commonly accepted element to begin dealing with the shock and noise of high-speed shooting.

You can feel the effect of a good stabilizer in your hand and arm, because it kills "riser buzz." (Scrape your fingernails down a blackboard. That resembles riser buzz.) Since after-shot noise is considerably diminished, you can essentially hear the effects of a good stabilizer, too.

COMBINING BALANCE AND SILENCE

In the mid 1990s, it seemed that the only thing any bowhunter wanted was a fast bow. A bow that only shot 225 fps was no longer regarded with respect. It was significant for bowhunting that the increasingly well-publicized cash payouts for 3-D shooting also helped make a faster, lighter arrow with a flatter trajectory desirable . . . and possible.

Millions of bowhunters bought into the high-energy, fast-bow, light-arrow syndrome, and manufacturers had to do something to ease the strain of high-energy shooting. Much of that energy was being delivered to the arrow, but a lot of it went into the bow, the accessories and the shooter's hand and arm.

This stabilizer is filled with powder. It comes in six- or eight-inch lengths in black or camo, and is an example of a stabilizer that primarily deadens shock in a straight-line direction, forward and back.

The old concept of a forgiving bow, one that would allow you to make a mistake in shooting form and still deliver an arrow in the vitals, was forgotten in the rush to faster arrow speed. Bowhunters soon found that their bows, although faster than ever, had become hard to handle and, especially as they grew shorter, almost impossible for finger shooters.

It suddenly occurred to America's free-enterprise system or to the bowhunters themselves, depending on whether you prefer the demand to the supply or vice versa, to study how to lessen this shock and noise. The idea was to add shock absorbers to the bow and the obvious place, at first, was the stabilizer.

Almost everyone realized that the available hollow tubes and solid-steel stabilizers were not getting the job done. Shock absorbers on automobiles were an obvious place to begin and manufacturers filled similar tubes with weights and springs, oils, sand, powders and, eventually, viscous gels and internal baffles. All of these are more effective than the earlier stabilizers, but all were in-line shock absorbers, channeling energy fore-and-aft.

In the early '90s, Bill Leven began to promote "Doinkers," and his concepts–stabilize and silence, disconnect the weight from the bow, dissipate vibration in multiple directions–caught on. His secret was to use thick rubber boots to prevent metal-to-metal contact, and it worked. It was the idea that had practically everyone asking, "Why didn't I think of that?"

Today, Doinker has a significant line of vibration- and noise-dampening items. Like other stabilizer manufacturers, well-traveled bowhunters endorse these products. Lately, several sizes and strengths of rubber have become available to serve as couplings and to hold different size and directional weights.

It is safe to say that if there is a spot on your bow and accessories that can successfully hold a shock- and noise-deadening unit or a silencing item, Doinker, Sims Vibration Laboratories or one of the numerous other companies in this field are working on a specialized attachment to make it more secure and more effective.

STABILIZER STACKERS

Several manufacturers offer stabilizers with ends shaped so that stackable weights can be added. This helps you customize weight distribution and vibration damping. Vibracheck, for instance, builds its gel-filled 6.5-inch, six-ounce rubber-coated Strikewave with a tip so that additional weights can be added to help you find the perfect balance, as well as deal with "stray" vibration not absorbed by the arrow or other vibration-absorbing elements.

Another handy stabilizer-related item is a quick disconnect. Screw this short, lightweight connector into the stabilizer bushing and leave it in place. Either screw or clip the disconnect plug onto the stabilizer. Muzzy and Carbon Impact disconnects let you add or remove a stabilizer in one, quick twist rather than screwing it all the way in and out each time you prepare to shoot or take down your bow. Vibracheck also has a ten-degree downward-angled disconnect that lowers the center of gravity of your bow slightly down and forward, and thereby helps you hold it steadier.

SOME STABILIZING ALTERNATIVES

Carbon Impact's camouflaged (or black) gel-filled series uses carbon-impregnated fiberglass tubes in 1.0- and 1.5-inch diameters. They call these their Fat and Super Fat stabilizers respectively. Mounting a rubber Sims to the front outside of the tube increases its shock dissipating abilities.

Saunders has a history of developing complex archery accessories. Saunders shock- and sound-deadening systems are outstanding for their apparent intricacy . . . and polished good looks. Beginning with their basic ShockTamer and adding the twin-chambered, screw-on Pro-Tamer or single chamber Tamer SS, and then "topping off" your stabilizer with a Pro-Bandit and adding a Bandit to your sight bracket . . . you have a system of a dozen or so metal and rubber parts. In typical Saunders fashion, their Pro-Angler knuckle has a whopping 312 total settings–13 vertical and 24 rotational–to counter-balance a bow quiver and any torque you add to your system. This Nebraska inventor and manufacturer introduced and advertised a unique stabilizer called the Torque Tamer as early as 1985!

Vibracheck responded to archery's increased interest in quiet, vibration-free shooting by using a thick gel, VibraSorb. A free-floating aluminum weight on the front of their gel-filled stabilizers is molded into the gel, not attached to the outer metal shell. When you shoot, vibration is transmitted to the weight; it rotates or "stirs" inside the gel and this dissipates vibration in all directions.

Stabilizers from TruGlo are available in many camo patterns. Their inexpensive, aluminum Solidifier is old-fashioned, solid aluminum. This stabilizer provides weight forward for balance, but does little to absorb shock. At four or six inches long, the Nullifier uses an internal weight in a fill of gel. The top-of-the-line Deadenator is one of many new stabilizers that uses a Doinker between its forward weight and a gel-filled aluminum tube. The Deadenator is available in sizes from 3.5 inches and 4.3 ounces to 6.5 inches and 9.3 ounces.

The Lore Stabilizer features six steel rods set into the outer perimeter of an anodized-aluminum base. Carolina Archery Products then wedged a sculptured rubber plug in the center. Carolina says the rods act like tuning forks to transmit the vibration of a shot into the rubber core. The Lore is 6.75 inches long and weighs 5.0 ounces.

The Global Resource ShockFin stabilizer begins with a wrapped carbon housing. A stiff rubber insert is inserted into the housing to absorb vibration. Adjustable, modular aluminum weights are then inserted in the center of the stabilizer to absorb and dissipate the vibration.

YOUR QUIVER

Three different quiver styles are available for bowhunting: hip quivers which hang from your belt; bow quivers which attach to your riser; and back quivers which are used by traditionalists and hunters who make extended stalking forays into wilderness areas.

Maybe a quiver is unglamorous, but it is important. It must hold arrows quietly and securely, so they are easy to retrieve when the time comes. You do not want arrows rattling or scraping against each other, and your sharp broadheads need to be fully covered to protect your fingers from terrible cuts.

Most bowhunters buy bow-mounted quivers. More of them are sold each year than all other styles put together. Bow-mounted quivers have been available since Fred Bear began experimenting with them in the '40s. Early bow quivers were more concerned with holding arrows than protection, and they often left a broadhead's cutting edges exposed.

Your quiver should be light but sturdy, and attach to the bow riser securely. You do not want anything rattling when you shoot, so it must hold arrows firm-

A two-piece bow quiver that mounts to your bow's riser, allows you to hold arrows nearer their head and fletching. This helps reduce the possibility of a bent arrow or noise from fletching scraping. Be sure the quiver cup and any foam insert will accommodate your chosen head (mechanical or fixed) and that the gripper will hold your particular size arrows securely but not so tightly that you can risk bending them.

ly inside the cup and the gripper, even after extended use. You do not want arrows vibrating after a shot and you do not want the arrow fletching scraping against other fletching. The farther down the shaft the gripper holds your arrows the better, although given the usual positioning of the quiver base above your grip and the length of your arrows, this causes practical design problems.

Your quiver should attach and detach easily and not interfere with the mounting of other accessories, such as your sights or a backward facing V-bar stabilizer or perhaps a Berger button to help mollify arrow wallowing.

Slots in the gripper should be sized to your arrows. Smaller holes are usually necessary for carbon than aluminum. The gripper needs to be made from a flexible product that holds the arrows securely, but not too tightly. The silent, flexible quiver gripper must work as well in cold weather as it does on a warm day.

The quiver hood should completely encase your broadheads and it should adapt to the kind of broadhead you are shooting. If you are shooting a large head like the two-blade Snuffer 125, which has a 1 5/16-inch cutting diameter, you want to be sure there is room in the cup to hold the heads. If you are shooting the mechanical Gold Tip Gladiator, though, be sure that pressing the blades into the quiver does not spring the blades open.

Bow-mounted quivers are either single- or two-piece. Single-piece quivers evolved from recurve days and they are still made today. The plastic Bear Hug Quiver from Escalade Sports has essentially been unchanged for decades. It holds seven arrows and attaches to a plastic bracket on your riser with just a twist. The generous cup fully protects your broadheads and the gripper holds your arrows at about their center, flaring them outward slightly so the fletching can be spaced apart. Many quivers are available in a similar style from Kwikee, Bohning and PSE.

The difficulties with these traditional one-piece quivers are arrow rattle, good arrow fit and a tendency to stand out from the bow riser by four to five inches. For novices or bowhunters who take their quiver off and hang or tie it on a branch, these are fine, economical quivers, however.

Manufacturers usually build several grippers and cup styles. Bear upgrades the Bear Hug to the Super 7. In place of the molded-rubber broadhead holder inside the hood is a block of foam. A thicker gripper designed to hold either aluminum or carbon shafts takes the place of the molded-rubber gripper. With a foam-filled hood, you must place the heads in the same blade orientation each time or you will soon chew up the foam and need to replace it.

If the simplicity of the one-piece quiver and its quick-detach benefit appeal to you, ask for one with a low-profile broadhead cup. In place of the bulky broadhead cup on the Super 7, bowhunters prefer a low-profile cup style available on a quiver like the Bohning Badger. With the arrows in a row, however, rather than in an oval around the stem the quiver, the Badger holds three less arrows than the Super 7.

How many arrows do you need, though? Unless you are one of those archers who like to carry a lot of ammo, four arrows should be plenty for a day of deer hunting.

Here are a few style differences that may help you make a decision about what elements are important for you. Martin's huge 10-Arrow features a built-in broadhead wrench, three storage compartments with snap-on lids, and holds arrows number nine and ten on special clips between the cup and your riser and limbs, thereby exposing you to the broadhead if you choose to use these. The Archer's Choice Pivoter Five is built with independent pivoting arrow holders for smooth, silent arrow release. Fine-Line's Hunter holds eight arrows. Twin center posts adjust to the length of your arrows. Push the broadheads into the foam-filled quiver cup and slip your arrow nocks over the bar at the bottom. Hot Shot's Quick Lock 7-Arrow has a metal frame that resists riser buzz and vibration. Kwikee's Mechanical 4 is designed for mechanical broadheads; it grips the arrows behind the head.

One debate about quivers centers around whether you are more accurate with one mounted on your bow or not. If you hunt from a treestand, it should be easy to remove it and lay it on the stand or hang it in the tree. You hear good arguments for removing the quiver and its load of arrows and broadheads from the side of your bow. Many bowhunters say that in the imperfect tension of drawing on a deer, a mounted quiver gives them problems with left-right placement because the bow is heavier and they must grip it tighter. Still, there does not seem to be a clear-cut answer to the question. You can learn to shoot just fine with a full quiver mounted on your bow riser. You just need to perform shot mechanics the same way each time.

In the early 1990s, many bowhunters switched to two-piece bow quivers. The two-piece quiver has a broadhead cup that attaches at the top of your riser with a gripper element near the bottom. These may either be held in place at special machined mounting holes or under the limb bolts. If your two-piece quiver fits under the limb bolts, you may need a pro shop to assist with the set-up because the bow will practically have to be disassembled before the quiver can be attached.

Out east, a bowhunter with a hip quiver is rare. In the wide-open west, however, hunters frequently use a spot-and-stalk method and hip quivers are relatively common. Certainly, they are excellent for recurve and longbow shooters.

Hip quivers fasten over your belt and tie around your leg. This prevents the quiver from flapping. Broadheads fit inside a standard, foam-filled hood and arrows are carried with the fletching pointed up and to the rear. Because most people are accustomed to bow-mounted quivers, the hip quiver may take some getting used to, especially the restricting feeling of the leg tie. On a hot day, this tie-on and the hip-hugging plastic backing can make a hip quiver uncomfortable to wear.

Neet makes several hip or side quivers just for bowhunters. Their six-arrow Bowhunter in

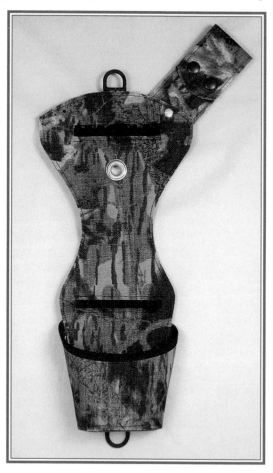

The Neet MB-107 Mechanical Broadhead hip quiver uses two molded grippers to hold four arrows. The swivel belt attachment makes this quiver useful by right- or left-hand bowhunters. A firm center stave gives this quiver rigidity. Hip quivers are especially useful when hunters are stalking or still-hunting.

Mossy Oak or Advantage camouflage comes with an adjustable strap to mount it to a stand or tree. Neet's Mechanical Broadhead side quiver holds four arrows with the heads in a fully enclosed cup.

Vista's Rustler holds seven aluminum or six carbon arrows inside a rigid, camouflaged shell that is protected and silenced with a fleece lining.

Traditionalists and hunters who are packing heavy enjoy back quivers. Leather seems just right for traditional hunters, and bowhunters preparing for an extended stay in the woods or who are covering rough terrain need their hands free for climbing and glassing. In the latter case, materials lighter than leather are the best choice.

Wyandotte Leather's Gerald Kaufman says their back and side quivers are used by traditional bowhunters and by people who just prefer the look and feel of leather. Leather has some positive characteristics that a bowhunter should favorably consider. It lasts longer, is quieter, and the older it is the better it looks. Compared to Cordura nylon, though, leather is heavy and it can be hot on the back when you are climbing or stalking.

The Arrow Incased System (AIS) holds five arrows securely and protectively via an inner rotational device, which is essentially a central spindle with a high-mount and a low-mount gripper. The patented AIS holds any type or size arrow or broadhead and weighs less than two pounds. It is available in 32- or 35-inch lengths and in black plus four popular camo patterns. The manufacturer sells an optional shoulder strap.

Rancho Safari markets several back quivers in tough saddle cloth or lightweight twill fabric. These quivers are designed with the broadhead down and the fletching up. The Cat Quiver Mini is worn like a single-strap back quiver. Its fletching hood and broadhead base are ABS plastic and are held together by an adjustable one-half-inch aluminum slide bar so arrows are held in by pressure. The seven-arrow Mini has a wide shoulder strap that is padded and adjustable.

The camouflaged, seven-arrow Cat Quiver VII combines a quiver with a large, versatile backpack and a fanny pack. The padded waist strap has two large side pockets and a water bottle pouch. The main compartment features padded back support and a private security pocket. A second bellows pocket has a side zipper opening. There are plenty of padded straps over the shoulders and around the waist to keep the packs and quiver tight. Arrows are drawn from the side.

RELEASE AIDS

Warriors and bowhunters have known for thousands of years that releasing the bowstring with their fingers caused some left-right placement problems. Hence, the popular Mongolian thumb ring which has been used for thousands of years. Using such a thumb ring would seem awkward today, but it should certainly work very well on traditional bows and on low-weight compounds.

Nevertheless, in something close to its modern form, the release aid has been around at least since the 1960s. The bowstring was wobbling forward, rather than moving forward in a smooth, straight line. This, they understood, caused arrows to wallow left-to-right and increased their difficulty of hitting their target, whether it was a deer or the gold circle at the heart of a Saunders Spartana-grass mat.

The function of a release aid is to remove 2 1/4 inches of finger spread, in the conventional one-finger-over/two-fingers-under shooting style from the bowstring. Even the fastest, smoothest archer has trouble releasing the string of a heavy bow in a straight line without it getting a head start and swinging out and around his or her fingertips.

A release removes the "out-and-around" misdirection by positioning a small, hard and smooth point of contact on the bowstring. When this point of contact is triggered, it releases instantaneously. There is no anticipation or sloppy string release even though you can torque the string if your release does not have a rotating barrel or trigger the release early, before you come to full draw.

Releases allow bowstrings to travel straight forward. The side-to-side movement of the arrow is minimized, perhaps eliminated. In its place, however, a vertical, up-and-down oscillation appears, caused by a nock point traveling erratically rather than horizontally. (Caused by cam roll-over synchronization, even with one-cam bows.) This effect can usually be overcome by tuning your bow for straight nock travel, adjusting the height of the nock point and the position and spring-weight of the arrow rest.

A mechanical release also helps you overcome target panic–at least one form of it–by teaching you how to eliminate flinching and freezing. Bowhunters are just as prone to this as are competitors. The inability to release with the pin on target (hair or paper) is just one form of target panic. A second form is flinching or jerking the string. In neither case will you hit what you are aiming at. A release, at least theoretically, is triggered quickly, but not in a jerky manner, like a good shotgun blast. You should not know when the release would go off so your mind can focus on perfecting your form and on holding steady.

Although no one knows why, it is accepted that releases triggered by the pinkie or thumb, rather than the index finger, are better for helping cure target panic. It is customary to trigger something or push a button with the index finger. Therefore, using the thumb or pinkie may establish a different set of muscular patterns, and this breaks a habit. Jerry Carter of Carter Releases says, "Today, I think 99 percent of all hunters and folks crossing over from gun hunting prefer an index-finger release."

ATTACHING A RELEASE

One way to understand the hand-held mechanical release aid is to look at the way it grips your bowstring or D-loop. There are three basic ways a release can draw your bowstring back: rope, jaws or caliper and ball bearing.

A rope release loops around your string and is held tight by a cocked and usually open-ended lever. The lever or jaw holds the rope in an open or in a closed manner, your choice. In the open style–Stanislawski's Avenger or Jim Fletcher's Fletchmatic–the lever does not close tight against the body of the release, and this can allow it to slip and fire prematurely. Some shooters prefer these because they believe they shoot faster and smoother as they have less distance to travel when the trigger is pulled or pushed. The closed-jaw release, like the venerable TruFire Crackshot, encircles the string with the jaw and the body of the release. Until you press the trigger, the string cannot pop out accidentally.

Rope releases typically cannot be left on the string; they will fall down the string and hang against your lower cam! They also take some practice getting used to, as they involve three steps: putting the release string around the bowstring, using your thumb to move the release string around the jaw, and locking the jaw.

Rope releases offer most of the advantages of other styles, will not damage your string and can be shot successfully without a D-loop. The rope loops compress to such a small dimension when you have drawn the bow that they almost cannot put any torquing pressure on your arrow.

Think about the operations required however to use this style release when you are hunting. The challenge can be formidable when you are faced with shooting quickly, too. So, a hand-held rope release will work for bowhunting, but it is not a preferred style.

Every modern release uses jaws or some type of rotating sear. On a rope release, the jaw holds the release rope rather than the string itself. On other styles, the jaws hold the bowstring or your D-loop directly.

Winn Archery's Freeflight Caliper has a single, rounded-edge stainless-steel movable jaw and is held deep in the hand, almost against the base of your thumb. This is unusual for release styles today, which usually make you reach for the trigger. This deep hold may give you more control and the single jaw caliper keeps the serving "on plane." What's more, these releases are designed to give you a natural, comfortable draw because the strap is more of a glove than just a wrist strap. The strap distributes the pull around your grip, hand and wrist, not just the wrist.

Bill Scott, founder of Scott's Archery, may have built the first caliper release. The Scott Shark has a dual moving jaw on a fully adjustable, aluminum pivoting head. The heat-treated steel jaws completely encircle your bowstring. This style dual caliper is perfect for a D-loop. If the calipers are attached directly to the string, they can quickly abrade the serving and put pressure on the nock. The beauty of the caliper is that it holds your string-loop immediately behind the base of your arrow. When you trigger the release, there is no sliding with a caliper. The jaw or jaws open and the string moves forward.

Popular in the early 1990s, a ball-bearing release draws the bowstring or D-loop back between the rounded surfaces of two ball bearings. This provides a crisp release of the bowstring because there is so little surface area holding it. Unfortunately, the small ball bearings crush or separate the serving over synthetic bowstring strands. With a D-loop, there is no reason a ball-bearing release cannot be entirely satisfactory.

TruFire makes a finely machined, ball bearing-mounted, swiveling release head. They mount it on releases in their SplitFire group: the finger-drawn Three Finger, the full-hand grip of the Custom and an economical hunting model, the Wrist Release. TruFire chamfers the ball bearings in an octagonal manner to present a flat surface to the bowstring. This eliminates the pinching and string crushing of round surfaces.

HUNTING RELEASES

Many hunters believe a release is something else to worry about at a time when there is enough pressure to perform already. Nevertheless, a mechanical release helps you hit what you are aiming at, and that may be worth the extra worry.

No specific release style is truly a "hunting release." A hunter's best release is probably one that attaches to a wrist strap. Hand- or finger-held releases are best left to target shooters.

There are other ways to think about releases, though. You could use a double-jaw James Greene Gator Jaws release with wrist strap to win Vegas . . . and use it to hunt javelina in the afternoon. Conversely, you can use a reverse closed-jaw Carter Insatiable 2 rope release to take deer . . . and then win all three legs of the IBO Triple Crown. 3-D Champion Jennie Richardson likes her Hicks XR7 because she can set the tension for 100 percent no-travel crispness. Bowhunter and NFAA competitor Dan Massimillo uses a back-tension release for all shooting.

Hunters tend to set their release with a little "give," while competitors like a release with a hair trigger. Winn Archery believes hunters need a little "play" or give in the trigger because they often wear gloves or mitts and are shooting from unusual heights and odd angles. Some play in the release trigger helps disguise the instant of the shot, and should thereby help avoid target panic as well.

These days, bowhunters prefer releases with wrist straps like the Copper John ME II rather than the older "concho" style. Popular in the '80s, conchos have a tubular connection to wrap your hand around. This changed because with all of the other things bowhunters have to worry about, dropping a release from your treestand is significant. Unless you have a backup in your fanny pack, you will have to crawl down and retrieve it.

Wrist straps by no means prevent all difficulties. When you make some last-minute adjustment, a dangling metal release on the end of a nylon strap can bang against your bow with terrible results in the quiet woods.

The wrist strap is important because your wrist absorbs all the pressure of drawing a bow. In a finger- or hand-held release like the TruFire Magnum, the weight is held by the grip of your fingers. This puts a great deal of strain on some of the smallest muscles and bones in your body. With a high-draw weight bow, that strain causes your hand and fingers to shake. Releases held solely with your fingers or hand are usually thumb activated and work best with light draw weight bows.

A wrist strap should have complete adjustability and room to fit over a glove. Most wrist straps are black with plastic buckles for adjustability and a Velcro strip for extra security. The best ones are also padded and have small side buckles to take up the slack of the nylon strips when you tighten the strap. You could get hurt if dangling straps get in the way of the bowstring, and if you expect to hunt with gloves, you should practice with gloves, because wearing them will change the feel of the release trigger and may be disturbing if you first experience it in the field!

There is one possible difficulty with a wrist-strap release. When a deer approaches unexpectedly, you must orient the release in your hand and then attach it on the string before you draw, without fumbling around. This could be the one true benefit of a finger-held release for bowhunting. Some finger-held releases can be snapped on the bowstring and left there. If you do

The Fletchunter release with wrist strap is a conventional index-finger-triggered bowhunting release. Patented self-locking action remains open until it is snapped on your bowstring. This release can be used right- or left-handed. On warm days, the heavy strap can be hot on your wrist and you may want to switch to the concho style. If you keep your finger away from the release lever, this is a versatile, safe, and accurate release style. Features an adjustable pull, from heavy to hair trigger.

not use a D-loop and shoot directly off the string, an extra nock on the string will keep the release from sliding.

It is possible to trigger your release too soon, and just one time can destroy a hunt. The safety feature on a release triggered with your index finger is mental: keep your trigger finger away from the trigger while you draw; move it forward consciously to trigger your shot.

THE STRING- OR D-LOOP

The string loop is a simple, effective addition to your bowstring for shooting a release. It removes the triggering element of the release from the bowstring, thereby eliminating a potential source of twist. It also eliminates the serving wear some releases cause and allows you to release from directly behind the arrow. Using a string loop will result in better arrow flight and more precise arrow impact.

Both rope and metal are used for string loops. Attaching a loop should be part of the bow set-up and tuning process, and you can easily cut and tie on your own loop. Simply make a knot and add a drop of glue or melt the loop ends tight above and below your nocking point. This puts your release directly behind your arrow and maintains positive peep alignment. Depending on the style of release or the manner in which it grips the string, you will need 1/2- to 3/4-inches of loop.

Metal loops like the Ultra Nok or the TRU Nok attach to your string with two tiny plates and screws. Before installing a metal loop, though, make sure your arrow's nock slides easily between the loop arms. The fit between some loops and arrow nocks can be too tight, forcing you to sand the sides and back of the plastic nock. You will lose a couple of feet per second when you attach a rigid metal nock to your bowstring.

The TRU Speed Loop is a two-part D-loop. It has a metal nock set that clips on the bowstring like a folding wing. The arrow nock fits in the center and is held securely. Around the metal clip is a conventional rope speed loop. The Speed Loop is designed to eliminate nock pinch at full draw, an aspect of extreme string angle on short speed bows.

One option for release shooters who prefer not to shoot with a string-loop or D-loop are small rubber buttons or cushions from Neet or TruFire that can be placed on the string above and below your arrow's nock. Your release touches the bottom cushion, not against your arrow nock. This keeps pinching and interference with arrow flight to a minimum. (You will need a bow press because your string must be removed for installation. That should be daunting enough to choose a string-loop or have a pro shop perform this operation.)

A typical set-up without a D-Loop for a caliper-style release aid. Holding on the string and serving below the nock, the pressure of the steel jaws is cushioned against the plastic nock by a rubber bumper. It is easy to see how a release can wear the serving and, when pulled to full draw on a short-axle-to-axle bow, can apply uneven pressures to your arrow.

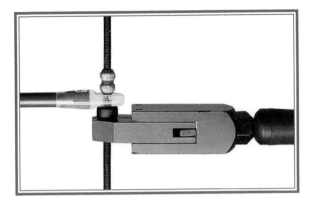

BACK-TENSION RELEASES

In spite of what you may imagine, bowhunters are afflicted with target panic. In Idiot Proof Archery, Bernie Pellerite writes that he cured rock and roller Ted Nugent and master whitetail hunter Myles Keller of this crippling archery malady.

Pellerite produces back-tension releases and he claims that if you want to hit what you are shooting at over a long period–hair or paper–you need to learn to shoot with back tension. This is not easy, but the results, he says, are well worth the effort.

According to Pellerite, everything we do repetitively we remember and store in our subconscious mind. Even though our conscious mind selects the program–blink or draw or release, for example–the subconscious tells muscles how to move and nerves what to feel. Otherwise, timely and consistent communication with each of our thousands of muscles and nerves would make movement almost impossible.

Your fingers and thumbs are extremely agile and sensitive, because they have thousands of tactile sensory receptors on the tips. You can feel the difference between holding one or two sheets of paper with your fingers and thumb, for instance, and that is only a couple thousandths of an inch! Fingers sense when your release trigger moves and tell the brain: "Ready to explode!" This makes us anticipate and flinch, lose our sight picture and then lose control of the shot.

Back muscles, on the other hand, perform gross motor functions only and are not equipped for such sensitivity.

We make a shot successfully when we practice because there is no pressure. There may only be a 3-D deer staked out on the range, but when the target really has hair, our heart pounds, our hands shake and we consciously think about what we are doing. That is the problem.

If you think about a shot consciously, you anticipate, and judge your form as you draw. You participate in the aiming and all the other details and try to correct anything that is not perfect. But perfection is almost impossible and so you choke; you pluck the string or punch the release early. You might or might not do this so readily on the range, where there is no pressure. Nevertheless, this is target panic and every bowhunter is subject to it.

Pellerite says to put your sight pin in the vitals and keep it there. Let your conscious mind focus on aiming and let your subconscious mind take care of the shot. A back-tension release is designed to do this.

Back-tension releases let you shoot an unanticipated shot, because there is no punching a trigger or even pulling a lever.

Few bowhunters shoot back-tension releases because they are difficult to learn and it means giving up control of releasing your arrow. For bowhunters who are interested and can persevere in learning back-tension shooting, there are a number of fine releases available: the Stanislawski (Mel Stanislawski is thought of as the father of the back-tension release), Jerry Carter's slim-line Atension (Hinge or Spike) and Colby 2 (Hinge or Spike), and Bernie Pellerite's Missing Link and unusual E-Z Back are but a few choices available. ■

CHAPTER SIX

Effectiveness at Any Speed

FAITHFULNESS HAS ITS PRICE

The old man took his fourth and final bear on the eve of the new millennium. Everyone figured this would at last be the end of the old fellow's black bear hunting. After all, he was almost 80, even by his own slippery accounting.

Year after year–nine, ten, eleven years in a row–he drove alone to Connecticut to see his sons the first week each June. A thousand lonely miles of Interstate stretched between them and his home near the Bear Archery factory in Gainesville, Florida, where he supervised Fred Bear's museum. In Connecticut, he would catch some pretzel-class puddle-jumper to Fredericton, New Brunswick, to meet his hunting guides. Just how much fun could that be at 80?

It was natural to assume he would have had a belly full of bears by number four, but everyone was wrong. We did not know him nearly as well as we thought. Perhaps no one truly knew him except Elly, his wife, and Fred Bear. "He" of course, was Archery Hall of Fame member Frank Scott.

By the year 2000, Frank Herbert Scott was a sure-enough curiosity. He was the exception that proved several rules, for he hunted long past the age when his mentor, Fred Bear, had his recurve strung only for ceremonial occasions. Even as his own path grew shorter, and dutifully aware of his approaching but still nameless commitment to the universal higher power, Scott was nonetheless serious about his bear hunting.

Moreover, few people have worked more years than Scott. Certainly, nobody ever worked longer at Bear Archery. Not even Fred Bear. Among his friends, it was commonly thought that Scott would die in the museum, long past the age most men and women retired to putter in their garden and bounce grandchildren on their knees.

Frank Scott was born Herbert Ross Mansfield in Elkin, Indiana, in 1921. His family specialized in throwing knives and shooting .22 rifles, usually at or in the general vicinity of each other. The Shooting Mansfields was his father's vaudeville act, performing at county fairs, and so it was that they met a lanky fellow who had a bow-and-arrow routine and needed someone to blow up balloons for him to shoot.

The "special something" that attracted people to Fred Bear throughout that man's life worked its magic on the young Hoosier, because the next year Scott left the family shooting act and went to work for Fred full time. Fred and Scott.

Frank Herbert Scott, a member of the Archery Hall of Fame and the Michigan Bowhunters Hall of Fame. For the final 40 years of his life and well beyond the age when most bowhunters hang up their bows, Frank hunted with a relatively lightweight recurve and traditional, one-piece broadheads.

Frank Scott was Fred Bear's first employee, deserting his vaudeville family "The Shooting Mansfields" to blow up balloons for Fred at the county fairs where Fred gave archery shooting exhibitions. Except for a few years in the US Army during World War II and a stint at Colt Firearms, he was a faithful Bear employee and worked in Fred's shadow until the day he died in November 2000, at 79 years old. Frank immediately began bear hunting in earnest after Fred passed away in April 1988. Frank poses on the Bear Archery grounds in Gainesville, Florida, with his final bear.

Except for two notable occasions, Scott took a paycheck from Fred's company for the rest of his life. World War II sent Scott to the South Pacific, where he collected a couple of Purple Hearts driving amphibious landing ships for the army. Later, in the '60s, he took a break to sell Colt firearms. Otherwise, he was a Bear man and always returned.

Norman Rockwell might have painted the scene best. The young veteran returning to Detroit after the war and presenting himself to Fred. Surely, he was much the wiser for being a little banged up and having seen the world, but what he had seen did not encourage him to see the rest.

Fred must have been surprised. After all, before the war Scott had been just another skinny, worshipful kid. By 1945, he must have figured the boy was dead or gone to see Paris. So when Scott slipped through the door again in Detroit, Fred looked up in surprise and, momentarily speechless, pointed toward the ceiling.

Years before, between waiting on customers, Scott had taken to shooting at the rats that ran along the antique building's rafters. Now he could have his job back, Fred indicated, but he first had to pull all those arrows out of the roof and patch the holes where water dripped. Scott said he would and Fred hired him again on the spot.

According to the National Shooting Sports Foundation, which keeps track of such things, the urge to hunt declines in a man's 40s. A 50-year-old who is actively on the trail of big game is rare. Somewhere in their 40s, men realize they will not live forever. This often results in the purchase of expensive sports cars or in finding someone younger to whom they can teach their craft, share their passion–bowhunting or fly fishing, for instance–someone who will eventually take their place in the field and then pass those skills on in their time.

When they were ready, neither Scott nor Fred Bear had young people in their lives. Perhaps Fred passed his legacy on to the millions of bowhunters who still recognize and revere his name. For Scott, that passage was more problematic.

Fred hunted in the spotlight with photographers and writers, salesmen and dealers, all of whom basked in his reflection. To the end of his life, he spoke to adoring crowds and signed autographs until he was ready to collapse from fatigue.

All that time, cloaked by the great bear's shadow, Scott watched and hungered for his own moment on stage.

As the strain of his fame mounted, Fred's hunting fevers cooled. He complained about the pressure to shoot record-book animals year after year. It wore him down.

So it was that when Fred Bear died in 1988, Scott came into his own. Not that he had wished for the old man's death. Never. Just that the flock needed a new shepherd and Scott perhaps thought that new shepherd might just as well be him. After all, he had waited his entire life. His father was gone. His mentor was gone. It was Scott's time.

The very next year, Scott began hunting black bears, and in spite of advancing age, his enthusiasm grew. Hunting those Canadian bears became more of a need than a simple desire, and although he had taken caribou and antelope and deer, after Fred died his only passions were bears and preserving the legacies enshrined in the museum.

Nevertheless, there were no camera crews or writers or photographers to surround him and, except for the odd speaking engagement, when and where Scott chose to tell his stories was his own business. It was then, I believe, that Scott's shadow began to merge with that of his famous mentor and employer . . . when he realized there was no escaping his fate.

Until the day he died, November 5, 2000, Scott was a master of the soft, winning smile and the perversely witty turn of phrase. As Director of the

Frank Scott worked at Bear Archery as Director of the Fred Bear Museum until the day he died. Before the Fred Bear Museum was sold to Bass Pro Shops, Frank supervised Fred's collections, including the elephant, brown bear and Yukon moose in the atrium. He would mention these huge trophies and then guide visitors upstairs and through the modest Frank Scott alcove before entering Fred's museum. He knew a story or two about every one of the thousands of artifacts in the museum. Frank planned his alcove personally, but opened it only after Fred passed away.

Fred Bear Museum in Gainesville, he put these talents to perfect use promoting Fred's exploits and inventions. Consequently, thousands of visitors found him to be such an enchanting guide, they scheduled their visits to coincide with his hours and his presumed availability.

He would show them Fred's Kodiak bear and moose, describe the Cape buffalo and the lion attacking it, all mounted life-size in the museum foyer. Then he would quietly usher them upstairs and into the second-floor alcove dedicated to himself and his rifle-shooting, knife-throwing vaudeville family. While extolling his own–and of course, Fred's special virtues and talents–the old boy was at his understated finest. He delivered a few laughs, told stories in a manner that made you believe you were the first person on earth to learn the truth, and then casually pointed to his photos and trophies.

Toward the end, Scott's snow-white hair and immaculate costume concealed a slight stoop. In spite of continually brushing his hair back with strong, bony fingers, a stray wisp of hair nonetheless curled down over his forehead, Tom Sawyer-like. Perhaps it was directing one's eye to the golden bear embedded in the gold-rimmed jade medallion that held the old veteran's bolo tie in place. Fred Bear gave him the bolo and the jade, but Scott selected the golden bear.

This kindly old man looked like a gentle grandfather, but looks were deceiving. Scott was a killer.

Scott was a master of the recurve bow. He knew its origins and its history. He said he preferred the recurve's "shooting signature" to a bow of more modern design and manufacture. Just like Fred.

Scott began shooting a bow before the Japanese bombed Pearl Harbor, and he estimated that he took more than 150 big-game animals with a recurve. As a competitor, he participated in the first-ever NFAA Outdoor National Championship in Allegan, Michigan, in 1946 and ultimately shot in the 50th Anniversary Championship in Warsaw, Wisconsin.

In 1971, Scott discovered a 60-inch Bear Kodiak take-down recurve. The die-cast magnesium handle fit him perfectly. This bow answered his shooting and hunting needs. At 27 inches, his draw length was short and his 50-pound draw weight was unimpressive. Nevertheless, except for a set or two of replacement limbs, the bow did not change for the next 30 years.

"It has always pleased me," he said of the Kodiak bow only a few months before he died. "I like the feel of the recurve in my hand. You know, when you are shooting, a bow that feels natural in your hand feels like an extension of yourself. If you find that bow, it will be the one you master to greatest effectiveness. I've carried that old Kodiak around so long that I almost forget it's there. If I switched to a compound with sights and a release, I would probably shoot better. I would be more accurate at long distance, but I don't take long shots. It wouldn't feel the same . . . and so it wouldn't be the same."

Too old to change and too young to quit, Scott did not think of himself as or particularly like to be called a "bare-bow shooter." Instead, he was an "instinctive archer." At full draw, he hesitated one or two seconds before releasing. During that moment of hold, he visualized a line between the arrow and his target.

"If I do it right, the arrow follows the line," he said. "This has taken some practice to learn, and while you would think I spend a lot of time estimating and pacing off shot distances, I almost never think about the yardage."

At only 50 pounds, the Kodiak was on the steep slope of acceptability for bears. "I would normally recommend something greater than 50 pounds for bowhunting, but I can't handle any more than that. Plus, I get tired a little easier these days." Fifty pounds had to do. Tipped with a 125-grain Bear Razorhead Lite broadhead, Scott understood his limitations.

Scott did not recall when, and would not say why he conceived such a passion for bear hunting, but he had one. His annual Canadian odyssey was, for many years, the old man's only hunting glory.

For a man only a year away from 80, though, bear hunting was easier than hunting elk or javelina. He would need some help field dressing, hauling and butchering a spring bear once it is down, because that is bloody, grimy hard work with a gazillion stinging bugs fighting over every inch of your skin.

If you are someone's guest or have hired a guide to do the scouting and baiting and hanging stands, there is hardly anything in bear hunting to complain about except the black flies and the mosquitoes.

When you are bear hunting, the days can progress lazily until you take your bruin. You may sleep late and gulp down your bacon and eggs at your leisure, followed by plenty of hot, black coffee. There is time to shoot a few arrows and go fishing. Around noon, you should fry up a few pike on the lakeshore. Then it is time for a nap. As the day begins to cool, around 3:00 p.m. or so, grab your gear and make your way out to your baited stand.

Once on stand, the deep Canadian forest will be as still as a corpse. It is peaceful among the sibilant firs and you will struggle to remain attentive. Soon the early northern darkness will begin to enfold you, as if the forest itself is quietly breathing, exhaling softly . . . and watching through heavy-lidded eyes. Drowsily, you listen through the flat, persistent drone of mosquitoes for the footfall you will never hear; you watch for the movement you will never see.

If a bear comes, your hunt could be over in a minute. If not, you hunt until dark at 9:00 p.m. and then, peering into the blackness and with your heart in your throat, stumble out through the dense brush. No, bear hunting is not a hard gig if you are 30, but Scott was about to turn 80.

Now, Steve Clark, Scott's friend and Canadian host, was a bowhunter and archery champion in his own right. Even after ten years of hosting their Florida guest, he and his wife Pat still enjoyed Scott's annual spring pilgrimage. That was a good thing, for 1999 marked Scott's 11th week-long bear hunt without missing a single year. On the previous ten hunts, he had taken three bears, the first two with Steve's help.

New Brunswick is not overrun with bears like Ontario, but neither are they in short supply. So on the afternoon of June 2nd, Scott and his 1999 guide, Lionel Gautreau, dove into the bush feeling optimistic.

"With an older hunter like Scott, I don't put their stands up much higher than ten or 12 feet," Gautreau said. "We take our time going in to the bait, because the woods are thick and rough. You can't see farther than a bear could lunge before you threw up an arm and screamed. In many places, the fir and spruce are so tight you have to crawl to get through, and the moss is so thick on the ground that you could not hear a bear walking right behind you."

Over the years, Lionel, like Steve, had become more Scott's friend than just his guide. Years before the 11th hunt, he had quit charging the old man for his guide services. "I have my guide license, but we're friends. I do it because I like it."

Lionel's New Brunswick bait sites were not different from successful bear baits anywhere. He hung meat in burlap bags eight to ten feet off the ground, "kind of in the open so the meat rots and stinks and the smell drifts," he said. Rancid is good for bear hunters. Days before the season opener, Gautreau switched to pastries and molasses-soaked loaves of bread. Chocolate. Honey. "Bears have a sweet tooth too," he grinned.

Lionel was the ideal bowhunting guide. With many bears of his own, he empathized with Scott's limitations as a bowhunter . . . and with his stubborn desire, as the oldest hunter he has ever guided. Moreover, he shot a longbow, having made the journey from a compound through a recurve.

On their way to the evening stand that June day in 1999, Lionel and Scott surprised a huge sow with an exceptionally small cub.

"When she saw us and 'woofed,' the cub went up the nearest tree," Lionel recalls. "She must have weighed 350 or 400 pounds. We talked in loud voices and slowly backed out of there. We gave her a lot of room!"

As soon as they climbed into their secondary stands that evening, another bear–he later proved to be a young boar–came to the bait. He approached silently through the ferns. Wary. Alert. Ears up. He seemed to float across the moist carpet of green moss on pudgy, padded feet, like fog slipping through the dark arboreal forest.

"He went directly to the bait, which Lionel had only hung about 15 yards from my stand," Scott said. He stood on his hind legs, ripped open the bag and sprawled out on the ground to pull food into his mouth. When he extended his front leg, I put an arrow through his lungs. The bear shot out of there like lightning, but ten, maybe 15 seconds later, we heard him crash."

No children ever held Frank Scott's hand while they walked to a hunting blind. No adoring grand kids came to Sunday dinner to listen to his gnarly stories. Perhaps Scott's legacy was the simple but heroic act of persevering. Perhaps that was what kept the old man going, year after year, until he was almost 80. Scott would have hunted bears until he was 100 or 200.

But what motivated him? What force drove him into the woods to hunt an animal that could kill him, long after everyone who knew him as a kid, everyone who accompanied him as a man, had hung up their bows? Was it some glory-bound death wish or some competitive fire from all the years of laboring, first in his father's and then in Fred Bear's shadow? We will never know. Perhaps we were not meant to know.

In the end, what matters is this fact: that he went into the field well beyond when he could honorably have retired. That whether or not he killed a bear each year, he respected the animals and the hunt. By remaining committed and filled with enthusiasm, he honored the tradition and he honored us.

Scott estimated that his fourth New Brunswick bear weighed 350 pounds. He mounted it life-size for the "Frank Scott Wing" of the Fred Bear Museum.

Less than six months after taking his fourth bear with Lionel Gautreau in New Brunswick, Scott was dead. It happened suddenly. As if the Great Bear he was chasing suddenly turned and beckoned to him. Ever the faithful employee and friend, Scott lay down his bow and crossed over.

TIMES CHANGE

To open a "fast and quiet" chapter with a story about a bowhunter who shoots a slow arrow, and was never heard to worry about silencing his shot, may seem odd. Scott's curious odyssey with Fred Bear and his upholding of the recurve tradition, however, illustrate how far the majority of bowhunters have evolved in just one generation.

When many of us began bowhunting, we served or tied a pair of Cat Whiskers into our string and tried not to step on dry sticks. We closed the car door quietly, sneezed into our jackets and that passed for silent hunting.

Of course, we were shooting arrows at 190 fps too, but even that was a big step from the recurves we chronographed at 165! Arrow speed was not something we gave any thought to. Hitting an eight-inch pie plate at 20

Installing a pair of rubber whiskers on your bowstring will help reduce noise and vibration. Tied or, better yet, served onto your string, these whiskers break up the dramatic, harmonic oscillation of the bowstring after you shoot.

yards was our big test. We were serious and we had fun.

Well, times changed. Our thinking evolved as bows launched faster arrows and the noise from a shot began to sound like gunfire. We decided we could have either a fast arrow or a quiet shot, probably not both.

Today, we know that is not true. Arrow speed and silent shooting are still very much on the minds of bowhunters. You can have it all.

Why should you care if you are shooting quietly, especially if your arrow streaks like lightning? We know that deer "jump the string," which just means that they flinch, contract their muscles tensing to run, when they hear an odd noise. This response happens even before they identify the source of an unexpected noise. While your bow shoots 300 fps, which is 200 mph, the noise of the shot is traveling at the speed of sound, 760 mph or thereabouts at sea level. But your target is close and so we are dealing in fractions of a second. Nevertheless, that slight dropping movement has saved thousands of deer from being skewered by arrows shot just a little high from treestands.

It is truly a sign of changing times when bow manufacturers talk more about the limb cups of new bows than they do IBO-rated arrow speed. By developing special pads that fit between the limbs and the riser, bow makers eliminated a source of vibration.

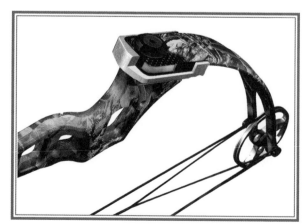

Attention to shooting a silent, accurate arrow will allow you to harvest good bucks like this mule deer from the prairies of South Dakota. Before you casually loose an arrow, you need to remember to pick a spot and breathe, but long before entering the field you should have made a commitment to taking big game with one well-placed arrow tipped with a razor-sharp broadhead. Make an effective, silent launch a priority. *(Photo courtesy SD Tourism)*

Noise in your shooting system is a sign that all is not well. Perhaps your arrow rest or your sight bar is loose, or when you removed your arrow from your quiver, the broadhead's blades twisted against the insert in the quiver cup and so the ferrule is no longer tight against the arrow insert.

Vibration and buzz indicate that you need to check your accessories, because these things do not self-correct. There is a universal tendency toward entropy. "Things fall apart," wrote the Irish poet William Blake. "The center does not hold." Indeed. Tighten up!

According to Eryleen Archery's Emery Loiselle in Burlington, Massachusetts, tuning a bow to shoot silently is not difficult. It helps to have an archery pro shop nearby, but silencing a shot is something you can do at home. There are only five steps, says the 84-year old bowhunter who still hunts, like Scott, with a 50-pound bow.

THINK ABOUT IT. Make silent shooting a priority. Select a bow built with some noise- and vibration-deadening elements, as well as speed and other performance characteristics.

THE RIGHT ARROW. Find the properly spined shaft for your set-up. You want the carbon or aluminum shaft that will fly best from your bow.

STABILIZER. Use a good stabilizer and wrist sling. Select a stabilizer that provides forward balancing and a wrist sling that gives you confidence the bow is not going to jump out of your hand when you shoot with a disciplined, but loose, grip. Stabilizers are not expensive, so buy one with some noise- and vibration-dampening properties.

STRING SILENCERS. Attach a pair of string silencers to your bowstring. They will not slow your shot in any meaningful manner and they do make a difference in noise levels.

ADD-ONS. Experiment with all-new accessories designed to dampen noise. Many of these do work as advertised and they are lightweight and simple to use. Limb Savers from Sims Vibration Labs or some comparable rubberized shock absorbers should certainly be part of your silencing equation.

Today, many bows have built-in advantages, designed specifically to address noise and vibration along with IBO speed and percentage of let-off and so on. In the "old days," there was less concern with shot noise because bows were slower and quieter. Nevertheless, even in the mid 1980s, every bowhunter tied or served Cat Whiskers onto his string nine to ten inches or so above and below the nocking point.

Selecting the proper type and spine for your arrow will help you achieve superior arrow flight and ensure that your arrow set-up absorbs the most energy possible from your bow. An improperly spined arrow will leave behind energy that is then transformed into riser buzz, vibration, and shock to your hand and elbow.

In the late 1990s, Sims Vibration Laboratories (SVL) kicked off a buying storm when it began selling its rubber Limb Savers. These inexpensive black buttons effectively took vibration out of a bow and dampened the noise of a shot. Bowhunters by the thousands testified that they could feel and hear (not hear?) the difference, and pro shops quickly sold out. SVL joined Doinker and a dozen other manufacturers introducing products to help bowhunters shoot silently and effectively. SVL now makes its dampening buttons for virtually every part of your bow—and accessories.

Because ultra-fast bows can be noise terrorists, some manufacturers incorporate silencing mechanisms into the bow itself. High-end Jennings and Fred Bear bows, like the Buckmasters G2 from Escalade Sports, include a rubber Shock Stop String Cushion on the cable slide. This bumper provides an intermediate string contact point between the cam and wheel that immediately diminishes string oscillation and noise after a shot. The G2 also has cut-outs in the machined riser equipped with Sims Limb Saver vibration dampeners.

The 40-inch Mathews Ovation is equipped with String Suppressors on the axles with its Straightline HP Cam and the ball bearing mounted idler wheel. These String Suppressors function like small rubber traps to physically retard and dampen string oscillation near the source. According to Mathews, that source is the contact point between the bow's cam and string. In addition, the Ovation has two removable, center-weighted rubber Harmonic Dampers plugged into the riser near the limb pivot points.

Pearson's Dagger has a built-in vibration-and-noise-reduction chamber manufactured into the riser. This chamber is filled with a rubberized gel plug called Vibasorb from Vibracheck (R&R Enterprises). Roger Templeton, chief of research and development, says this system, called VIB~X, has been tested at the University of Alabama and eliminates 40 percent of noise and vibration following a shot. It also eliminates metal-to-metal contact between your bow riser and your stabilizer.

While it is debatable whether they are actually built-in or factory add-ons, both PSE and Martin address shot silencing directly. The PSE Primos STL with NRG One-Cam features Sims Limb Savers designed into a special aluminum donut—the NV or no-vibration system—at each limb pivot. Martin's Razor-X with twin Dyna-Cam positions patented Vibration Escape

Modules toward the ends and on the sides of the riser to help dissipate riser buzz.

Next, Loiselle says to select the arrow shaft that is most suitably spined for your bow. The proper shaft is the one that will shoot most efficiently for you. It will absorb most–but not all, it can never absorb all–of the energy of a shot, allowing the bow to transform its stored energy into deliverable penetration and killing power. Theoretically, the more energy an arrow shaft absorbs from the bowstring, the less troubling noise and vibration will remain in your shooting system . . . the less of a pounding your arm and shoulder will take . . . and the less of a problem you will have with target panic!

All arrow manufacturers provide information in the form of catalogs and reams of brochures to help you make a proper shaft selection. You should spend some time studying these fascinating documents, especially the arrow selection charts, to learn your full range of options, because shooting the proper arrow is critically important to your success.

For example, assume that your draw length is 29 inches, your draw weight is 75 pounds and you have what is considered a "medium" cam on your CP Oneida ESC Black Eagle. You still have to know what weight broadhead you are shoot before you can make the best aluminum or carbon shaft selection. If you decide on an 100-grain Razortip Mechanical from Grim Reaper, your sophisticated set-up suggests that you will want a carbon shaft, even though Easton could offer properly spined #2512s, #2514s or 2317s. Their 3-71 ACC, carbon-wrapped aluminum would work, or perhaps their carbon #300 ST Axis. If you become confused, you are normal. Get help at a pro shop or from a veteran bowhunter.

For additional carbon possibilities, Carbon Impact offers the seamless, wrapped XLT Fat Shaft 6500. The green division has a straightness/weight range measured from + .001/+ 1 grain per dozen shafts and Carbon Impact rates it for "pro hunters or 3-D competitors." The blue division Fat Shaft 6500 has a straightness/weight range measured from + .006/+ 4 grains per dozen and is recommended as an economical hunting shaft.

Two rarely-asked questions are, "Why can't an arrow absorb all of the energy a bow can produce?" and "Is the arrow that absorbs the most energy the best one for me?"

Imagine that your bow is alive. Just lying on the back seat of your car, it possesses potential energy because you have cranked the limb bolts down and the limbs are stressed. When you draw, you further stress the essential parts of the bow: riser, limbs, axles and string. When you release, about half way to brace height, the arrow separates from the string. The arrow speeds away, but the bow is still in motion, still breathing and surging with power.

High-speed photography proves that all parts of and accessories attached to a bow respond to the shot. The riser flexes. Your sight and rest

Selecting a bow with built-in noise and vibration dampening elements and then adding a good stabilizer is a great first start toward silent shooting. A built-in sound-and-vibration-dampening chamber called Vib~X is filled with a visco-elastic (rubber) plug. When you screw a stabilizer onto the threaded steel rod in the rubber plug, this set-up guarantees there will be no metal-to-metal contact with the bow.

wobble crazily. Immediately, the strain and tension in your arms and back turns into an instant of shock and, within a few microseconds, the bow returns to a state of readiness, straining to fulfill its purpose once again. Unless you destroy your bow by disassembling it, unless it dies, it cannot release all of its energy and it still has potential.

Whatever the various arrow charts suggest, the best arrow is the one that flies best out of your set-up. Nevertheless, extensive testing has arrived at the shaft selection tables you use to select your arrow.

You cannot assume that the arrow that flies best is the one that absorbs the most energy (KE) or that there is necessarily a connection between the amount of KE it absorbs and its penetrating ability. Because heavier arrows absorb more energy than light arrows, it stands to reason that solid fiberglass or aluminum shafts absorb more energy than a hollow aluminum or carbon shaft.

Part of the dynamic of arrow flight, though, is how well or how effectively, from our bowhunter's point of view, the arrow uses the energy you give it. The best arrow flies straightest and truest to its intended target. If the target is 20 feet away, as it is in bowfishing, then a solid shaft is just right. If it is 20 yards away, the solid shaft requires more energy to maintain its velocity than a hollow shaft. While the solid shafts accepts more energy from the bow, our hollow hunting shafts use the energy they have and maintain it more effectively down range.

The next factor in silencing your shot is to find a noise- and vibration-damping stabilizer and a wrist sling or strap. Bowhunters have at last accepted the need for a shock-absorbing stabilizer to help dissipate leftover energy from a shot, but the use of a wrist strap is still far from common.

A modern stabilizer, such as a seven-inch, seven-ounce Vibracheck Icon, will provide forward balancing–hence the variation in stabilizer lengths and weights–and effective assistance dampening of stray system energy as well. Stabilizers that isolate metal-to-metal connections or have rubberized ele-

Bowhunters have not widely accepted the fact that a bowsling, like a release, will make them a better shot. Use a sling properly and your bow cannot jump or fall out of your hand. This means you do not have to grip the riser so tight, thus torquing it, to control your shot. This bowsling is made from one-inch wide polypropylene webbing. It includes a mount for a stabilizer or bow-fishing bracket.

ments, help dampen the buzz of contact.

The second part of this equation is a wrist strap or sling. Nine out of ten bowhunters look down on a sling as unnecessary. They think of it as something used by target archers or just another thing that gets in the way. It is true that competition archers shoot with a sling. It is also true that they can take their time and execute their shot without the distractions of wind-borne odors or tree branches or the elevation of a treestand or a moving, flesh-and-blood target. If you have ever competed seriously in any sport, though, you understand how fierce competition is when money is on the line. Competitors use wrist slings because they have released thousands upon thousands of arrows and they recognize the benefit of excellent shooting form. That, after all, actually means good hitting form, or putting your arrow precisely in the vitals of a game animal.

With a deer in your sights, the natural tendency is to tense, shorten your breath, grab your bow and shorten your draw as you become conscious of the antlers. You want to do just the opposite. Relax and focus. This is very difficult, and this is why you need a wrist sling. It helps you position your hand on the bow grip the same way every shot. It reminds you to take a relaxed hold, because the only thing your hand should do is provide a pivot point. A sling also prevents the bow from bouncing out of your grasp in the explosion of release. So think of a sling as a tiny insurance policy that reminds you to position your hand properly and not squeeze the bow in your excitement.

The next step in silencing your bow is to attach something in your strings that breaks up post-shot string oscillation. The negative side of a quieter shot may be a slightly slower arrow because anything (anything except speed nocks, apparently) attached to a bowstring slows down your arrow.

U-nique makes a number of items to help silence your shot, beginning with its Spider Leggs rubber string silencers that will not absorb water or pick up stickers or seeds. Its 100 percent Teflon cable slides and Teflon

Indiana bowhunter Greg Pyle says that a quiet bow shooting at a moderate speed is all you need to take whitetail bucks successfully year after year . . . well, that and a theory to guide your efforts. A former partner in an archery pro shop, Greg scouts heavily and sets up at intersections of fence rows and other topographic features, and he typically harvests magnificent deer. In the second photograph, Greg holds half-a-dozen racks that were, he says, "just a little too small to mount."

silencing sleeves use the "slickest material known to man" to provide friction-free contact in your shooting system.

Numerous varieties of string silencers are available–Tarantulas, NEET's Maxi Mufflers and Puffs–but some of these work best on traditional or round wheel bows, as the string tension of BCY's 450 Plus, 452 or Brownell's Fast Flight strings (advertised as "stronger than steel") can quickly destroy some brands.

(The above-mentioned speed buttons might be extra nock sets securely attached to your string or even specially designed speed buttons. Positioned a few inches from your cam and/or wheel on both ends of your string, they can both dampen string oscillation and increase your arrow speed by as much as 12 fps!)

To reduce a small amount of bow torque, you can remove the cable slide and place a strip of Teflon tape along the guard arm. This brings the cables closer to centerline and, with an adjustable cable guard, allows you to fine-tune for fletching clearance. The Teflon tape makes the trip down the cable guard as friction-free as possible, but Teflon is soft and does wear, so this must be monitored. (Some bow set-ups do not permit this tuning procedure.)

Emery Loiselle's final silencing tactic is to look at options coming on the market from innovative companies such as Sims Vibration Laboratory, Doinker and Global Research. Bowhunter interest in quiet shooting has allowed many new products to find a place in the market. For instance, rubber vibration dampening sleeves and nodules are now found in many of the machined holes in risers and even on your accessories themselves.

A couple of years ago, Sims Limb Saver technology was a tremendously in-demand bowhunting accessory. Since the introduction of the original Limb Savers, Sims has expanded its offering to fit practically every type of bow and bow-limb design. The small Sims String Leech string silencer that, SVL claims, cuts 80 percent of string resonance with "minimal if any speed loss" is an inexpensive silencing product, and it works well with modern synthetic string materials.

Can you totally silence your shot? Can you shoot so that an alert deer, standing within range, will not hear it? The possibility of completely eliminating noise from a shot is not based in the physical reality we live in. You can come close, though, and you can certainly expect to hit deer at close range before they react to the quiet, but audible, "thunk" of a shot.

There is a big difference in what we as humans and elk or deer perceive as noisy. We are accustomed to noise, but should remember that a low decibel level to us may be penetratingly loud to a bull elk. Your computer CPU sits beside you humming all day and overhead fluorescent lights add a buzz that we have become accustomed to. We believe that dogs barking, children running, and the television playing while the dishwasher is running in our home is relatively peaceful. So how can we judge what a deer may hear or think except by observation?

Massachusetts' Emery Loiselle says longbow shooters testify that deer jumped their string. Of all hunting bows, the longbow is exceptionally quiet. That does not give bowhunters who are shooting ultra-hot bows a whole lot of hope except to make their shot as accurate and silent as possible . . . and expect that their super-sharp broadhead will do its job as intended.

FAST OR FORGIVING?

Bowhunters used to talk about a "forgiving bow." It was one of those concepts like "art." While we could not define it, we knew it when we saw it.

A "forgiving bow" lets us make minor shooting-form errors and would still put an arrow on target. A minor error in form could be plucking the string, or releasing before we reached full draw, or even gripping the riser so hard we torqued the bow, which normally caused left-right impact problems due to drawing a heavy weight.

A commonly accepted standard for a forgiving bow was one with a seven-inch or greater brace height, the distance from the low point of the grip to the string when the bow was at rest. With the long, vertical limbs of the '80s, this had a lot more to do with the axle-to-axle length of the bow than it did with any inherent ability to absorb and patiently look the other way when we screwed-up. What "forgiveness" meant was that a particular bow shot a slow arrow.

The benefit of longer brace height is thought of as improved bow efficiency. A longer brace height would allow you to shoot lighter, thinner-walled arrows for increased speed. But with advances in designing fast, quiet, short axle-to-axle bows, the traditional thinking about brace height is no longer true across the board.

While we talk arrow speed, we really want arrows with flat trajectories. At 240 to 260 fps, which is a fine speed range for consistent, no-problem shooting, you can mis-estimate the distance to a 40-yard deer by several yards and still place your broadhead in its vitals. At 300 or more fps, you can mis-estimate by twice as much and still collect your trophy!

Of course, there is a "down side." Faster means you will have more tuning problems, a less "forgiving" bow and a bow that is less efficient. Energy not transmitted to the arrow becomes noise and vibration . . . and maybe a sore shoulder and elbow as well.

The average bowhunter can reliably tune and shoot between 240 and 260 fps, even with a release aid. Faster than that, the stress on your bow is so great that things might happen for which the average hunter cannot prepare: risers can twist, axles bend and so on. At very high speeds, typical force-and-motion streams sometimes react in a chaotic manner. This, in part, accounts for the switch to mechanical heads, which do fly with the precision of field points.

If you want to shoot a fast arrow, but do not want to spend hours tuning, you should use a rangefinder. This device can make the difference between hours tuning and hours enjoying shooting. If you like to tinker with equipment, you may enjoy the challenge of achieving higher arrow speeds. But for most of us who simply enjoy the pleasure of hunting with a bow, the secret to

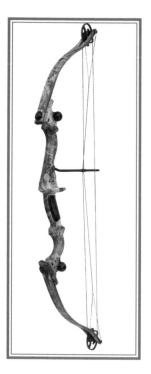

Fast or Forgiving? This older twin-cam bow measures 43 3/8 inches, axle to axle. Available with two cams and in both camo and colorful competition versions, the Scepter III has a long 8 3/8-inch brace height. Equipped with Nitrous cams, Martin states that its peak speed is 300 fps and that should make this long, axle-to-axle bow both fast and forgiving. The bow comes equipped with two Martin Vibration Escape Modules, one at each end of the riser.

longevity is to tune a little and shoot a lot.

Speed freaks want a short axle-to-axle bow with a hard, aggressive eccentric(s). You will shoot with a caliper-style release aid and use short, lightweight carbon arrows tipped with 75-gr. mechanical broadheads and fletched in a semi-helical manner with three-inch plastic vanes. You will want to draw as much weight as possible without dislocating your shoulder. You will want to spend your spare time fine-tuning and programming your arrows to fly like the super-darts they have become.

Your fast arrow set-up will eliminate some pin guessing errors and flatten your trajectory. This will minimize errors in distance estimation. You might consider adding a short overdraw that incorporates an arrow rest so that you can pull your arrow back behind the riser at full draw. This will give you an incredibly short, lightweight arrow! Make sure you install speed nocks on your bowstring four to five inches away from the cams on your twin, hatchet cam bow, for an equivalent speed increase of three to six feet per second. Position any rubber Limb Saver dampeners as far out on the end of your limbs as possible.

A general caution about fast set-ups. You will only achieve peak performance from your equipment if you practice and perfect peak-performance shooting form. This means you must study good shooting form–perhaps take lessons from an archery coach–and your practice sessions must be disciplined.

If you are shooting a bow that is quiet and efficient, arrow speed should be irrelevant. Your arrows will arrive on target precisely and predictably. ■

CHAPTER SEVEN

How to Scout Effectively for Big Deer

Now it is time to put your knowledge together into an effective bowhunting set-up. After reading this book, you know more about your bow, for instance, and about your reason for choosing among the styles available: compound or traditional or even a crossbow. There are quite a few parts of the success equation that we did not discuss, however: camouflage, treestands, GPS units, boots or even selecting an outfitter.

Nevertheless, you should have a good understanding of your choices of archery gear and, with a little trial and error, should be able to fling arrows in the general direction of a pie plate at 20 yards. Don't stop there, though! The pie-plate-test is no longer considered "state-of-the-art" because we know that with the right equipment and proper practice, perhaps even some professional coaching, you can shoot quarters out of the air. Accept that accuracy is your birthright . . . and your responsibility.

As you begin to pull everything together, you will soon tire of shooting hay bales at the park or even the 3-D deer in your back yard. That means your neck is beginning to swell and it is time to get serious about the coming deer season.

Just as fine-tuning your gear and experimenting with new shooting techniques and new accessories is a year-round hobby for serious bowhunters, we also know that scouting for deer (You could think of it as scouting for success.) is a year-round hobby, too. For years, passionate and accomplished bowhunters–Bob Fratzke, Peter Fiduccia, M.R. James, Myles Keller, Rob Evans, Greg Miller, Bill Winke–have preached that the deer season lasts 365 days a year.

Of course, a 365-day deer season can cause problems with the job, the family and soon enough, one's own enthusiasm. Assuming your deer season is between 60 and 90 days long, you have between 275 and 305 days in the year to locate your trophy–before it becomes time to draw, aim, and release.

You want to be totally committed to the shot before opening day.

Our final chapter reviews effective year-round scouting. Based on techniques developed by Michigan bowhunter and television producer Tim Hooey, it outlines a scouting regimen that makes maximum effective use of your time and effort. Indeed, it actually minimizes the time you spend walking around in and disturbing the territory you are planning to hunt in the fall. This program will work for bear, elk, and pronghorns as well as for the trophy deer that live in your neighborhood.

Hooey's program depends upon two things: that you have made a true and

The result of effective scouting is a fine trophy buck: venison in the freezer and antlers for the wall. Michigan's Tim Hooey says bowhunters too often limit their scouting to a few concentrated days looking at the same old scrapes, rubs, and trails in the same old hunting areas. Expand your horizons and make a plan for success.

personal bowhunting commitment and that you have put together a bowhunting equipment set-up that, from a technical and performance point of view, supports your commitment. The commitment and the set-up work together.

The internal and the external are a team. Nothing is worse than performing your scouting, locating the deer you want to take and then blowing the shot. Conversely, winning club trophies is delightful, but if you cannot get out of bed in time to have your award-winning set-up in position to kill your trophy, you need to do some self-examination.

This last chapter on effective scouting is designed to place your effort and energy precisely on point, where steel meets leather, and thus completes the bowhunting circle.

For us bowhunters, scouting is not only an institution for young people. It is our way of searching for deer sign, understanding deer-herd dynamics, and thereby locating places to ambush deer within a hunting area.

If we are to be effective deer hunters with the bow and arrow, we must scout year-round. This is because success rates with bow and arrow are usually much less than for gun hunters, perhaps 10 to 15 percent nationwide.

Conventional wisdom requires that we make frequent outings to study food sources and deer movement, to pick up shed antlers, look for active scrapes and rubs, and walk the land. This conventional wisdom is mostly wrong.

The most effective approach to finding deer requires a three-part plan. Part one is to "unlearn" years of bad advice. Part two is to gather all of the available information and write it down to find the best area to hunt. Finally, part three is to carefully put your boots on the ground inside your selected hunting area.

UNLEARNING BAD ADVICE

In this chapter, we want to identify and unlearn the bad advice that has prevented us from taking big, mature deer every year . . . and replace it with a fresh approach and a habit of success. We have received bad advice from many sources: perhaps from the people who introduced us to hunting, from our hunting buddies and from years of retread magazine articles about scouting.

At least two elements have misdirected millions of bowhunters:

Overemphasis on the hunting "record books." The big-game record books published by the Pope & Young and Boone & Crockett clubs have an honored and historic place in hunting. They are fun to study, but they cannot be used successfully to guide your day-to-day hunting decisions.

Overemphasis on walking our hunting turf. For a serious hunter, effective scouting is a year-round activity, but it rarely requires that we invade the sanctuary of the deer we are going to kill.

Regardless of where we live, on any given Saturday in the fall, we will only go so far from our home to hunt deer. This may be an area circumscribed by a half-hour drive or even an hour. Generally, we spend most of our hunting energy and satisfy most of our hunting desires within an hour of our house. To travel farther than this requires a special occasion.

Anyone can visit the Pope & Young Internet site at www.pope-young.org and order volumes of North American big-game trophy data. This is interesting and sometimes fascinating material. Pope & Young has even separated the whitetail data into a secondary printed volume, and all game entries made during the most recently completed recording period, the 23rd, covering entries in 2001-2002 as of this writing, are available in a statistical summary.

In spite of the abundant data in the long lists of trophy kills, however, a national or even a statewide book about big-game trophies is practically useless for your specific hunting situation. The data will not help you discover the best specific hunting location within the distance you are routinely willing to travel.

The fallacy of studying the record books, even those of the prestigious Boone & Crockett Club (www.boone-crockett.org) for game taken with any legal weapon, gun or bow, is that the information you discover will not help you find and harvest a trophy deer.

We imagine that record-book entries reflect, for instance, the deer population in any county or region, but there is only anecdotal evidence that this is true. There are simply too many variables to make record-book entries more than a general statistical guide: food availability fluctuates over time, often because of international economic conditions; individual hunters may not be inclined to enter their trophy or identify correctly the specific hunting location; and the American landscape is undergoing rapid and accelerating sub-urbanization.

If you can chart the sources of deer food in your chosen hunting areas by season, you can narrow your hunting focus. Bowhunters of today have limited time available; use it wisely!

In 2006, more large, trophy deer will be taken in Pike County, Illinois, than in Leon County, Florida. Even though Pike County is a relative hotspot, 99.9 percent of America's bowhunters do not live within easy driving distance and are not willing to pay the thousands of dollars necessary to travel there and book a hunt with a lodge or outfitter. And should they wish to hunt in Pike County but not choose to hunt with a commercial outfitter, the chance of finding property to lease with deer on it will be small.

For a generation, we have accepted on faith that we should walk our hunting grounds throughout the year. This activity is supposed to tell us what the deer are eating, where they are bedding and where they drop their antlers and their fawns. Writers and seminar speakers even suggest walking a grid through woods to discover deer travel and escape routes. This boots-on-the-ground approach calls upon us to locate specific mast-bearing oak trees, overgrown apple trees, honeysuckle thickets and heavily used trails. It would have us select and prepare hunting stands months in advance.

Regardless of what we hear about bowhunters generally not being good shots and how difficult it is to judge distance accurately, these are not the primary reasons we fail to kill a deer every year. The old-fashioned boots-on-the-ground scouting strategy is the reason that we either take no deer or drag out young does and skinny yearlings rather than the big, mature animals we want.

When you are in the woods, your size 10½ boots disturb the natural order and rhythm; they change the wildlife dynamic. You break things and cut things; you urinate; you leave your scent where it is not welcome. Of course, timber cruisers, kids with BB guns, stray dogs and feral housecats, disrupt a deer's natural patterns all the time. Mature animals smell you and change their routes of travel. Big bucks become increasingly nocturnal or at least travel more often during off-peak hours at dawn and dusk.

Few bowhunters would argue that disrupting the natural order of the deer woods is good. Temporary disruption is not the primary reason to reject the walk-in-the-woods approach to scouting, though.

The primary reason to reject it is that a stroll in the woods is not effective scouting. Has it worked consistently for you? No, because you are putting the proverbial cart before the horse. You are not in the woods with a plan or a specific learning objective.

PRACTICAL SCOUTING

We know what does not work. What does work?

Begin here. Conventional wisdom says you should scout every month. Excellent. Plan to do that.

Americans pioneered the "busy life" syndrome, however. We carry our cell phones when we attend a concert. A laptop computer with wireless Internet, modem and fax sit on our lap at the beach.

Unless we live on our own hunting land, no one has the luxury of driving to his or her hunting area and tramping around for a couple hours every month. Expecting that you will honor this scouting strategy is a sure way to become anxious, feel guilty . . . and quit scouting completely. Fortunately, there is a more effective plan.

Unless you routinely harvest big, mature deer, you are hunting in the wrong location. Questioning where you choose to hunt is step number one of effective scouting, according to whitetail hunting authority, Peter Fiduccia (aka The Deer Doctor).

This is big because, just like the deer we hunt, we humans are creatures of habit. We do not end up in a particular hunting spot by accident. Our traditional spot is convenient or the place where "the guys" like to "get together" or "near where Joe said his cousin's brother saw a humongous buck last year."

If you bowhunt for convenience, it is easier to drink

Photos taken from the ground and from the air will give you a terrific perspective on areas you are interested in scouting. Flying over your hunting areas can give you a unique view and help you discover patterns that you might never otherwise find when scouting only on the ground.

beer and watch football. If you bowhunt so you can "hang out with the guys," it will be moresaisfying to invite them over to mow the lawn. If you hunt to kill a trophy deer every year, develop a scouting plan that works. In other words, scout right.

"Scout right." It does not sound as literate as "make a proper scouting plan," but it works. All it means is that you will take personal responsibility for your time, effort and results in the woods and out.

If you already knew the best place to hunt, you would be there now and you would be hanging trophy deer on the wall. Because you do not, you must organize your search by obtaining a good road map of your potential hunting area . . . not of your state. If you will drive an hour to bowhunt deer, you need a map of the area circumscribed by an hour's drive at 4:00 a.m. (not at rush hour) with your home at the center of the circle. Most counties have good road maps available.

The next step is to go to the telephone book for a list of the sporting goods stores, taxidermists, pro shops and hunting clubs in your area. Visit them and see what they have to offer. You should not attempt to do this in a single day, because it will become a chore or task rather than a process of discovery. This scouting is a year-round activity.

Locally owned sporting goods stores that carry hunting supplies are veritable warehouses of information (you can also search for dealers across North America on the web through www.archerysearch.com). As well as being specialists who can help you solve equipment problems and make appropriate selections, store personnel know their regulars. These stores maintain bulletin boards with success pictures and names of hunters. If the store offers league shooting, you should consider getting involved. Successful hunters around the world, and perhaps from prehistoric times, like to relive their experience. You can be there to listen and learn from them.

And for heaven's sake, spend a little money in each of the stores you visit. After all, you need what they sell. You can buy gear cheaper from a mass merchandiser or over the Internet, but this is not lawn service or new tires for the car. This is personal. This is pride. The few extra dollars you save shopping at BoxMart are not worth what you learn and the friends you make at these stores. Support them and they will support you.

A taxidermist is the second person a hunter calls . . . after asking the best friend to help find and drag a downed deer. Consequently, taxidermists see every trophy taken in your area and meet the successful hunters.

If you scout and hunt effectively, you will need a taxidermist. These men and women know who takes big deer. They know the good places to hunt. Since you are eager to begin spending money with them, it is in their best interest to share a little of what they know. How much they share depends on each individual.

Consider your trip to a taxidermist's studio or lunch with a newspaper columnist or conversation with a bow salesman to be scouting.

At one time, newspapers happily printed photos of hunters with their trophies. Today, unless you live in a rural area, your local newspaper probably features little or no useful hunting information. You find newspapers that will benefit your search for the right place to hunt near the checkout at convenience stores. They are called "tabloids." They may not be fancy, but they are literally bursting with specific information–who, what, when, where and how–about your specific hunting areas. In my experience, tabloid editors and writers are flattered by your call, especially if you offer to buy lunch. What a small price to pay for a new friend and a hot tip!

As you expand your circle of informed sources, you narrow the parameters of your search. Do not expect to set aside one month or even two to meet the presidents of local rod and gun clubs or official record-book scorers. This is a continuing but occasional process. Meeting and interviewing one or two new individuals every month is a reasonable goal. Save their business cards and always make a few notes about what you learn. If you fail to take notes–after the meeting, not during–you will forget important details.

From experience, some "informed sources" will be interesting, but will not readily share information. Allow these individuals to buy their own lunch. State game employees, including enforcement personnel ("game wardens"), fall into this category, as do well-known local trophy hunters. Nevertheless, talk to anyone who may have a clue for your puzzle, including school bus drivers, UPS and other postal drivers, etc.

WHAT TO EXPECT

Effective scouting is identifying the Best Place to find deer (or elk or even feral hogs), but beware. Almost anyone can direct you to some hunting area or other, but you must piece together the information and fit it into your map to find the Best Area.

Do not ask anyone, "Where can I go to kill a big deer?" and expect a helpful response. Bowhunters are typically careful with such information and even seeing another bowhunter in the same wilderness area makes the best of us grouchy.

When you talk to your informed sources–taxidermists and writers, sporting-goods store salesmen and county trash haulers–you want to learn about their specialty. The more you learn from them, and appreciate their knowledge, about caring for a deer's cape before you take it to their studio, or how to write a story for a regional magazine, or what their favorite style of broadhead is, the more they will share with you. "Yep. I killed it down along Old Dodd Road." Or "Davey Crockett shot a big deer over on the Gum Ridge with an expandable head."

Even the people who will not readily share information have a story to tell. If you can get a state big-game biologist on the phone, ask him or her where the deer herd is densest. Perhaps they will tell you about depredation

When you flew over your hunting area, you identified a small marsh that you had never before identified and you made this sketch. It occurs to you that deer may bed in the low, thick brush on the southeast corner of the small pool of open water. Now it is time to get a feel for the ground on the ground. If the prevailing winds were from the west, how and where would you set up a stand for the best chance at the buck bedding in the marsh?

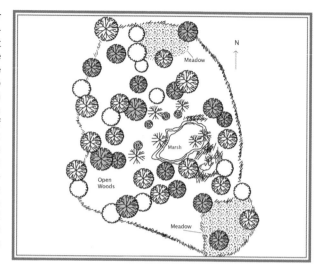

permits. Ask about buck-doe ratios and see what they know. Perhaps they will direct you to scientific papers in the state archives or on the Internet.

As you begin to build your database–and it will come together quickly if you are the least bit diligent–please remember to respect the rights of others, certainly other hunters. Successful well-known hunters often testify that people park in front of their homes at three o'clock in the morning. Kansas' Russell Hull thought a group of hunters camped in his yard one night and then followed him to his treestand the next morning. No matter how much we desire to take trophy big game, the true satisfaction is to develop and execute our own strategy. To interview a trophy hunter, and question him as diligently as he will allow, is appropriate. To invade his privacy is cheating and will lessen your pride in your eventual accomplishments.

OUTSIDE-IN SCOUTING: DRIVE AND FLY

By this time, you will have found several possibilities for excellent hunting areas within your home range. The next step in finding the Best Area, the one you want to hunt. Now, it is time to drive the roads and study the area through the windshield.

You have maps and can make enlargements of the sections you choose for closer study. Sketch in the fields and woodlots. Mark the stream beds, the woody draws and the overgrown fence lines. Shade in saddles between ridges. Note the planted fields and what is growing there. Peas, corn, clover, soybeans and especially, grown-over weedy fields all attract deer.

You can learn a great deal without getting out of your car. Early in the process, it may not seem like much, but you are building an atlas of a mature deer's world. In each of these areas, a few bucks will be dominant and you are mapping their bedrooms, their groceries and the paths they take between them.

As you map an area, working from the outside-in, you will see and meet people along the way. Farmers and ranchers living there. County grader operators smoothing the dirt roads. Deputy Sheriffs asking for your driver's license. Garbage haulers stopping for a quick smoke. Each of these people is a source of information, especially the farmers, because you want to know what they are planting, what they are going to plant next, what fields will lay fallow, which areas are in a government set-aside program and will not be planted, AND if they would consider letting you hunt on their land. You want to know where the deputy most frequently picks up deer killed along the road, if this is his job. You want to know where the heavy equipment operator routinely sees deer tracks. All of this information helps build your deer census.

At some point, you will identify the one or two areas in which to concentrate your search. It is time to fly over them and take pictures. Of course, government sources are available for some aerial photos, but they are often years out of date or the resolution is poor. Unless you live deep in the heart of rural America, an aerial photo older than one year is probably useless. In addition, since 9-11, several government agencies have restricted access to their highest quality photos. Okay, take your own.

Unless you invest $7,000 to earn your private pilot's license, you will want to rent an airplane . . . and a pilot. This will cost $100 an hour, but if you split the cost with a friend, you can fly longer. Your objective is not solely to enjoy an hour of aerobatics over your hometown or check out your neighbor's back yard. Your objective is to fly specific areas and take their picture.

You must sit down with your pilot and carefully explain what you are doing. The pilot must understand what results you want, so use your map and show him or her exactly where to fly. Flying during the middle of the day eliminates confusing shadows, but it tends to flatten out the landscape. You need to fly low and slow on a day when there is no air disturbance and when the air is exceptionally clear.

Ask your pilot (or your closest photo laboratory, not the photo technician at the neighborhood drugstore) about film selections, processing labs and perhaps special films, such as infrared. Take several cameras, because one will certainly jam or the battery will fail, and it helps to use two kinds of film and polarizing filters. Whether you shoot digital or film does not matter, but you want the highest resolution possible, even if you must rent a high-quality camera.

Try to rent a plane with passenger-side windows that roll down or detach. Otherwise, steady your camera against the window if you cannot hold it outside. Often, pilots of experimental (homemade) planes or pilots who enjoy aerobatics will be your best source of rides, and crop-duster pilots are accustomed to flying low and slow.

Take as many pictures as possible, because in some of them the ground

A bowhunter is sneaking toward his stand near the conjunction of a food plot, a fence line and nearby woody cover. In an early morning approach, deer may be bedded in the woods, however, so this may not be his best approach or his best stand site. Perhaps an approach to the woods from his left and a stand at least 100 yards in the woods would be a better choice.

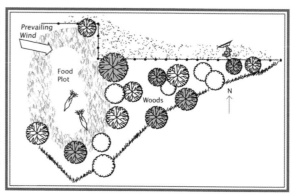

will be blurry, in others the strut will obscure the point of interest, or your air sickness bag will flop in front of the lens. Ask your pilot to bank the plane onto its side so that you are facing the ground rather than having to take pictures at an acute angle.

If your flight is successful–and you may want to fly a couple of times a year–you will have superb overhead photos of high-quality hunting areas. Aerial photos will show what you may not be able to see from the road. From the cab of your truck, a ditch appears to head north from the road toward a ridgeline and bend around a wooded hill. From the air, you see that it actually bifurcates, one branch ending on either side of a sloping finger of woods snaking down from the hilltop. Now, there is a place to investigate!

FACE-TO-FACE OR BOOTS-ON-THE-GROUND SCOUTING

Once you have identified one or two specific areas that hold good deer, you need to get out and meet the landowners face-to-face and, finally, walk the ground. Meeting the landowners and obtaining their permission may be the trickiest part of your scouting mission. Walking the land, on the other hand, may be the easiest, because you have been mapping cover and seasonal food sources as you progressed. In-the-woods scouting, slow and unobtrusive, simply helps you connect the dots–first, from your treestand and second, with your broadhead.

Often, it will be obvious who owns property, but if it is not, a few friendly inquiries in the neighborhood should point you in the right direction. If this fails, your county or township property appraiser's office will solve the question. In addition, plat books indicating property lines and owners are available. Today, much of this information is online on government Internet sites.

Understand that with 16 million hunters in the US, landowners receive frequent requests for hunting privileges. If their property holds deer, chances are they have hunters already. That should not matter. Landowners can only say, "Yes," "No" or "Maybe." If they say no, leave your business card or make sure they have your name. Send a "Thank You" note anyway and stay in touch. The next year may be entirely different.

Even if a landowner gives permission, there may be strings attached. These days, an increasing number of landowners are asking hunters to pay for access to their property and to sign waivers of liability. Just 25 years ago, most rural landowners were generous with hunting privileges on their property. They were primarily oriented to firearms hunting and just becoming familiar with bowhunting. These things also have changed.

However, bowhunters still have an easier time gaining access to private land than do gun hunters because the bow season typically begins earlier and lasts longer; because of our self-limiting shooting range; and because of our self-limiting (perhaps unfortunately) success rate. Do not be surprised if the landowner has already committed his property to local gun hunters–about five times as many people hunt with a gun than a bow–and your ability to hunt there during the gun season is curtailed. Because you have scouted back-up locations, however, this will not be a problem. You have alternative places to hunt depending, perhaps, on the wind or even on your alarm going off on time.

A landowner waiver, by the way, helps protect the landowner. For conscientious bowhunters, it should not be a problem even if it loads you with responsibilities. You will hunt safely. You will leave gates as you find them and police your area. You will use stands that do not damage trees and trim shooting lanes minimally. You will notify significant others where you are hunting and when to expect you to return. You will park in an agreed-upon spot. You will respect the landowner's property and livestock. You will never shoot without being able to identify your target clearly. Therefore, you will not have a problem and you will be able to hunt this farmer's land year after year.

There is a slowly growing trend to require hunters to pay to hunt private land. A financial transaction changes the legal nature of the hunter-landowner relationship, however, so if you have any questions regarding a document that you are asked to sign, you should consult an attorney to resolve any ambiguities. For instance, if you pay to hunt property, does the landowner have a responsibility to provide a safe hunting environment? Who pays for your injuries and your "pain and suffering" if you fall into an old well? What is a "safe hunting environment" and how much of it is your own responsibility? The point is that both you and the landowner need to be aware of your actions . . . and the possibilities.

Once you have worked through the mapping and talking, you want to find the best site to erect your stand or blind. By this time, you will know what the deer are primarily eating and should have a few good clues about where they are bedding. Conventional wisdom says to position your stand between the two, perhaps even close to their bedding area if a single spot can be identified–and often it cannot. Most bowhunters want to be in the way when bucks

Some tools to make your scouting and your hunting easier. The laser rangefinder on the left has an effective range of 10 to 700 yards with an accuracy of plus/minus one yard and an adjustable 6x eyepiece. The option (not pictured) is a Model 75 coincident image rangefinder from Ranging (American Visionwear), which has a 2x eyepiece, an effective range of 10 to 75 yards and an accuracy of plus/minus one yard at 50 yards. Typically, bowhunters are advised to purchase a compact set of roof prism binoculars for use in the woods. The author, on the other hand, prefers a large set of porro prism binoculars with a wide field of view. Heavier, but what you see in its context is supremely better than with a tiny set of optics.

are returning to their bedroom from a night out. In practice, with real, live deer, it is rarely this simple, but this is the strategy.

Hooey, says there are a number of things to keep in mind when you are scouting:

Leave your camo and your bow home. You are not actually hunting, so save your camo. Wear clean, rugged clothes. And even if the small-game season is open, take your bow only when you expect to harvest a deer. Keep your deer-hunting area "clean": no shooting at squirrels, taking the family on picnics or searching for mushrooms there.

Do not leave a treestand up year-round or think that you will become more woods-wise by sitting on it in an off-month. Finish your "honey do" projects before September so that you can build a savings account of good will for hunting. No stand is designed to stay in the woods year-round. It will deteriorate and will be a distraction to others who may have business in the woods.

Forget scouting for shed antlers. They are curiosities, but you are only interested in live deer. Because you have scouted effectively, you know big deer live where you are going to hunt. Blundering around in search of sheds only disrupts the environment. Leave the sheds for the little critters that need the minerals.

Select stands and blinds based on your knowledge of typical wind direction and food sources. Trim selectively and do not hesitate to move in response to observed deer movement. It is better to move than to alter the landscape by trimming too much. As you clear shooting lanes, remember that treestand hunters shoot from 20 to 25 feet above the ground, not from the base of the tree.

Do not rely on memory to locate your hunting stand in the dark. Mark your trail clearly and as close to the ground as possible. Reflective tacks or even fluorescent orange surveyor's tape are essential, because you want to cause as little disturbance as possible. Erecting your stand will be disturbance enough. And do not be a tenderfoot: Keep your trail markers low so that you are not shining your flashlight in all directions at eye level.

Along with necessary scouting tools–knife, pocket saw, no-scent bug suit–take pencil and paper. If you are able to make a note immediately about an irregularity or some surprise find, the new element will become a permanent part of your hunting equation. How many times have you forgotten . . . "oh, I should have asked" . . . or "why didn't I remember?" We are human. We forget. Jot it down.

Lightweight binoculars and a camera are always useful. Expensive is nice, but lightweight with a wide field of view is best. In the heavily wooded east, trade magnification for field of view. Today, a camera with a zoom lens will fit in your shirt pocket. Cameras are wonderful for recording change of food sources, rubs, scrapes and your hunting adventures.

Coincident rangefinders are a wonderful addition to the fanny pack. Lightweight and inexpensive, these rangefinders give accurate, plus/minus one-yard estimates within bowhunting distances without batteries. They work by aligning interior mirrors. They can easily be realigned if dropped and are not susceptible to changing or challenging weather conditions. Laser rangefinders are expensive, bulkier and measure distance accurately, but far beyond your effective bowhunting range. If you also hunt with a gun, however, they are probably the better choice.

Be safe. Put a whistle in your fanny pack or hang one around your neck. There are too many stories about bowhunters injured in the woods who do not have a whistle for signaling. If you become disoriented, a compass will help you maintain direction and it is always useful for updating your maps. Keep the compass with a canteen of fresh water and an energy bar or two . . . just in case. "It" can happen to you.

If you do not carry a cellular telephone, someone needs to know that you are going to be in the woods, when you will be home and where to look for your car. Otherwise, if anything happens, you are on your own. Leave your spouse a map and, although we hunt to "get away from it all," I know more than one bowhunter whose life has been saved because he carried a cell phone in his fanny pack.

THE EXCEPTION: PUBLIC LAND

Hooey believes that you must treat public land a little differently than private land if you want to kill a mature deer every year. After all, you have far less control over the typical wildlife management area than you (or a landowner) have over a set of woodlots, fields and pastures. The basic rules of effective scouting apply to public land, too.

• Open your mind to the possibilities for clues and information.

- Expect that you will take a deer that you will make you proud.
- Make scouting a year-round hobby . . . and not just the first year.
- Take notes and build a hunting map.
- Talk to everyone who may have insights into area herd dynamics.
- Study the food sources and hunt accordingly.

The difference between hunting public land and private land is that you will have more company in a public place, especially one without designated seasonal uses. Pheasant hunters stumble through following their dogs. Squirrel hunters rise the same time you do. Hikers litter the trails with granola wrappers. Snowmobilers leave a trail of blue smog through hardwood hammocks. Unlike a privately owned woodlot, the deer on public lands are accustomed to greater diversity of human traffic and disturbance at almost any time of day. That does not mean they necessarily like it, though.

Hooey's approach to scouting and hunting public land pays close attention to what he calls the "topographic advantage." Hooey believes that deer are smart enough to use natural and man-made features to their benefit when traveling to and from feeding and bedding zones.

Natural or man-made funnels, for instance, do channel deer movements. A funnel is the tongue of a hill protruding into a plowed field. It is the point of a wood with a stream angling sharply around it or a break in a brushy fence-line by the woods. A funnel is any feature that constrains deer movement along their normal routes. These are wonderful places to set up, Hooey says. Discover what the deer are eating at either end and you have a natural ambush site.

What Hooey calls "spider webs" are intersections of ditches or overgrown fencerows. Deer are likely to ghost along these at any time of day or night. Spider webs provide the illusion of cover for movement and the weedy browse that wildlife biologists claim deer prefer to corn or clover.

Although most bowhunters argue that deer find thick cover to bed and give birth to fawns, the author has often found deer beds (sometimes with deer in them!) on relatively barren hilltops and in corners of open woods. Perhaps these spots give deer a sense of security because they can see anything moving, but they should not be ignored when you scout public land.

According to Hooey, deer walk logging roads in thick woods and will travel across saddles and parallel to ridges in hilly country. While he has taken several deer off logging roads, perhaps because they are eating the weedy browse there, he feels that the difficulty of setting up may offset any natural advantage. Walking the road to your stand deposits your scent throughout the area you want to hunt, but walking noisily through the woods to reach a spot in the road may be self-defeating.

Deer are no more immune to the effect of gravity than are bowhunters, so in hill country, look for natural ramps and saddles. These natural features give deer time- and energy-saving advantages when moving through the hills, and are excellent places for an ambush. ■

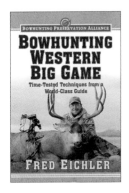

Bowhunting Western Big Game
Time-Tested Techniques from a World-Class Guide
by Fred Eichler

A master guide shares his secrets and tactics to successful bowhunting for big game in the Rocky Mountains in this essential hunting handbook.

$22.95 Paperback • ISBN 978-1-62087-226-0

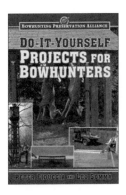

Do-It-Yourself Projects for Bowhunters
by Peter Fiduccia and Leo Somma

Do-It-Yourself Projects for Bowhunters is a detailed reference book including dozens of useful woodworking, antler, bone, and hide projects that are practical for camp and home. This guide also features articles, diagrams, and illustrations on field dressing, skinning, and quartering deer as well as information on planting successful food plots to attract game to your property.

$24.95 Paperback • ISBN 978-1-61608-816-3